# Systems Practice in the Information Society

As a collection of ideas and methodologies, systems thinking has made an impact in organizations, particularly in the information systems field. However, this main emphasis on organizations limits the scope of systems thinking and practice. There is a need first to use systems thinking in addressing societal problems, and second to enable people involved in developing the information society to reflect on the impacts of systems and technologies in society as a whole. Thus, there are opportunities to review the scope and potential of systems thinking and practice to deal with information society-related issues.

*Systems Practice in the Information Society* provides students of information systems as well as practicing IS managers with concepts and strategies to enable them to understand and use systems thinking methodologies and address challenges posed by the development of information-based societies. The book brings experiences, ideas, and applications of systemic thinking in designing and evaluating socio-technological initiatives. Using a number of cultural contexts, the book explores how organizations, including governments, can enable better access to information and communication technologies and improve the quality of life of individuals.

**José-Rodrigo Córdoba-Pachón** (MA, PhD) is a senior lecturer in the School of Management, Royal Holloway, University of London in the UK. He is the current director of the Master of Science in Business Information Systems.

**Routledge Series in Information Systems**
Edited by Steve Clarke (Hull University Business School, UK),
M. Adam Mahmood (University of Texas at El Paso, USA), and
Morten Thanning Vendelø (Copenhagen Business School, Denmark)

The overall aim of the series is to provide a range of textbooks for advanced undergraduate and postgraduate study and to satisfy the advanced undergraduate and postgraduate markets, with a focus on key areas of those curricula.

The key to success lies in delivering the correct balance between organizational, managerial, technological, theoretical, and practical aspects. In particular, the interaction between, and interdependence of, these often different perspectives is an important theme. All texts demonstrate a 'theory into practice' perspective, whereby the relevant theory is discussed only in so far as it contributes to the applied nature of the domain. The objective here is to offer a balanced approach to theory and practice.

Information Systems is a rapidly developing and changing domain, and any book series needs to reflect current developments. It is also a global domain, and a specific aim of this series, as reflected in the international composition of the editorial team, is to reflect its global nature. The purpose is to combine state-of-the-art topics with global perspectives.

**Information Systems Strategic Management: An Integrated Approach, 2nd edition**
*Steve Clarke*

**Managing Information and Knowledge in Organizations: A Literacy Approach**
*Alistair Mutch*

**Knowledge Management Primer**
*Rajeev K. Bali, Nilmini Wickramasinghe, Brian Lehaney*

**Healthcare Knowledge Management Primer**
*Nilmini Wickramasinghe, Rajeev K. Bali, Brian Lehaney, Jonathan L. Schaffer, M. Chris Gibbons*

**Systems Practice in the Information Society**
*José-Rodrigo Córdoba-Pachón*

# Systems Practice in the Information Society

José-Rodrigo Córdoba-Pachón

Routledge
Taylor & Francis Group

NEW YORK AND LONDON

First published 2010
by Routledge
270 Madison Ave, New York, NY 10016

Simultaneously published in the UK
by Routledge
2 Park Square, Milton Park, Abingdon, Oxon OX14 4RN

*Routledge is an imprint of the Taylor & Francis Group, an informa business*

© 2010 José-Rodrigo Córdoba-Pachón

Typeset in Garamond by
HWA Text and Data Management, London
Printed and bound in the United States of America on acid-free paper

*Library of Congress Cataloging in Publication Data*
Córdoba-Pachón, José-Rodrigo.
　Systems practice in the information society / José-Rodrigo Córdoba-Pachón.
　　p. cm.
　Includes bibliographical references and index.
　Information technology. 2. System analysis. 3. Information society. I. Title.
　HC79.I55C6747 2009
　658.4'038011–dc22　　　　　　　　　　　　　　　　2009003529

ISBN10: 0-415-99230-3 (hbk)
ISBN10: 0-415-99231-1 (pbk)
ISBN10: 0-203-89315-8 (ebk)

ISBN13: 978-0-415-99230-5 (hbk)
ISBN13: 978-0-415-99231-2 (pbk)
ISBN13: 978-0-203-89315-9 (ebk)

To my brother Juan-Carlos and the rest of my family

"Caminante no hay camino, se hace camino al andar"
(Serrat)

# Contents

# Tables

# Figures

# Permissions

The author and publisher gratefully acknowledge permission to reproduce the follow material.

Figure 2.1: reprinted from C. Shannon "A mathematical theory of communication", *The Bell Systems Technical Journal,* Vol 27, p. 380. © 1948 with permission of John Wiley & Sons, Inc; Figure 2.2: reprinted from Y. Masuda *The Information Society as Post-Industrial Society,* p. 13. © 1982 with permission from Transaction Publishers; Figure 2.3: reprinted from C. Perez, "Structural change and assimilation of new technologies in the economic and social systems", *Futures,* Vol 15 Issue 5, p. 363. © 1983 with permission from Elsevier; Figure 3.3: reprinted from Humberto R. Maturana, and Francisco J. Varela *The Tree of Knowledge* p. 74. ©1987 Humberto R. Maturana and Francisco J. Varela. By arrangement with Shambhala Publications, Inc., Boston, MA. www.shambhala.com; Figure 4.1: reprinted from R. Mason, and I. Mitroff *Challenging Strategic Planning Assumptions: Theory, Cases and Techniques,* p. 48. © 1981. This material is reproduced with permission from John Wiley & Sons Inc, Hoboken, NJ; Figures 4.2 and 4.3: reprinted from P. Checkland and J. Poulter *Learning for Action: A Short Definitive Account of Soft Systems Methodology and Its Use for Practitioners, Teachers and Students,* p. 21 and p. 75. © 2006, with permission from Wiley-Blackwell (UK); Figure 4.5: reprinted from G. Midgley *Systemic Intervention: Philosophy, Methodology and Practice,* p. 144. © 2000, with permission from Springer; Figures 5.8, 6.6 and 6.7: from J.R. Córdoba "A critical systems approach for the planning of information and communications technologies in the information society", pp. 201, 231 and 251, unpublished PhD thesis, Hull University. With permission from Hull University Library, UK; Figure 6.1: adapted from Edward De Bono *Teaching Thinking,* Penguin Books,p. 96, with permission of the author; Figure 6.4: reprinted and adapted from R. Heeks "E-government as a carrier of context", *Journal of Public Policy,* Vol 25 Issue 1, p. 55. © 2005, with permission from Cambridge University Press; Figure 6.10: reprinted from J.R. Córdoba, and G. Midgley "Beyond organisational agendas: using boundary critique to facilitate the inclusion of societal concerns in information systems planning", *European Journal of Information Systems,* Vol 17 Issue 2, p. 137. © 2008, with permission from Macmillan Publishers Ltd; Table 6.2: from J.R. Córdoba "A critical systems approach for the planning of information and communications technologies in the information society", pp. 238–240, unpublished PhD thesis, Hull University. With permission from Hull University Library, UK.

# Preface

This book is about systems practice in the information society and the information society as a system. It presents a number of ways in which this practice can be directed to offer better opportunities to societies with the help of information systems (IS) and information and communication technologies (ICTs). Practice is about what we do in our work as information systems planners, developers, designers, policy makers or users. The book is for those individuals who work in these or other areas, or want to learn about systems-thinking applied to them in the context of the information society. More importantly, the book is conceived for people who want to improve how we live and work nowadays in our societies.

Throughout the book the meaning of the term 'practice' encompasses the activities of practitioners. As an information systems and systems-thinking practitioner I find that these two areas have many similarities when it comes to addressing complex situations. Nowadays, information systems practitioners have to deal with the complexities of designing and implementing systems that need to be interconnected with other systems, the internet and across geographical regions. They have to deal with the complexities of norms and standards, let alone codes of conduct, ethics and practice. Moreover, they have to deal with different groups of people. There is no more one group of 'systems users'. Users have become more sophisticated, demanding and clever. Practitioners have many systems and technologies at their disposal. They do their best to make sure 'users' understand and use these in the best possible ways. There is still a long way to go in the information society.

Systems practitioners also face complexities. The popularity of systems-thinking can be reflected in the number of books written in the subject, and the vast amount of resources that one can find on the internet (e.g. by typing 'systems-thinking' in the Google search engine). In organizations people are becoming aware of the importance of looking at the 'big picture', seeing the 'inter-connectedness' of situations, and working on 'relationships'. A range of methodologies is available. But we still work within the confines of organizations, within their norms, culture and ways of doing things. This can sometimes help when it comes to change, but in many situations we find that our 'users' are cleverer than expected, and they do not surrender to change without a good fight. Users still surprise us! There is plenty of scope to work effectively with them and other stakeholders involved in a situation.

This book suggests ways of developing systems practice with the information society in mind. It considers that the information society contains different types of phenomena which we need to look at and intervene in if we want to make our societies better to live in. With the information technology revolution that has changed our ways of working and communicating, it is essential to reflect on how we think about situations, and how we can improve them. These situations often (and in the future inevitably will) involve the use of systems and technologies.

This book suggests focusing on our thinking as a way of guiding our actions in the information society. Thinking can be helped by systems ideas and methodologies.

## Motivation for the Book

In 1997, as a member of the High Technology Forum (Foro de Alta Tecnologia) in Colombia, South America (my home country), I became involved in a series of conversations with the central government planning office to define how to use information and communication technologies (ICTs) for economic and social purposes. The term 'information society' was of interest to planners and politicians. Also, policy makers were very keen to follow what other countries (Europe, the US and Japan amongst others) had been doing in this respect. The result of conversations with government officers, ICT providers, educators, consultants and entrepreneurs was a set of guidelines to orient the formulation of policies and plans (Ministerio de Comunicaciones, 1997). It seemed that as a so-called developing country, Colombia could take advantage of the development of ICTs to 'catch up' through their incorporation in different sectors. Without knowing exactly what it really meant, the term information society became significant to me and my future career.

During 1999, as a PhD student, I attended another meeting organized by the Forum. This time the aim was to generate awareness about the benefits of electronic commerce for the national industry; the term 'information society' had been losing ground to 'knowledge society' but still was of interest to policy makers. Policies to put the information society into place were being implemented. These included generating awareness about new information technologies and educating people in their use. One type of technology which was emerging at that time was electronic commerce. During that meeting, I remember a very successful business woman asking a speaker about the usefulness of internet-based commerce: "What is the internet? Is it a place? Can I visit it?"

The innocence of the woman's question and the consultant's disconcerted reaction encouraged me to research ways in which the use of information systems and technologies can be better understood and managed by non-experts. We seem to forget that information society developments are a long way from benefiting a wide spectrum of groups. As soon as we start thinking about how we can make the information society more inclusive, a number of challenges appear.

In modern societies we face the challenge of language. The more 'professional' or specialized people become, the less able we are to talk to other professionals or the lay person. We keep inventing new terms (our children do it faster on their mobile telephones!). Technologies help us to do this and the terms make it easier for us to communicate. We have gained a better appreciation of our human condition and our limited ability to make sense of the world around us. We have produced technologies to help us in this regard. But we have not overcome the problem of human language when it comes to expressing what we think about the world. Our conversations with people, the ones we seem to value most in societies, are about economics, profits, efficiencies, redundancies, ventures, self-interests and the like. We have become 'economic' people, and unfortunately most of the benefits of the information society seem to have been in this area.

Then there is the challenge of 'problem solving'. In our societies and the global world we keep encountering and solving problems. Problems of hunger, war, illnesses and epidemics, egalitarianism and human rights, crime and terrorism are part of daily news and daily concerns, but we do not seem to be able to address them. Moreover, if we think we can escape from problems at work we are wrong. The life blood of organizations has become solving problems to become better than yesterday and better than competitors. Problems of efficiency, quality, relocation, supply, connectivity and customer satisfaction take up our time as managers or employees. We find ourselves solving problems to which we see no connection with bigger problems in society. The challenge is to go beyond organizational boundaries.

Connected to the above challenges is the challenge of 'narrow thinking' or 'thinking inside organizations' as we will call it. Despite claiming that we live in a global village, we do not seem to learn from our mistakes. Organizations keep making basic mistakes, because they concentrate on their own business and the short term, forgetting any potential consequences for the 'outside'. Corporate social responsibility has thrown a life-line to organizations and societies, and we are beginning to recognize the importance of considering the needs of stakeholders, not only those of shareholders.

In the so-called non-developed regions of our planet, we find ways of living and working that have not become industrialized but which have shown us how to make community life more bearable and important for organizations. Our thinking needs to widen and consider other forms of working. More importantly, it needs to bring our human values and concerns back to the workplace, so that we become human beings again, we become 'whole' systems in search for higher goals. Again, we need to examine how we actually think about situations, to rescue the possibility of talking to each other, to envision a joint future with different people, and to make sure we retain certain values for the benefit of present and future generations.

Throughout this book we revisit these and other challenges which seem to be part of the information society. Our aim is to address them with the help of systems-thinking and systems methodologies. Systems-thinking can give us an idea of society as a system which aims to ensure people's realization and development. It can help us to recognize ourselves as part of this system. With systems methodologies we can enquire about situations with a view to improving them and society as a whole.

## What This Book Is About

This book is neither a theoretical nor a practical account of the practice of policy making, information systems or systems-thinking. It is more about practice when these and other areas come to be used in exploring phenomena in the information society. It offers a number of 'middle-ground' ways of thinking about and acting on challenges that emerge when we have to deal with information society developments. Each of these offers something useful that we can put into practice. We will call these ways of thinking and acting 'patterns'. The book aims to help practitioners, policy makers and citizens in general to engage with a number of challenges and issues which emerge when we consider different ways of thinking about the information society, and how systems-thinking and methodologies can respond to them.

I have tried to articulate what my practice as a project manager, software developer, researcher and academic has been in the last fifteen years. In this journey, systems-thinking has been my best friend. It has enabled me to find my true vocation, and to help other people to think about their own. It has also helped me to make sense of the changes that we as individuals have experienced in the last decade with globalization and technology revolutions.

This may or may not be the case for the reader. An information systems practitioner might find that the book conveys in simpler (non-technical) language reflections from practice in each chapter, and some practical implications derived from novel ways of thinking about the information society. The book offers a perspective of how the information society can be better developed using systems-thinking and systems methodologies. The latter play a greater part, although I have attempted to show how complex, unpredictable and ultimately humane the information society could become if we decide to contribute to it. In developing the information society, policy makers, information technology suppliers, consultants, academics and other 'experts' have taken the lead. It is time for other people (practitioners) to help us to make this society more understandable, inclusive, participative and helpful in our lives. It is also time for other people to use the information society for their own purposes.

An 'expert' in systems-thinking may find this book somewhat basic. In countries like the UK the debate in systems-thinking has taken many different directions. As will be seen in the introductory chapter, the debate has become very sophisticated, with people arguing for the need to arrive at the 'true' nature of issues of pluralism, a single theory to inform systems methodology use, generic principles systems practice or reflective modes of methodology application.

Whilst these and other developments no doubt ensure that systems-thinking is alive and kicking, in practice we find that *time* is an issue that we need to consider; not only our time to reflect and debate on these issues (which in some countries is provided by academia), but also the time of people who are to benefit from methodology use. From our experience we find that people who are interested in improving situations in the information society also have to deal with the pressures of work, problem-solving orientation and narrow thinking, amongst others. They need to continually 'think on their feet'. And so should systems practitioners. I think that the door is open for systems practitioners to search for new opportunities to engage audiences; to leave aside considerations about big, well-paid crusades and to become simpler and accessible to those who would like to talk to us. We can learn from them too.

This is why I focus on developing ways of thinking to support our practice in the information society, wherever this practice might take place. This also led me to pass over other developments in systems-thinking including the work of colleagues in Venezuela on interpretive systemology and of others in Mexico, Colombia and the USA on producing systems theory applicable to information systems. I present my perspectives on the main tenets of theories including autopoiesis, complexity and general systems theory. I value their insights into understanding how we as individuals are challenged to make society a better place to live. I focus on using existing methodologies to enquire about how we can arrive at societal improvements, and how information systems and technologies can become supporting elements in achieving these improvements. To me this should also be a way forward for systems thinkers who want to go beyond the boundaries of their current practice. As the reader will see, many of the experiences of practice neither start with information-systems related issues nor end with them.

Therefore this book can be of relevance to practitioners, policy makers or anyone else interested in learning about the information society as a 'whole' and what to do about it. I provide a number of examples, ideas, exercises and further reading to make the book accessible to different audiences. I have also used the term 'we' to invite the reader to join me or to report on experiences in which I have collaborated with other systems thinkers, information systems practitioners or stakeholders.

There is one last thing to be mentioned. Throughout the book I use the term 'systems methodology' when other people may prefer to use the term 'systems method' or 'systems practice'. I make the distinction between methodology and method in Chapter 4, but then continue using the term methodology. For me, using a systems methodology encompasses the principles and aims of what we want to achieve. Even if we use the term systems method, we are still much guided by the principles and 'spirit' of the methodology that a method belongs to. I interpret my experiences as based on systems methodology use. I hope the reader will see my point.

# Acknowledgments

I am indebted to a number of people who in one way or another have helped me shape the ideas contained in this book.

First of all, I would like to thank my family for loving me and inspiring me to work hard and be grateful for life. My father and mother (Carlos and Clara-Inés) who tried their best to educate me and inspire my reading and writing. My brothers (Juan-Carlos, Ricardo-Augusto) and my sisters (Claudia-Pilar and Clara-Ximena), you always valued my interest in reading and studying. Thank you for making me feel special!

Ernesto Lleras at Universidad de los Andes inspired me to pursue research in systems-thinking. His challenging approach really touched me when I was doing my first degree in computer science engineering. I always remember his first intriguing words: "You think you know something, but you need to wake up!" I think I know now what he meant. In looking at the world, we as information systems practitioners are often unaware of society as a whole, its complexities, its problems and its possibilities. This book is a first attempt to become fully awake as a citizen of the information society. I hope to inspire other people as Ernesto has inspired me.

Cesar Cabrejo and Rodrigo Paredes from Fundación Social (my first bosses) offered me key opportunities to become involved in working with people outside technological areas whilst still being an information technology analyst. I was also involved in a number of government forums aimed at discussing the future of information and communication technologies in Colombia.

Fundación Colfuturo of Colombia gave me a scholarship-loan to come to the UK and study a masters' degree in systems-thinking at Hull University. I have not gone back as expected. However, I hope this book shows how much I have gone 'astray'.

Dr. Gerald Midgley and Dr. Wendy Gregory mentored me in my first years at Hull. They also believed that I could be a good researcher and teacher, and I hope I have lived up to their expectations. This book aims to pay tribute to their dedication to me as a student.

Javeriana University in Colombia gave me the opportunity to put ideas in practice. As a 'foreign expert', they valued my contribution to their initiatives. I would also like to thank them for the opportunity to teach my first course on systems-thinking.

Various people at the centre for systems studies at Hull and the business school have contributed to make Hull my home in the last five years. Wendy Robson, Amanda Gregory, Jennifer Wilby, Steve Clarke, Tim Butcher, Ashish Dwivedi, Michael Jackson, Zhichang Zhu, and many others have helped to shape these ideas.

Many thanks also to everyone at School of Management, Royal Holloway, University of London. It is now my new home and I thank them for giving me their time and the new responsibilities which I have enjoyed so far. I have found that I can be an information systems academic and practitioner here.

Thank you also to my students on systems-thinking courses, for believing that it is possible to think in different ways and that we can be better at challenging ourselves.

And finally I would like to thank Cecilia, my wife, for being there as a friend and a companion when I have needed her the most.

**José-Rodrigo Córdoba-Pachón**
Royal Holloway, University of London
December 2008

# 1 Introduction

This chapter lays out the context of use of systems-thinking and systems methodologies in terms of what is happening in the information society. It presents a number of challenges for practitioner audiences and suggests how these can be tackled. Finally it lays out the general structure of the book.

## Objectives

- To describe a number of assumptions that inform the implementation of the information society in different realms of activity.
- To highlight the importance of being aware about unintended consequences on the information society.
- To introduce systems-thinking as a set of ideas and methodologies that can be used to support information society developments.

## The Information Society

As individuals, we now live in a world surrounded by information and communication technologies or ICTs. Life without computers is for many a thing of the past or something that they did not experience at all. Mobile phones, computers and other devices have come to stay in our lives. They are essential for our lives (just remember the last time you needed the internet and it was not available!).

For some people not only technologies but also *information* is a key to success. They have built companies and new ways of working based on the possibility of electronically exchanging information. Wireless technologies also make exchange of information faster and immediate. Ability to process large amounts of data in real time and communicate it efficiently to other parties can give companies the edge over their competitors. It can also make life easier for citizens and their governments.

These and other possibilities and opportunities are not entirely new but not easily made available. Governments and many organizations strive to bring the benefits of ICTs and information to people in societies. In different parts of the world, plans have been defined and implemented to exploit the potential offered by technologies at economic, cultural and social levels. Skills and knowledge are required from information systems practitioners, planners and policy makers. We see a number of policies and initiatives, plans and investments being laid out, some of which we have contributed to in our practice without us fully knowing why they need to be done. Their effects can now be seen but remain to be fully assessed.

What is emerging, to some, is a 'new societal order', in which almost every aspect of life will be based on the use of information. They have called this the 'information society'. This type of society promises to offer a greater benefit than any being foreseen before: *improving the quality of life of individuals*. To achieve such improvement, a number of 'preconditions' need to be achieved. These include for instance:

- deregulating markets of information-based products and services, as well as that of telecommunications, to enable companies to compete with cheaper and better information offers, and ultimately to benefit the end user;
- building communication infrastructures capable of enabling fast and reliable electronic information exchange;
- promoting development of electronic content industries;
- encouraging use of ICTs in different sectors (education, health, logistics, etc);
- enabling the acquisition of knowledge to master technologies and offer opportunities for employment and with it the renewal of knowledge.

Information systems practitioners, students or policy makers might consider that their activity has little to do with enabling these preconditions to take place. Nevertheless, and with the pervasiveness of ICTs in different realms of life, preconditions and plans are now part of our *daily* agendas. Among other activities that constitute our practice, we are called to initiate projects, select appropriate software, build databases, set up communication networks; formulate policies for enabling access to information and protect it; facilitate the creation of companies operating on and with the internet; etc. These examples should give us a flavor of our practice as being part of the development of the information society.

This book is about improving our practice in the information society. As the reader will discover, it not only has to do with facilitating the implementation of information systems and technologies but also is about working with people in exploring activities to facilitate societal improvements, so that the use of technologies and systems becomes more effective and sustainable in the long term. In this book we aim to provide ideas and experiences to help the reader appreciate and deal with the complexity of implementing projects, plans and initiatives related to the information society.

We begin by conceiving of the information society as a 'system', i.e. with a number of elements, issues, stakeholders and their needs; these elements are interconnected and interacting together. This leads us to formulate a number of questions: What is the purpose of such a system? What is it generating and what should it produce? How can we engage with this system? We intend to provide some answers to these and other fundamental questions with the help of systems-thinking.

A brief account of the information society as a system highlights a number of phenomena to be observed. These are:

- transformations
- engagement(s)
- unintended consequences.

## Transformations

Castells (2001) provides a very comprehensive analysis of the development of the network society as a *new and radical* way of relating people. This comes about due to the technological revolution experienced worldwide during the 1990s. There are similarities between the information society and the network society, but in the latter, the negative aspects are made more explicit. For Castells, the network society comes about because old hierarchies in organizations are being flattened. What matters now, according to Castells, is not traditional bureaucracies that allow production and service to occur but the flows of information that emerge in these processes, with the additional feature that many processes occur in the virtual world. Goods and services are now assembled around and with information flows, requiring the participation of people across widespread geographical locations. Societies are being relocated geographically as people move to be part of 'nodes' of production and servicing of these information flows. As individuals living in the information society, we need to understand these transformations, and inform our practice by the possibility to contribute to (or challenge) them.

## Engagement(s)

Those individuals and organizations participating in any of the types of information flows described above (e.g. by storing, producing, or mediating in their exchange) can access 'knowledge' and gain other benefits derived from being part of a network. Those being excluded can find it difficult to benefit. Governments are called to ensure that people get access to education, knowledge and skills to participate fully on the information society (CEC, 1997). However, the continuous development of new technologies, their accessibility via markets of information-related products and services, and existing socioeconomic conditions can all contribute to perpetuate existing gaps between those who have the resources and knowledge required to survive and those who do not.

This continuous perpetuation has been called *marginalization* (Beck *et al.*, 2004) and could be manifested in various forms. It can have features to be considered a macro-phenomenon (structural conditions of societies that make marginalization a consequence of the economy, the education, and the formulation of policies). It can also have a more 'micro' set of features in which organizations and individuals experience difficulties with or lack of access to information services, products and technologies. At this micro level, inclusion and marginalization in the information society is very dynamic, as Beck *et al.* (2004) portray. Because of this dynamic nature, any plan or policy to facilitate access to the information society should considered that through time, those being excluded from access might be included, and those being included might be excluded later on.

This shows the importance of continually engaging with people in the information society. Not only are there opportunities to offer new products and services with information systems and technologies, but also these opportunities need to be revisited continually to assess who is benefiting and who could benefit in the near future.

About the potential existence of situations of marginalization, Castells (2001: 282) sees that the use of information systems and technologies needs a *political act* from individuals. He says:

> So, either we enact political change (whatever that means in its various forms), or you and I will have to take care of reconfiguring the networks of our world around the projects of our lives … If you do not care about the networks, the networks will care about you. (original parenthesis)

This should encourage individuals (in different realms of practice) to become aware of how this new order is affecting them, and what they need to do about it. As practitioners, citizens or policy makers, we need to prepare ourselves and others to be able to engage with possibilities of inclusion and marginalization generated by information society initiatives. In this book, we will look at different types of strategies that have been used to engage with others to bring the information society to place. Some of these, it will be argued, can help people to start thinking about more inclusive and effective ways of planning.

## Unintended Consequences

As mentioned above, situations of use of information systems and technologies in the information society continually change, and we need to be prepared to act on the face of unintended consequences. Castells (2001) speaks about the dynamics of the information society and how change often takes place in unintended directions. He shows how the internet was initially conceived of to suit military purposes, but then became a tool to facilitate communication around the world and later on a medium to generate business and education opportunities. Changes develop as individuals engage with the use of information systems and technologies to address their own concerns as business entrepreneurs, community members or citizens.

One of Castells' examples is the Zapatista movement in Mexico, where the Zapatistas (left-wing guerrillas) used the internet to get their cause known and respected, and gained international support for it. These individuals managed to create an image of their group which appealed to worldwide audiences. Another example is that of a group of individuals in the city of Amsterdam in the Netherlands, who established an online community to provide advice and support. After a few years, this community became embedded into a private organization and thus lost most of their community-oriented goals.

The above two examples also show that the use of information systems and technologies by different groups in society becomes embedded in a kind of network of relations whose direction and purpose change continually. We need to help people to understand the dynamics of these networks, so that as Castells suggest, we can take appropriate action according to our own purposes. As much as we can exert (political) action in the information society, we also need to consider some intended and unintended consequences that it could bring, and be able to act within existing networks of relations between people. Information systems and technologies can facilitate and take action to new domains. We need concepts and ideas to help us understand and improve our practice in relation to what can be done in networks of relations. In such networks there might be plans which produce intended and unintended uses and impacts of systems and technologies. We need to embrace both in our practice.

## Issues of Concern About the Information Society

The information society is not a new phenomenon. It has generated benefits in the use of electronic information and related systems and technologies. However, a number of issues need to inform our practice and as will be seen in later chapters, they lead us to define a number of challenges for systems practice. The issues are:

1   *Economic focus*. Planning to simply adopt ICTs in societies becomes a process driven by economic concerns. With several examples of corporate scandals and bankruptcies, we are now seeing that too much emphasis on these concerns results in negative effects in the long run. Use of information systems and technologies has also contributed to what is happening now.

2   *Dominance of expertise*. The formulation of plans and implementation of initiatives to bring the information society into different countries has been almost entirely left to 'experts'

(i.e. policy-makers, technology experts). The prevalence of expertise has generated demands for well-prepared practitioners, but if not carefully managed, this can produce exclusion of some groups from participating in the formulation of plans and ideas about the information society. This applies in particular to citizens and community organizations. Governments contribute to reinforce this situation given their limited degree of knowledge about what technologies can do, and their own inability to deal with change. Where partnerships are formed with private investors (for instance ICT providers), knowledge of how to manage and implement ICT is not transferred to governments (Dunleavy *et al.*, 2006), let alone to citizens or community groups. Lack of participation produces resistance to change. In the best of cases, where different stakeholders are involved, technical and economic interests seem to prevail.

3    *Thinking inside organizations.* Information technology has become a necessity rather than a luxury in organizations, and this generates a pressure to contribute without fully foreseeing consequences outside them. With new technological developments in mobile and ubiquitous computing, internet-based processes, intelligent database management and telecommunications, organizations continually find opportunities to make their processes more efficient. Employees and government officers are encouraged to use their creativity to generate opportunities in the use of information and technologies to generate competitive advantages for their organizations, without looking too much at getting the best for society as a whole. With such a continuous pressure and narrow focus, it becomes difficult (if not impossible) to consider the impacts *beyond* organizational boundaries and interests. Issues of quality of work and quality of life are simply not part of the agenda.

4    *Leaving out human values.* Even in countries where information society implementations are most advanced, there is an emerging preoccupation with enabling new generations to keep a set of core human values in society. Violence and intolerance, religious hatred, corruption and other issues have not disappeared because of the use of information and communication systems and technologies. Some of these continue resurfacing even more strongly nowadays. The information society is about improving the quality of life, and if we as practitioners are going to contribute to this end, we need to think of ways of addressing these issues too.

Practitioners in public-sector management will find that the above challenges are part of the day-to-day concerns of organizations in this sector. Those in business management or information systems will find that involvement of people in the formulation of plans is a nice idea, but there are many difficulties in running discussions; in some cases participation becomes a 'hassle' and it is better to get on with the technical 'stuff' than interacting with other people. In other cases, the 'public' or the 'customer' is either not interested in formulating or validating plans or policies, or we lack any methodological resources to help us to overcome difficulties in getting people on board.

## Systems-thinking

Systems-thinking means a collection of ideas, concepts and methodologies that enable people to review the scope and impact of their assumptions and perspectives about a situation and thus improve social interventions. For some people systems-thinking is a discipline, for others it is science, for others it is an international movement.

What is common among these perspectives is the use of the idea of a system in different realms from biology to management and even spirituality. The idea is that a system is a collection of interconnected parts which produce emergent properties. The system is part of bigger systems, and there are also interconnections among them. Systems could be conceived of as existing 'out there' in the world, or could be defined as mental constructions that we can use to promote understanding and collective action. In addition to the basic idea of a system, there are many other features depending on what 'school of thought' one adopts. Both interconnectedness and nesting are used as features to investigate and *improve* situations, in other words systems-thinking offers some ideas which can illuminate ways of going about situations with an ethical perspective in mind.

Systems-thinking, with its ideas and methodologies, has addressed social change by encouraging the appreciation of different stakeholders' perspectives prior to the selection and implementation of planning methods (Midgley, 2000). It can also be a vehicle to bring the ethical dimension of improvement to the fore so that different strategies to bring improvement can be reviewed, debated and implemented.

The development of systems-thinking has been multi-fold and worldwide, and we can trace its origins to the origins of philosophy in both Western and Eastern contexts. The West has been particularly good at providing a number of methodologies that put into practice the principles of systems-thinking so that we can use them to solve problems. Jackson (2003) provides a comprehensive review of these different methodologies with a view of facilitating their use in a variety of 'problem contexts'. Jackson refers to *messy* situations, where there is a diversity of views on what the problems are and hence what solutions can be designed to improve the situations. He adopts some of the ideas of Russell Ackoff (1981) who promoted the use of systems concepts to improve situations. At different times through the history of science (and perhaps with different linguistic terms), systems-thinking has surfaced to allow us to think about our way of thinking about situations.

Systems-thinking is now a mature area of research. For some people it is a discipline on its own which can even contribute to the development of other disciplines in social science and other areas. This claim is still debatable for a number of reasons, one of them being that systems-thinking imports ideas from other social science disciplines whilst still benefiting them, making this claim unnecessary or unpractical for the purpose of contributing to knowledge. To some people the claim still holds because some developments in systems-thinking could provide insights for other disciplines' developments. One of these developments is what has been called 'pluralism' or 'complementarism'.

Pluralism or complementarism means that in systems-thinking there is a variety of frameworks that would support the use of different systems methodologies and methods to intervene in situations. As long as we are aware of the theoretical assumptions of methodologies and methods, we could combine them in practice with a view to improving people's lives. The debate is insightful, but claims to what is the true approach to pluralism seem to have taken it to areas in which practitioners might not find it useful or relevant to spend time. In our experience and considering that we are dealing with a complex global phenomenon such as the information society, it is better if we use a variety of methods and methodologies according to what we think are relevant phenomena in the information society (transformations, engagements and unintended consequences), and learn from this use. This is the strategy of this book and we hope that our reflections will inform other developments in systems-thinking.

Therefore this book provides contributions to systems-thinking that arise from the practice of using a number of systems methodologies and methods. A methodology contains principles and a method defines steps to be followed (Midgley, 2000). These are used to promote thinking and action in the information society. With methodologies and/or methods we address the issues of concern about the information society whenever possible. We consider phenomena of the information society and present our ways of thinking and acting upon them.

In using systems methodologies and methods, we also want to address a number of challenges that have arisen from our experience in practice. In our view, these challenges have little to do with pluralism or complementarism; they have to do with working with people who are not systems thinkers and often would disregard the use of systems methodologies and methods at their full length. These people are normally busy, under different pressures and often with an understanding of the information society which is not their own.[1] At different levels (senior, middle or junior) and in different types of organizations, people have to plan and do things to react to the information society without fully realizing its impacts. Issues of concern about the information society make us consider a number of possibilities to improve systems-thinking practice.

## Possibilities to Improve Systems-thinking Practice

At the heart of systems-thinking as a discipline today, there is the idea that things are interrelated, and that any situation can be better understood as being part of a context (wider system). Different elements (human and non-human) influence and are being influenced by the actions of those people involved and affected. Systems-thinking can be used to address societal problems (Midgley, 2000), and this book is an attempt to go in this direction. There are a number of key challenges for systems-thinking to consider in relation to how systems-thinking is currently developing:

- *Language*. The language of systems-thinking can often be confusing and not engaging. Efforts need to be made to make systems more available to 'lay' audiences. For instance, and in a way contradictorily, some developments in complexity theory or applied systems-thinking in the last few years have become very sophisticated whilst at the same time difficult to understand. The language of 'holism', 'process philosophy', 'meta-methodology', 'pluralism', 'edge of chaos', 'variety' and other terms needs to be translated into friendlier, simpler and appealing terms.
- *Methodological focus on 'problem solving'*. Systems-thinking is now a victim of its own success. In areas like operational research and information systems, the idea of a system is becoming popular to help structuring problems, and with it, contributing to their solution. But systems-thinking has much more to offer; it also offers a way of looking at the whole world and by doing so it brings a number of imperatives on how to improve situations.
- *Time*. Many audiences (including those of practitioners) do not have enough time, resources or authority to commit to long periods of work or to make decisions. Time is also an issue where systems thinkers need to 'leave' their context of practice.

## The Purpose of This Book

Considering the above account of the information society in terms of phenomena to be observed, emerging issues of concern and possibilities to improve use of systems-thinking in practice, the purpose of this book is not to offer very descriptive, unattainable or impractical descriptions of both the information society and/or systems-thinking. Rather, it is to show how existing ideas and methodologies in both of these camps can be combined to inform the practice of different audiences including those of information systems practitioners, policy makers, systems thinkers, managers and citizens (yes, there can be a practice of citizenship too!).

We propose to guide the use of systems-thinking by thinking about ways in which the information society can be developed. These ways will be called 'patterns'. A pattern is *a set of assumptions, beliefs and ideas which inform the thinking behind the definition of any improvement in society.* It is not an entirely philosophical or theoretical concept. It is rather a way of thinking which aims to bring elements from the context in which it is used. From our thinking, action follows, and therefore a pattern influences the types of actions we develop in our practice.

We think the idea of patterns can help us to understand better the ways in which the information society is being developed across the globe. A pattern of thinking can also be shared across governments, institutions, groups and individuals. Its level of abstraction does not preclude anyone from reflecting about it. Neither does it preclude the possibility of linking our thinking with the ways in which we apply systems-thinking and helping improve the information society developments. Throughout the book we will identify a number of patterns that we think guide these developments, and examine their strengths and weaknesses in dealing with the above challenges in the information society. This will mean articulating ways of using systems ideas and methodologies to support the practice of different audiences.

## The Structure of the Book

With the definition of patterns that guide implementation of information society initiatives and thus could guide the use of systems-thinking methodologies and concepts, it should be clear to readers now that we are proposing a 'middle ground' use of systems-thinking (between theory and practice) to address the information society. We would like to convey ideas in a simpler and friendlier way than just theory or practice alone, and use these ideas to inform practice in government, information systems and technologies or academic professions.

Chapters 2 and 3 provide an overview of the information society and systems-thinking so that those in charge of policy formulation and implementation can guide a more detailed appreciation of issues of concern and possibilities to improve. Both of these chapters provide a historical account of the information society and systems-thinking in information systems which shows a number of discontinuities and possibilities. Readers interested in government or policy formulation can gain an appreciation of some of the perspectives adopted about society from information society and systems-thinking lenses.

Chapter 4 provides an account of applied systems-thinking. It reviews a number of systems methodologies that facilitate the identification of stakeholder perspectives prior to the selection and implementation of (systems) planning approaches. The review is made with consideration of phenomena in the information society (transformations, engagement, unintended consequences), issues of concern (economic focus, dominance of expertise, thinking inside organizations, leaving out values), as well as opportunities to improve systems-thinking practice with some challenges in mind (complex language, focus on problem solving, time).

In order to build a common ground to inform both systems and information society practice, Chapter 5 introduces the identification of patterns of thinking. It presents an 'idealist' pattern to help in the transformations required. The pattern suggests developing visions and supporting transformations related to the information society. The use of this pattern can help to 'kick off' initiatives and gather stakeholders around a common goal (implementing a vision). Systems methodologies can support the formulation and re-definition of a vision, giving people opportunities to learn about the development of plans to take a vision to completion. Some experiences of using systems methodologies under this pattern of thinking are offered.

Chapter 6 presents a strategic pattern of developing the information society which considers the issue of engagement in the information society. The pattern can help us establish dialogue and participation of stakeholder groups at different levels of formulation and implementation of policies and plans. Examples show how systems methodologies can help us to structure dialogue and participation activities and link these with the development of plans to bring about the information society. Here the challenges of applied systems-thinking are discussed and used to generate the possibility of considering systems-thinking as a form of generating knowledge that needs to co-exist with other forms that belong to a particular context of intervention.

Chapter 7 introduces ideas from power and ethics in order to articulate a more grounded type of thinking pattern which would enable critical reflection about ethics in the information society. By doing so, it can help combining previous patterns. Within this pattern we need to consider phenomena of unintended consequences in the information society. Doing this will lead us to suggest thinking about issues of *power* that in our view cannot be separated from ethics. This is important because these and other perspectives influence and are influenced by relations among people, something that we have discussed as a key element in the information society. A focus on relations will allow us to suggest new ways of developing critical thinking about using systems methodologies, and to reflect on the ethics of bringing improvements in a particular context of intervention. This is suggested as an area for further research in both the information society and systems-thinking.

Chapters 5, 6 and 7 conclude with some reflections from practice. It is important to offer practitioners our own account of how the use of each pattern can help practice. We revisit the challenges laid out for systems-thinking in each of the chapters and we give our view of other issues that emerge.

Chapter 8 defines a framework for the use of different patterns of thinking in systems practice. The framework facilitates the use of systems methodologies in future practice in the information society. It also helps people to define the sort of individuals they want to become in such a society.

Chapter 9 concludes the book by presenting implications for the use of patterns, and a number of doubts, hopes and ideas for the future of systems practice and the information society.

Each chapter offers a number of objectives to be achieved, examples from practice, a chapter summary, key messages and questions or exercises to help the reader reflect on and use the chapter's content. In some chapters we also include a further reading list.

## Chapter Summary

This chapter has introduced the information society as a context in which there are phenomena of transformations, engagement and unintended consequences in the use of information systems and technologies to improve the quality of life of individuals. A number of issues of concern have also been identified. These are:

- economic focus
- dominance of expertise
- thinking inside organizations
- leaving out values.

Systems-thinking is a set of ideas and methodologies that help people tackle complex phenomena. It could help to address the information society, and in doing so it can also gain insights as to how best it can be used in practice. The use of systems-thinking and methodologies implies challenges to be considered in practice. These challenges have to do with the language of systems, a focus on problem solving and time. We will explore these in more detail later on.

## Key Messages

- The information society proposes a new 'order' based on the use of information, to improve people's quality of life, but the definition of such quality is left to experts.
- Engagement by practitioners with different phenomena is required to improve the ways in which the information society is developing.
- In the use of information systems and technologies, we need to consider potential consequences. That can be developed if we consider the information society as a whole system with different phenomena being interrelated.

## Questions / Exercises

- Which of the issues of concern described about the information society do you find most relevant? Why?
- Are there any other issues of interest which you think need to be addressed? For example, generational, cultural, legal, etc?

## Further Reading

Castells (1996) presents a thorough overview of what he calls the 'network society', a new order in which the production of knowledge becomes the main asset of societies. This has influenced definitions of the information society in the policy-making arena.

# 2 The Information Society

The information society is a complex phenomenon. It did not emerge overnight; it has it been with us in different parts of the world for no longer than two decades. We need to attempt to explain it. The purpose of this chapter is to account for its following phenomena: (a) *transformations*, (b) *engagement(s)* and (c) *unintended consequences* as presented in Chapter 1. In describing these phenomena, we will revisit a number of challenges for information systems practice so that readers could gain a better appreciation of the things they have to deal with when engaging with information society initiatives, plans or projects.

Some current perspectives about the information society describe it as a revolutionary change, a type of change that appears to stay due to the conception of information as an asset in the lives of individuals. Other perspectives regard the emergence of the information society as a continuous change which can be shaped; in these accounts the claim about information as an essential commodity in societies is diminished. A third possibility is that of seeing the information society as a by-product of a number of interests and possibilities, in which the paths to follow are uncertain in terms of opportunities and constraints (Mansell and Steinmueller, 2000). These possibilities need to be considered in the light of where we think action can be taken forward (at the level of policy, at the level of organizations, at the individual level, or maybe at all these levels!).

## Objectives

- To appreciate a historical account of the emergence of the phenomenon called the information society from three different perspectives, including those talking about radical transformations, those emphasizing engagement, and those accounting for unintended consequences in the development of plans, projects and initiatives.
- To offer guidance as to how these perspectives can help address challenges of the information society.

The chapter starts by describing the general context of society today as a result of technological developments related to information and its communication between humans or machines.

## Communication Technologies and Information Today

Today, the capacities of mainframes of the 1950s and 1960s can be well emulated by a powerful *personal computer* if not by an enhanced mini computer. Computers now can process large amounts of data in practically nanoseconds. It has been calculated that since the 1980s the cost of computers has reduced by a factor of 8,000 and the time taken for one electronic operation has fallen by a factor of 80 million. Nowadays, computers are seen as part of our lives, and the *information* they store has become invaluable. From our bank account records to financial statements; from family pictures and videos to key work documents; from software packages that we use in our work to those that we keep at home for entertainment purposes. The computer is a key device to help us manipulate information.

But where did the term information come from? How did we become used to thinking that information is a key element of our lives? How did the worldwide information society emerge?

## Origins of the Term 'Information'

The term 'information' has been loosely associated with things that we can know or need to know. One of the first appearances of the term was linked to communication processes. Shannon (1948) developed a mathematical theory to explain how communication transmits information in channels and suggested the possibility of quantifying information.

For Shannon, information becomes a measure of 'possibilities' of messages that can be encoded, transmitted from a sender to a receiver in a particular channel and decoded (taking into account noise in the channel and in the transmission). Information can be quantified in terms of 'bits' being effectively selected and transmitted from a range of possibilities, for instance "… a device with two stable positions, such as a relay or a flip-flop circuit, can store one bit of information" (Shannon, 1948: 380). The association between communication and information gave information a subordinate character to ensure communication in the light of potential sources of noise. As Shannon (1948) argued:

> The fundamental problem of communication is that of reproducing at one point either exactly or approximately a message selected at another point … The semantic [meaning] aspects of communication are irrelevant to the engineering problem [of ensuring adequate communication of a message].
>
> (p. 379, brackets added)

Concern with information at that time was not about the meaning of information. Shannon's model of communication leads to a model of communication processes as suggested in Figure 2.1.

Figure 2.1 shows how communication was conceived of as a process, and how for people like Shannon the main concern was ensuring the accuracy of transmission rather than interpreting the message being transmitted. Information then became associated with a measure of the number of possible messages to be transmitted (all possibilities being equal) through a communication channel, in other words with a measure of one's freedom of choice when selecting a message, "… all choices being equally likely" (Shannon, 1948: 379).

Despite focusing only on the accuracy of transmission, Shannon was talking about 'freedom of choice', for people communicating. This possibly means that individuals could have more choices to communicate and transmit any type of message to other people. Historians of the information society can see that this attempt to give freedom of choice to people has been repeated through time. Individuals could enrich their knowledge, and ultimately their lives, with the information being transmitted, contributing to and being impacted by society as the medium in which knowledge was to flourish.

## Transformations

No doubt Shannon's ideas were very influential and are still relevant us today. Advances in data (information) processing use the concepts of feedback and control to facilitate connection of computing and networking systems. During the late 1940s and 1950s, a similar development

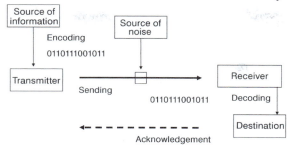

*Figure 2.1* A model of a communication process

took place when scientists engaged in studying and modeling communication processes in human beings, animals and machines. Among other things, this would lead later to the development of cybernetics, which would apply to management,[1] the implementation of communication networks leading to the birth of the internet, and the availability of a number of automated control systems in industry powered by autonomous and intelligent computers. Communication is also with us today when better systems are designed to facilitate interaction between humans and machines.

In particular, the notion of information and the availability of technologies to process it was to be used to imagine a new type of society.

### Transformations in Japan

According to Masuda (1980), Japan was one of the pioneers of the information society. During the 1970s, the government established a nationwide initiative to facilitate the exchange of information between people and public institutions. The initiative contained a number of projects in different areas of activity. With the advent of new technological advances, it was considered that society needed to transform itself in order to accommodate them.

By enabling continuous information exchange, it was said that society could reach a state of *flourishing* of human intellectual creativity, instead of simply catering for the affluence of material consumption. A new type of society according to Masuda (1980) would be one "where people may draw future designs on an invisible canvas and pursue and realize individual lives worth living" (p. 3). Individuals would be able to access information to make their lives more rich, interesting, innovative and productive.

The Japanese initiative set up key projects, many of which were ahead of their time. Projects included: (1) an administrative data bank to share statistics between government institutions; (2) development of an automated transportation networks to serve citizens and businesses (by supplying materials and products); (3) a regional remote control medical system; (4) a computer-centered educational school; (5) a management information system to support small businesses; (6) a training initiative to support staff development; and (7) an aid initiative to bring computers to developing countries (Figure 2.2).

This initiative was inspirational in portraying a new type of society: one in which the quality of life would be improved. With the information society, Masuda (1980) foresaw by the year 2000, "there will be a personal terminal in each household, used to solve day-to-day problems and determine the direction of one's future life … the goal would be for everyone to enjoy a worthwhile life in the pursuit of greater future possibilities" (pp. 39, 33). This was to bring profound transformations in the lives of individuals. They would not only be able to participate in a space of information flows but to fulfill their own needs as human beings, which included contributing to the success of projects.[2]

Information society projects in Japan (commenced 1972)

| Name of project | Degree of realization (1980) |
|---|:---:|
| Administration Data Bank | ◯ |
| Computopolis Plan | ◐ |
| Broad Area Remote Medical Care Systems | ◕ |
| Computer-Oriented Education in an Experimental School | ◖ |
| Pollution Prevention System in a Broad Region | ● |
| Think Tank Center | ◖ |
| MIS for Small Enterprises | ● |
| Labor Re-Development Center | ◯ |
| Computer Peace Corps | ◐ |

● Already realized   ◕ In practical application   ◖ In model tests   ◯ To be undertaken

*Figure 2.2* Initiatives in the Japanese information society

Masuda was envisaging an *organic* type of society, able to quickly, flexibly and appropriately respond to environmental changes thanks to the commitments and energies of its citizens. This society was to generate *feed-forward* loops showing new opportunities to define and pursue individual goals towards self-realization. Communication channels would allow individuals to learn from each other, their achievements and mistakes, and decide on better ways to live their lives, as they possessed a stock of knowledge to help them in their affairs.

The new view of society had to do with transformations which were characterized by:

> a span of time during which there is an innovation in information technology that becomes the latent power of societal transformation that can bring about an expansion in the quantity and quality of information and a large-scale increase in the stock of information.
>
> (p. 49)

In Masuda's view, societal transformations have to do with seeking new sources of growth and responding to environmental changes, the main one being the availability of information through technological advances; information was to be a key resource that would enable societies to get to know their environment and to design ways to facilitate individuals' adaptation to it.

In the West, together with advances in technology, transformations were to take place by the economic quantification of information (Porat, 1977), and by an emerging concern with the contribution that technology and information as commodities could provide to national economies.

### Techno-economic Transformations in the West

In the West, Perez (1983) was one of the first to provide us with some ideas of the dynamics and interplay between economic, technological and institutional changes in society as a possible alternative to explain how the information society as such was developing. An organic expansion view of society as foreseen by Masuda was replaced by one of cycles of disruption and accommodation in the creation and use of technologies. Instead of an 'epoch', we had several components interacting together in a techno-economic paradigm.

There were a number of key components of a techno-economic paradigm in Perez's (1983) account:

- A *key factor* is a technological advance which is perceived as having low and descending relative cost, with unlimited supply for all practical purposes, with potential all-pervasiveness. The key factor has a capacity to reduce the costs of capital, labor and products as well as to change (Perez, 1983: 361). A key factor appears in the downswing of economic (Kondratiev) cycles as a response to the 'exhaustion' of previous technologies, which leads to its widespread use. Perez saw the 'microelectronics revolution' during the 1980s as a key factor that would then determine a new economic upswing and a corresponding social and institutional set of transformations.
- A *technological style* is a form of organization based on the use of technological factors which becomes 'best practice' (Perez, 1983: 361) and challenges the existing array of technology use for economic and social purposes. The micro-computer enabled the emergence of forms of organizations based on distributed data processing, which challenged other ways of processing and working (e.g. mainframe based).
- *Investment patterns* appear when economic resources are shifted from areas best adapted to the 'old' technological style towards those most amenable to the new style. The key factor is then incorporated into a number of areas of economic activity. Some of these areas include those of research and development, others of technology dissemination or recombination into products and services.
- An *upswing* is a situation characterized by changes in economic, social and institutional spheres around a technological style at local, national and trans-national levels. With new technological styles, changes occur in many domains including occupational structures, the roles of governments and unions, educational institutions and market demands (see Figure 2.3).
- A *downswing* due to emergence of potentially new key technological factors, there are disruptions, because existing institutional mechanisms to support them become obsolete and counterproductive. Investment is needed to find and develop alternative key factors or to boost existing ones which had not generated technological styles.

Perez's account suggests that technological advances bring a number of economic and organizational transformations. A certain type of technology becomes pervasive and is adopted, and its use could (in principle) bring better income, better possibilities for consumption and ultimately better quality of life. Policy makers could look at the different aspects of the above model and take appropriate action by considering 'where' a country's economic system

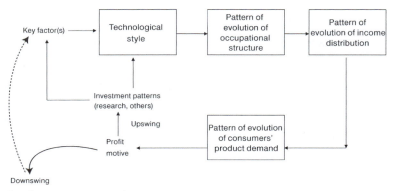

*Figure 2.3* A techno-economic paradigm

and related activities (for instance research and development, or the adoption of particular technologies) might be in terms of an 'upswing' or 'downswing'.

However, in the process of adoption, Perez's (1983) techno-economic perspective does not fully consider the *social* conditions[3] that surround the appearance of key factors and of technological styles other than a drive for profit, as seen in Figure 2.3. Neither is the detailed nature of changes in organizations discussed. To compensate for this, we now offer a brief account of transformations in organizations.

### Transformations in Organizations

At about the same time that Perez proposed the above explanation of transformations in societies (1980s), we begin to notice descriptions of the value of information in organizations, and how information systems and technologies can help enhance such value for the benefit of the customer. Organizational transformations are about flattening of existing hierarchies and structures. Technologies began to be incorporated in profit and non-profit organizations where before they were mostly used in the military sector.

The 1990s saw more widespread use of technologies and restructuration in organizations. The idea of 'value' gained by the use of information became a core concern. To allow value to be gained from information, structures needed to be redesigned and connected to facilitate generation and use of information. Customers became the focus of transformations. As stated by Porter and Millar (1985), the value of information was to be found in customer satisfaction, and to be gained by the use of information systems and technologies:

> The value a company creates is measured by the amount that buyers are willing to pay for a product or service ... Information technology is permeating the value chain at every point ... A company's value chain is a system of interdependent activities, which are connected by linkages ... Every value activity has both a physical and an information processing component ... The information processing component encompasses the steps required to capture, manipulate and channel the *data* necessary to perform the activity.
>
> (pp. 150, 152, italics added)

Interestingly, information and data are used in the same way. What seemed to matter was that people needed to be prepared to share information for the benefit of the business. Organizations would rethink their core activities so they could provide better services and ultimately better value to the customer. And the end product of transformations was aimed to be alignment between technologies, strategies and operations (Henderson and Venkatraman, 1999), and a reengineering of business processes (Hammer and Champy, 1995). For the individual, changes required sacrifice but were to pay off as they could have more autonomy in their work, and possibly more time to do other things alongside keeping their jobs.

Some quality of work life was envisaged but still subsumed within the achievement of competitive advantage with the use of information. The fact that people can be made redundant is the 'price' that we have to pay in order to get our organizations serving their true purpose: that of producing the products and services that the customer wants. The notion of value has gained supremacy at the expense of people, and the fear of 'survival' fuels the use of information technology.

With more sophisticated developments in the field of strategy during the late 1990s and the beginning of the new millennium, the use of information technology has pervaded many organizational activities. The new millennium has seen further developments in the use of information for strategic purposes in organizations. With information being continually available, individuals can generate opportunities for information use, and generate possibilities for organizations to develop sustainable advantages. Generating appropriate information sharing activities requires having organizational environments where the value of information is collectively shared and developed.

To date, it is often still assumed that the purpose of transformations is to help organizations (and people) to gain more from information systems, technologies and related investments so they can better serve their customers. It is also assumed that customers are more demanding by the day. More importantly, it is assumed that people are committed to support organizational purposes (based on gaining and giving value). The meaning of information (or knowledge) is still loosely defined and associated to action to meet organizational purposes. It is supposed that by linking information, value, organizational purposes and technologies, people will also gain (by possibly improving their quality of life). This *narrow* thinking needs to be reconsidered when thinking about plans or initiatives. As will be suggested later in the chapter, this type of thinking requires us to engage with plans or initiatives related to the implementation and use of information systems and technologies in the workplace.

### *The Network Society*

The above transformations seem to be one-sided, and guided by economic concerns only. To account for and justify the diversity of changes that allow transformations to develop, Castells (1996, 2001) proposes a new paradigm called *informatization*.[4] For Castells (1996), it is possible to identify a number of key developments within society, because "technology *is* society, and society cannot be understood or represented without its technological tools" (p. 5). Castells (1996) suggests that more *social* emphasis is now being put in the production of *knowledge*, and that also includes knowledge about knowledge. He says:

> In the new informational mode of development the source of productivity lies in the technology of knowledge [statements of facts] generation, information processing and symbol communication ... [knowledge] is transmitted to others through some communication medium.
>
> (Castells, 1996: 17, brackets added)

With the above, Castells is suggesting that changes are being absorbed in different spheres of society. The physical spaces of production, decision making and participation in society are being shifted, and therefore our view of a society is becoming that of a network. Societies becomes spaces of information flows which travel across institutions, regions, cities and countries, regardless of who generates this information (knowledge is only about stating something). In economic terms, the space of flows enables the generation of knowledge-related products; it also generates producers and consumers. In cultural terms, people can access different types of knowledge in the form of symbols, practices, heritages, etc.

### Engagement(s)

All transformations take place in a particular context. They cannot occur in a vacuum. Historians on the information society stress that the need to facilitate communication and information transmission has taken place several times in the history of humankind. Technological advances (the steam machine, the telegraph, the telephone) have brought changes in the way we work and communicate. This time, with the information society, there is concern with the content of communication. If this is the case, people need to be engaged as it is they (us) who are able to interpret such content, select it and use it in their lives.

The information that has already been available to us has come about because of people and our relationships that allow us to engage with each other and exchange knowledge. To many, information has a social nature that speaks about engagement. It is created in a particular context, used and transmitted. People need to be engaged to create and use information, to make it a social commodity.

People are part of communities in which they engage and interact, driven by particular needs, concerns or interests. Communities could be part of the transformations that information society initiatives drive. They are often neglected but increasingly recognized as essential.[5] As practitioners, we need to engage with people, their relations, their communities, their values.

For Castells, there is a *social substratum that precedes* technological advances and societal changes, whilst being affected by them. There is a set of cultural values, supported by individuals and organizations (including the state) that has helped societies to adopt information technologies and to emphasize production of knowledge as a core activity in the network society. Moreover, technology emerges in a particular cultural milieu, and then spreads its influence to other spheres of society. With technologies being available, other societies can generate new sources of wealth based on the manipulation of knowledge symbols, products and services. They can help their people by fostering opportunities to become part of a 'new' and global economic system.

It is people in communities, organizations and governments who have taken forward visions, plans and policies to bring the information society to reality. It is people who are now using the products of the new knowledge economies. It is people who provide the social substratum that allows these products to flourish. And it is people who can challenge and shape the new types of society that the information society envisages.

In Castells view, the 'new' economic system generated by the information (network) society is in fact a restructuring of the existing one(s). Transformations reinforce existing power of traditional economic and urban centers (nodes), as they attract people with skills and motivation to be part of new spaces of flows. Only a few geographical pockets enjoy the benefits of concentrating jobs and skills. Other places and people need to fight to keep their identity and ultimately for their own existence.

Partly motivated by the above and the potential offered by information systems and technologies worldwide, governments issue policies to take advantage of technology use whilst attempting to diminish potential negative effects of transformations on their citizens. In the US and some countries of Europe for example, policies have aimed at enabling markets of information products and services to flourish, whilst tackling potential exclusions of citizens' groups from access to information or education in the use of technologies. Different strategies have been adopted to implement policies including public and private partnerships to engage with consumers, communities and marginalized groups. Other countries have formulated national plans to make use of information and communication technologies in different industrial sectors. Worldwide, there is awareness of the need to "bridge the digital divide, invest in people, and promote global access and participation" (DOT Force, 2000).

However, the situation is far from resolved. Many people are being left out and the pace of technological change is greater than that of policy making or policy implementation. As Table 2.1 shows, a number of issues arise in the implementation of information society initiatives. Some solutions have been proposed to address these issues.

Table 2.1 should encourage practitioners to engage with initiatives and review their purpose in bringing information, systems and technologies to people, and facilitating individuals'

*Table 2.1* Emerging issues of concern in the information society

| Initiative and region | Issues and proposed solutions |
| --- | --- |
| The Information Highway (US) | The information society is generating processes of 'uprooting' of people from their culture (they are losing their cultural identity). More democratic stances are needed to include people's own culture. Community action is also needed to regain the value orientation of social life and with it the use of information. |
| Liberalization of markets for information services and products (North America) | Organizational structures reinforce inequalities between employees, and the power of some people over others; information should be considered a free commodity to be used by anyone. |
| The information society initiative (South Africa) | Lack of physical communications infrastructure, information access, institutional support to policies and implementation. Gap between 'information poor' and 'information rich' people. Need to generate local policies more sensitive to the realities of the country, and transform institutions to support implementation of policies. |
| Implementation of deregulated markets in Ireland, Italy and other European countries | A 'unique vision' for the European Information Society is proving difficult to implement. The state is now reinforcing and centralizing control over access to information. Institutional transformations are a long way of including technologies to facilitate interaction with citizens. Policy definitions are being left to experts and technology providers. Experts need to be challenged; citizens need to become more active in policy formulation and initiative implementation. |
| Provision of internet access in Malaysia and China | Limited regulatory environment and participation possibilities; access conditions solely driven by free markets or authorities; growing inequalities in the use of internet. More locally sensitive initiatives need development and adequate integration with existing cultures. |
| Development of technological parks in India | Disparities between urban and sub-urban areas where parks are being developed. Exclusion to access and information is dynamic and changes through time. Continuous awareness and intervention is needed to deal with emerging exclusions of people. |

participation in the information society. From the table the following issues of concern need to be addressed when dealing with initiatives or projects aiming to bring the information society to reality:

- *Economic focus.* The majority of initiatives on the information society, or at least the dominant ones in countries, seem to be those aiming to support the development of 'new' information-based economies through products and services. Whilst initiatives might have helped some people, other effects (exclusion) have led governments to consider regulative actions to mitigate some effects including widening the gaps between the rich and poor.
- *Dominance of expertise.* It is the so-called experts in policy making and information technology who have been the protagonists in defining information society plans. This also includes visionaries and people who have predicted radical transformations and who have visions to be implemented across the globe. Whilst the ideas contained in visions are valuable, societies find that their policies, plans or visions often need to be firmed up in local realities and circumstances in order to work and produce expected benefits.
- *Thinking inside organizations.* Information society plans have lacked ways to ensure better and more co-ordinated work between organizations. In some countries, there have been initiatives in areas like education, industry sectors, technology manufacturing, digital content, and infrastructure. However, the dominant thinking is about existing organizations

generating or adopting new technology rather than rethinking how organizations should work more openly with society in mind. In particular, government institutions are acknowledged as inhibiting rather than facilitating changes. Initiatives aim to encourage organizations to generate information-based services and products for consumers, without thinking about non-consumers.

- *Leaving out values.* As reported in Table 2.1, community groups and other stakeholders have raised concerns about the information society initiatives generating fragmentations between groups. In countries where the information society initiatives are well advanced, it is not clear which values are now core societal values to be preserved. In other countries, efforts are made to get in tune with what advanced countries are doing. Local values, practices, and traditions could be forgotten in attempts to focus on catching up with technologies.

The above challenges lead us to suggest that people in general and at different levels need to become more active and engage with transformations in order to avoid being excluded. Exclusion in the information society is not only about being left out from access to information and its economic benefits, it is also about losing one's own identity in society. Engagement is about taking action and using information technologies to support it.[6] About engagement, Castells says (2001: 282):

> 'Why don't you leave me alone? I want no part on your Internet, of your technological civilization, or your network society! I just want to live my life!' Well, if this is your position, I have bad news for you. If you do not care about the networks, the networks will care about you anyway. For as long as you want to live in society, at this time and in this place, you will have to deal with the network society.

The information society is developing worldwide, and we had better engage with it, doing our best as practitioners, policy makers and citizens to include ourselves and others in its development.

How we engage depends on our particular circumstances as participants of our societies. In many societies, engagement is directly related to democratic participation, given that the conditions in such societies allow individuals to voice their concerns openly and be part of decision making activities. This could be the case of Scandinavian countries, in which trade unions and other organizations are empowered to be an important part of decisions. In other societies, some degree of participation is allowed in the form of consultation, and views are gathered to be taken into account in expert-driven processes of planning. This includes, for example, countries where the information society is just starting to be developed.

In other societies, there is neither the interest nor explicit forms of participation for engagement to be considered important. There is no 'tradition' of participation, or participation takes place in different forms which to outsiders could be considered non-democratic. All the above and other circumstances should be considered by practitioners when deciding to promote engagement. As will be seen in later chapters, the use of systems methodologies can help engage people but will never be a substitute for forms of participation or engagement that are rooted in the context where people live.

## Unintended Consequences

It would be difficult to argue that despite the above issues of concern and challenges, most of us as individuals have not benefited from what is happening in the development of the information society worldwide. Thanks to the implementation of electronic and telecommunication structures, the development of intensive markets of information-based products and services and the use of information and communication technologies, our lives have experienced positive change in one way or another. In daily activities, we can send electronic emails; we can talk on our mobile phones to almost anywhere in the world; we can connect remotely through the internet and work whilst at home; we can organize our time; we can book trips, browse and shop around for whatever we need, chat to friends and family and have more choices in getting what we want or need (we can watch a movie at home or in the cinema). Our children are now grasping the use of technologies as if they had been born with them.

However, this positive change has come with a price. Balancing work with life is difficult for some people, as they have to continually interact with others electronically whilst being physically in only one place. Organizations give their employees autonomy but in return expect good performance. The continuous and often desperate search for energy resources becomes part of the agendas of countries, as more people who turn into consumers demand more. With more technologies, there are more demands.

In terms of information, its availability as a resource is valuable but also protective. In some countries, the capturing and digitalization of information has generated concern about its property and confidentiality, and with this a whole new set of activities to ensure protection of information. The economic drive to use information to boost economies has generated parallel or marginal economies based on piracy and misuse of confidential data. The availability of communication channels has enabled people to connect, but also has allowed criminals to find a new market in pornography and child abuse. Again, this might have not been foreseen, but some people are suffering from the unintended use or misuse of information systems and communication technologies.

The above could prompt some skeptics to consider the drivers behind the information society. They would argue that the 'network' idea of a society had existed long before. There are several examples which one could associate with (for instance the telegraph, the telephone, the car). In them, the network view of society (e.g. everyone being connected) could have been conceived as a way of domesticating space and enabling the values of freedom, equality and democracy (even in communist-type societies) mainly to support the development of *economic* systems. With the information society, communication is being standardized, and with this, individuals become depersonalized, becoming 'cogs' in the global economic order machinery. Given the current economic climate where any decision in one country will affect or be affected by other decisions in other countries, we could feel powerless in the face of the changes that are being developed, and conscious of an 'invisible' hand that intervenes in the shaping of the information society. Skeptics would subordinate the information society to economic globalization, and by doing so they would subordinate us to it.

However, to these skeptics it is important to say that changes that have taken place are being influenced by the social substratum of societies and that despite the 'global' nature of the information society there are many different configurations, manifestations, and ultimately consequences which not even those in charge of economic policy or those interested in economic goals had foreseen. It is people, their purposes and their relations which shape and are shaped by technological advances. As individuals who shape such advances, we can become aware of a variety of consequences, and in the midst of them, try to do something about these consequences. Other people who are not so skeptic would suggest focusing on understanding the social stratum that enables the information society to flourish, and working from there to develop gradual changes to incorporate the use of systems and technologies in our daily lives.

The above diversity of views (skeptic, not so skeptic) point to the holistic nature of the information society. Not only planned and expected impacts are generated, but there is a degree of uncertainty about other impacts as being shaped by ourselves. The best thing we could do as individuals who live and work in the information society is to try and appreciate this holistic nature of changes, whilst we still live in their presence by trying to influence them as we see fit. This would mean taking advantage of transformations being developed, engaging with them, whilst we plan for possible consequences that both transformations and engagement would bring to ourselves and our societies. This suggests adopting a holistic attitude towards the information society; to see it as a 'whole system', where different phenomena are interrelated, producing a number of consequences that we need to understand and possibly manage.

## Implications for Practice

Adopting a holistic attitude to the information society would lead us to value and contribute to transformations; to engage with other people in addressing issues of concern related to consequences; and to accept that we will never be able to foresee completely the future of our actions. In other words, a holistic attitude to the information society is about dealing with all these three phenomena (transformations, engagements, unintended consequences) in our practice. It is important to be able to support transformations; to facilitate people's engagement; and to make the best of consequences as we see fit and appropriate. As individuals, we need to continually think on our feet in the information society. This book will suggest ways in which we can deal with all these three phenomena with the help of systems-thinking. The information society is what we want it to be.

If we adopt a holistic attitude, it might be possible to learn more about the information society. Figure 2.4 suggests a map of the information society as a system in which transformations, engagements and unintended consequences interact together. We can be part of that system and part of the information society development worldwide. The system considers particular circumstances of the context in which we are interacting and considers us part of it.

Figure 2.4 summarizes the description of the information society that will be used in the rest of the book to guide the reader in dealing with different phenomena. Both information technologies and the social substratum (left-hand side of the figure) generate opportunities and challenges to improve the information society. These opportunities and challenges will be further explored when we talk about dealing with transformations, engagements and unintended consequences (right-hand side of the figure) with the use of systems-thinking.

## Chapter Summary

This chapter has presented an overview of the development of the information society. With this review we have come to appreciate the complexities and issues that emerge when humankind develops new ways to communicate and manage information (whatever the meaning of information is).

We have also identified three different phenomena which are related to the information society and which deserve our attention. First, the information society brings a number of transformations (social, economic, cultural). These transformations take place as a 'new' societal order is promulgated. Within these transformations, a dominant view of information (or knowledge) is that which subsumes it under communication to meet certain purposes (profit, contribution, value). People and their concerns need to be included more explicitly when designing ways of transforming our societies to become information-based.

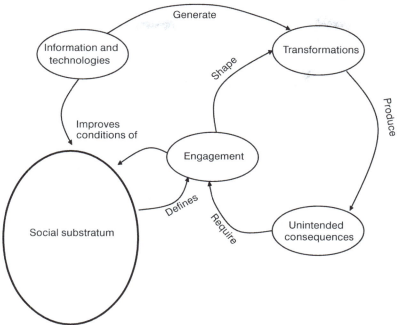

*Figure 2.4* The information society as a 'system'

Second and following from the above, each of us as people living in information societies has the possibility (and responsibility) of engagement with these transformations. Not engaging with the information society means not participating, and possibly being excluded or not taken into account. Engagement can take different forms, and is commonly associated with political action. In contexts or countries where participation and engagement cannot be seen with a political or democratic lens, we need to look for alternatives. Whatever the case, if we want to make the information society our own, we need to engage as practitioners, policy makers or citizens.

Third, a number of unintended consequences have been put forward as a result of the development of initiatives to bring the information society into place, technological advances, or ultimately societal dynamics. These consequences lead us to think that we need to be more holistic in appreciating not only benefits or negative impacts of the information society, but also other things that escape our thinking. We need to see what we can do about change within its dynamics. These dynamics are complex and it would be very difficult if not impossible to manage them. We would need to understand these dynamics and act within the realm of our possibilities.

Given the above phenomena, the book will now proceed to review systems-thinking as a discipline which also describes society as a 'whole' system, and provides ways in which we can use systems-thinking to improve societal situations. These two themes will be explored in the next two chapters.

## Key Messages

- The information society is the result of a number of developments in the use of information and communication technologies (ICTs) together with the emergence of 'information and knowledge' as key assets.
- Transformations, engagements and unintended consequences together relate to produce the information society as a continuous process of change in societies.
- The 'network society' is a latest manifestation of societal change.

## Questions / Exercises

- How do you think the information society brings quality of life to people?
- Which of the above phenomena (transformations, engagements, unintended consequences) do you think dominates nowadays in your society?
- Based on these phenomena, find some examples of policies for the information society in a particular country. Which of the following aspects do they emphasize or take into account?
    technological and economic transformations
    social dynamics
    inclusion
    participation.

## Further Reading

Mansell and Steinmueller (2000). This is a comprehensive review and critique of developments of the information society. Mansell (2002) presents other interesting cases about how the information society is unfolding worldwide.

# 3 Systems-thinking

In the previous chapter we have described the information society as a 'whole' system in which phenomena of transformations, engagements and unintended consequences were identified as important. But where did the notion of a 'system' come from? Can this notion be used to improve our understanding about the information society?

This chapter presents systems-thinking as a set of ideas and theories which have helped individuals to understand the world around them through different times in history. In saying this, we have to highlight that there are more detailed accounts of the history of systems-thinking and we do not aim to substitute any of them. Rather, our aim is to show how we can use some of these ideas to deal with transformations, engagements and unintended consequences in the information society.

We use the term systems-thinking to describe a 'whole' body of knowledge, which also means not only thinking about situations, but also acting on them. Therefore, the ideas identified will lead us to highlight a number of implications and challenges for practice. These have to do with how we use systems-thinking and what we expect to achieve. This is part of the ethical commitment that systems-thinking brings with it.

## Objectives

- To gain an appreciation of the origins and development of systems-thinking.
- To identify a number of current challenges that systems thinkers will have to deal with when it comes to thinking and acting in the context of information society initiatives.

## By Way of Introduction

In our daily life, we often complain about transport, pollution, insecurity, war and, recently, about economic recession issues. Often we find ourselves saying: "It is the system that needs to change", without reflecting in depth on what we mean by the word 'system'. We often associate it with how we organize the delivery of public services, the operation of markets, and the use of information and communication technologies (ICTs). The language of systems is part of our daily language. But where did these ideas come from? What do we think about a system when we use this notion?

It is difficult to point out exactly the origins of our thinking in terms of systems. But we can trace some ideas to Plato and Aristotle. From them we know that after humankind decided to seek explanations about the universe beyond mythology, man became part of a universe, and both were seen as 'whole' and interdependent systems, composed of parts whose interaction was to produce harmony. There were some differences between human beings and their surrounding environments, but it was acknowledged that in the cycle of life these were to progress towards their self-realization as beings.

The view of things as 'wholes' transcended explanations about physical phenomena and was taken forward to account for the formation of collectives (cities), and the role of individuals in them. We also see that cities were conceived of as organized systems in which different people (politicians, tradesmen, and the military) performed specific functions in order for such systems to survive. Failure in the operation of any of these elements could lead the city to be thrown into chaos or less appropriate forms of government rather than democracy.

Individuals were also encouraged to look after themselves as 'whole' living systems, so that harmony between body and soul could be maintained and human beings could achieve happiness. We see now a purpose for humans as systems, as society had a purpose of enabling them to achieve it collectively. Socrates (Plato's hero) speaks about caring for oneself as a condition to being able to care for others. Care was to take different dimensions from the physical to the intellectual, the spiritual and the political.

The interdependence between elements of a 'system' can also be seen in the East, where philosophies like the Ying and Yang portray opposites as complementary: Day and Night, Cold and Hot, Good and Bad. There is *interdependence* between things (they cannot be separated) as Figure 3.1 shows.

What is interesting about this interdependence between parts of a system is that it produces something new that cannot be brought about by only one part. For instance, a full day is produced by daylight and darkness. A full day means balance between both. It is not enough to think of only one part, or how it affects the other(s); we need to consider the whole of the system and the whole of relationships between parts to produce the whole. The co-production between parts has been described as the emergent properties of a system, what a system does or its teleology.

A common trait in the history of systems-thinking is that it emerges as a *reaction* to thinking that is focused on single causes and effects, what people regard as *mechanistic or reductionist thinking* because it mechanizes reactions to causes focused on effects. In both the East and the West we see that time and time again people stress the importance of balancing such reactions by promoting more holistic behavior so that as a result, individuals can live harmoniously in society and be recognized as 'good' individuals (citizens included). In ancient Greece, it was said that failure to achieve balance would convert individuals into machines, driven by passions,

*Figure 3.1* Interdependence of the Ying and Yang

vices or bad habits. Excessive mechanistic-thinking in one's own life would lead to vice and thus act against the soul, and ultimately against society as a collective system to fulfill people's needs. Systems-thinking was to appear again to react against excessive mechanistic-thinking in science, and also to explain how the world out there was transforming itself. We now move to a different time in history in which this reaction appeared again.

## Rationalism and the Loss of the 'Soul'

According to Kapra (1997), excessive trust in the Cartesian and Newtonian ways of thinking – which aim to explain things in terms of cause–effect and divide something to be studied into smaller parts, was depriving science of its more holistic, uniting and perhaps more humble attitude to what human beings were observing and explaining. In the Middle Ages, the emergence of scientific disciplines and awareness of their successes was driving scholars to discover regularities and laws that allowed them to predict different types of phenomena. Thanks to the availability of knowledge, new worlds were being discovered and new machines were being invented. We know of the success achieved by engineers like Leonardo da Vinci, and interestingly we also know of his success in arts.

Later on in history, romanticism became a reaction to the notion of human reason as a capacity to discover and predict. This was a new type of mechanistic thinking. Kapra (1997: 21) summarizes this by quoting William Blake, a poet and painter of the English Romantic movement, who said: "May God us keep / From single vision and Newton's sleep". Blake's plea was to avoid reducing a phenomenon to be studied to its constituent parts; it was called *reductionism*. With reductionism, it was argued that the essential nature of things as 'wholes' would be lost.

Systems-thinking became a reaction to reductionism and an invitation to think of knowledge as a joint creation by different elements. For example, the German philosopher Immanuel Kant examined how knowledge was being produced and concluded that reason could do well with (and needed) a number of other aspects (for instance knowledge categories) so that knowledge could be considered a new 'whole' element. Moreover, knowledge production and life in general should have a purpose, and for Kant it was that of treating every man as an end, not as a means.

Kant's ideas were part of the philosophical movement of the Enlightenment. As an invitation to 'dare to know', it was taken forward in many different ways. Activities of knowledge generation could then be undertaken in either reductionist or 'systemic' ways, given that the claim to knowledge could generate insights using any of them. These ways are with us today. If we think about the information society, a systems-thinking view would invite us to look at it as a 'whole' system rather than as a collection of different parts to be studied or improved separately. Following Kant, adopting different ways of thinking about the information society would also mean considering the human being as a means to the ends of society or as an end itself.

The claim to systems-thinking in knowledge generation was to regain importance later on in history with general systems theory.

## General Systems Theory (GST)

In the mid-twentieth century and with advances in science, a similar reaction to mechanistic/reductionist thinking (focusing on the study of parts rather than on the whole) was to be developed by those scientists who observed similar behavior of systems/phenomena in biology, psychology, economics and other disciplines. The result of this reaction was the development of a theory called *general systems theory* (*GST*), pioneered by Ludwig von Bertalanffy. The theory has been a key building block for systems-thinking in the past and in this century. We now present some basic features of the theory.

Von Bertalanffy proposed a theory to explain the behavior of different types of systems, a theory which would become the cornerstone of a new science of 'wholeness'. Originating from his work in exploring biological phenomena, the idea was to describe general properties which could be exhibited by any molecule, individual, living being, organization or society. Von Bertalanffy observed that living systems were in continuous evolution and trying to maintain equilibrium with both their internal and external environments. This could not be described only in terms of causes and effects because of the nature of phenomena. For instance describing human behavior in terms of stimulus and response was proving inadequate in some cases where people reacted differently to the same stimulus. Working towards maintaining 'equilibrium' implied for systems a continuous exchange of energy between their constituent parts, and required them to organize themselves into hierarchies to enable them to deal with different degrees of complexity. Furthermore, systems had exhibited cycles and they were able to reproduce themselves thanks to their own capacities which enable them to self-organize (maintain their identity), reproduce, live and die.

By observing the behavior of such systems as well as by being aware of other scientists' findings, von Bertalanffy (1968) suggested that different sciences were all "forced to deal with complexities, with 'wholes', or 'systems' in all fields of knowledge" (p. 5), and hence some commonalities could be established to enable people to communicate their findings to each other more easily. The claim was echoed by other scientists who welcomed the possibility of facilitating communication between them with the help of a common theory. The main component of the theory was the notion of an 'open system', which von Bertalanffy described as one which (1968: 39, 41)

> maintains itself in a continuous inflow and outflow, a building up and breaking down of components, never being, so long as it is alive, in a state of chemical and thermodynamic equilibrium but maintained in a so-called state which is different from the latter … Thus, living systems, maintaining themselves in a steady state, can avoid the increase of entropy, and may even develop towards states of increased order and organization.

The above portrays systems as entities that can be well defined (for instance molecules or animals) and which are in continuous transformations. Such transformations require them to continue relationships with their environment so as to maintain their own features, in order to allow systems to evolve and/or change.

- In general systems theory, *openness* (or permeability, represented by the dashed character of the systems boundary in Figure 3.2) was considered a key property to enable change to happen. To support this notion of openness, other features included (von Bertalanffy, 1968):
- *Feedback* is about obtaining information from the environment so as to alter the system's behavior. Systems use feedback mechanisms to assess the deviation of their goals according to what happens in their environment as a result of their actions. General systems theory incorporated developments in cybernetics about the use of feedback mechanisms by living beings to change their behavior.
- *Equifinality*: Living systems (using feedback), could reach a desired final stated (often a steady one) in many ways according to different initial conditions. This concept aimed to rescue the idea that systems had a defined teleology rather than responding to a cause or stimuli.

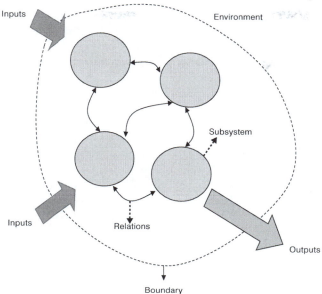

*Figure 3.2* An open system

- *Entropy* is a measure of stability (equilibrium) of a system in relation to its environment. The more negative the entropy, the more order a system has and more stable its environment. Entropy can be measured by looking at information about different 'states' that stability could yield. Information becomes a measure of the 'deviation' from a goal which is obtained by feedback mechanisms.

Using these properties, general systems theory encouraged scientists to observe a variety of phenomena in different areas of science. In their search for systems 'out there', it could be that people decided to look for common phenomena across sciences, or that using the above concepts they could build theoretical models to explain the behavior of more complex systems. Some of suggested phenomena to study included:

- Populations and their evolution.
- Interactions between an 'individual' and its environment (physically internal or external to the individual). Later developments in psychology and psychiatry considered an individual as an 'active personality system' in continuous need of developing such personality in appropriate environments.
- Growth of individuals (e.g. crystals, embryos and societies).
- Information and communication in the interrelationships among 'individuals' of a population. The findings of Shannon's theory of communication (presented in Chapter 2) were seen as a good reference to explore this phenomenon in different types of systems.

With the study of these and other phenomena, systems could then be classified according to their degree of complexity. Some scientists like Kenneth Boulding (an economist) suggested a hierarchy of systems according to their physical structure. Boulding's hierarchy ranged from frameworks (patterns of formation of systems) to clockworks (machine type self-regulated systems) to more autonomous systems (cybernetic machines), self-maintaining and self-reproductive ones (organisms, individuals) and to those with a particular teleology (goal or purpose), self-aware, organized (human beings and societies). The purpose of proposing hierarchies like Boulding's was to challenge scientists own ways of thinking about phenomena, and ultimately encourage them to explore society as a whole.

This echoed von Bertalanffy's claims against a way of thinking that was compelling scientists to "approach everything we study as composed of separate, discrete parts or factors which we must try to isolate and identify as potent causes" (von Bertalanffy, 1968: 16). Equipped with the notion of open systems and their features, general systems theorists were proposing both ways of transforming society (by following the principles of open systems) as well as engaging people (including scientists) in contributing to the betterment of society. Their efforts were to contrast with those of other scientists which continued developing their thinking along the lines of reductionism. The end result is what we have today: two ways of thinking about phenomena. We now present *an example* of systems-thinking applied to the information society.

As an 'open' system, the information society continually evolves, thanks to the interactions within its internal environment (for instance, economical, legal, social activities) and its external environment (other societies, external technology suppliers, community in general).

The information society *produces outputs*, one of which is quality of life for individuals. Some of the system's outputs are intended (for instance providing access to information as a valuable resource). Other outputs might be unintended. These can include for instance, exclusions of sectors of the population from access, the continuous marginalization of groups, or the generation of technological waste as a result of acquisition or implementation of information and communication technologies.

The above unintended impacts can be considered internal to the system, in which case the system's different functions (or subsystems), their purposes and interactions between them would need to be reviewed so as to avoid this inadequate degree of 'entropy'. Appropriate communications would need to be designed to allow appropriate selection and flow of energy and information between systems, to facilitate permeability between them and the external environment.

Alternatively, the unintended impacts can be seen as part of the outputs of the system generated towards its environment, in which case the information society is generating undesirable outputs to its bigger system (society as a whole). This undesirability could mean that the system is far from equilibrium with its 'outside' (the rest of society). To work towards equilibrium and to evolve or change towards its own teleology (or purpose), the system needs to use its own feedback mechanisms, for example the media (Gregory, 2007). Feedback will detect problems and will call the attention of different subsystems (economy, law, education) so as to realign their work and contribute to the achievement of a 'good' or harmonious society as the finality or teleology of the whole system.

Following the above example, it can now be said that the ideas of general systems theory provide useful insights about the information society and its phenomena. In particular, its use could help explain:

- Society as a system that is in continuous change, partly motivated by aiming at or deviating from states of equilibrium in relation to society's environment (what is external to each subsystem such as economic, social, technological).
- Transformations as a result of a system balancing its own internal operations with external demands.

- Engagements arising from the need of systems to balance their internal operations, and include groups of people in society's activities. People could then contribute to improve communication between systems, and to generate other communications for society as a whole to examine itself and improve.
- Unintended consequences arising from the dynamics of the system, in particular of the interactions between its subsystems, which could motivate some people within the system to realign these dynamics in order to fulfill society's overall purpose of aiming to satisfy everyone's needs. Alternatively, consequences might appear to be unintended but be part of the system to reach a desired state of equilibrium in the long term.

These can give us some insights on the nature of change in society, as well as how best to manage it. The ideas of general systems theory have been taken forward and we now explain how.

## GST Taken Forward

After the popularity of general systems theory in the 1950s and 1960s, different developments occurred. The notion of a system and its features inspired people to use them in two ways:

1   For some people the aim was to identify systems 'out there' and thus continue advancing the study of their properties, in order to formulate theories which could help dealing with complex phenomena (including society as a whole). This would include also studying phenomena of self-organization of complex systems.
2   Others used the notion of systems to inquire about situations with the aim of helping people intervene in and improve such situations.

We now turn our attention to these developments with a perspective of exploring how they can contribute to explaining information society phenomena.

### Systems Out There and Self-organization

Using ideas about how systems worked, many scientists engaged in proposing new theories and explanations about them. Developments in biology were followed by those in cybernetics, communication and sociology. The German sociologist Niklas Luhmann proposed a theory of *autopoiesis* to refer to how society becomes organized to deal with complexity. Luhmann was using the term autopoiesis from the biologists Maturana and Varela (whose ideas we will explore later).

Basically, Luhmann (1996) argues that society was the result of the operation of self-production of systems that composed it. For Luhmann, society is a closed system that is composed of autopoietic systems which only look after what is relevant for them and nothing else. These systems are open to their environments (which include other systems), but selectively filter information in the form of communications. These systems are (Luhmann, 1996):

- The Economy
- Politics
- The Law
- Science
- Religion
- Education.

Each of the above systems is only able to 'see' what it is able to recognize, and it uses binary distinctions to classify situations in its own terms. So for instance,

> The legal system functions wherever one works with the schema *legal/illegal*. This schema serves to differentiate a specific kind of acquisition of information; it does not serve, at least not primarily, to find out anything about actions, to explain or to predict them … As a functionally important characteristic, the legal process itself does not decide which cognitions it needs, and it can even make decisions without cognition (e.g. can proscribe denying justice) – just like an *immune system*. The legal system's cognitions are concerned with their *own* complications.
>
> (Luhmann, 1996: 374–375, italics added)

With the above distinction Luhmann suggests that it is not individuals but *communication* processes which enable such self-reproduction. Such communication processes entail not only the act of selecting information, but also uttering distinctions about (expression, action) and understanding (comprehending) it. Through communications, systems maintain a self-referential network so that communications refer to each other and between them they decide what to attend (select, utter, understand) and what to ignore.

In this account of autopoiesis we see similarities with general systems theory. Both describe mechanisms by which systems reproduce and evolve, and how society can be conceived as a continuous by-product of the interactions (in this case via communication) between them. Interestingly though, the role of individuals in autopoiesis according to Luhmann is not prominent. This is different from another variant of the same systems theory to be explored later.

### Potential Implications of Luhmann's Autopoiesis for Practice in the Information Society

For practitioners, the above use of systems notion can lead them to consider the issue of how society evolves and self-organizes. Some researchers have taken autopoiesis ideas to formulate claims or analysis about the excess in self-production as detrimental to society. By this they mean that excessive importance given to one subsystem (e.g. the law, the economic system) by those in charge of society is to the detriment of other subsystems (Gregory, 2007).

This calls for a critical attitude towards the impact of systems in society. Such systems include technological ones, in other words all activities and interconnections between them which promote the adoption of information and communication technologies in society. A critical attitude concerns how they self-reproduce to the detriment of society as a whole. Too much technology could alter the balance of other systems; this can partly explain why technology without education, economic and legal support fails to benefit society.

Other researchers have looked at how organizations exhibit autopoietic behavior. Self-production is conceived of as an appropriate measure of an organization's capacity to survive and adapt. However, self-production can also be detrimental to introduce new innovations, if some subsystems become autopoietic on their own. If we look at organizations as part of a wider system (society), we need to start considering what effects they are causing on other parts of the system (e.g. the community). Again, autopoiesis *as a mechanism* calls for attention to the impacts of excessive self-production on the part of some subsystems. Self-production could be a response to changes in the information society. Furthermore, with the information society as a complex phenomenon, any change could be 'absorbed' by certain subsystems (i.e. economic) to prevail and take control over others.

What then should we do to avoid excess in self-production? Although the role of individuals is not prominent, in Luhmann's autopoiesis there is a mechanism called 'irritation', which is about flagging the attention of different subsystems to respond to what is happening. This would allow subsystems to improve communication between them, and create new ways of interacting together so that they better co-ordinate their action. Through irritations, it might be possible to take action to force subsystems (economic, cultural, legal, etc) to influence each other to bring about change. Some of these 'irritating' communications come from communications that are not binary, for instance those of the media (Gregory, 2007). With irritation, change could be effected in society, and some communications can play key roles there. How we can contribute to irritation from our individual practice (our individual lives) becomes a challenge to address.

For phenomena of transformations, engagements and unintended consequences in the information society, self-production and irritation could become an opportunity. The idea of improving the quality of life could be raised for the attention of different systems. From different types of practice, one could promote action that could be attended at different levels. One could also examine how change does (not) happen, and promote new types of interactions so that we all become attentive to the need for change.

Overall, it can be said that autopoiesis could help us explain societal change. But change is the result of individual and/or collective action. We are part of the systems we observe, and it seems up to us to engage with other people in order to generate useful irritations if we want positive change. It remains to be seen *how* we can do it.

Moreover, it remains to be seen what motivations or intentions drive us to act in relation to change. There is another variant of autopoiesis that makes some suggestions about the ethics of acting as individuals.

### Autopoiesis, Co-ordination, and Love

The original coiners of the word autopoiesis were Maturana and Varela (1987). They studied how biological systems (e.g. the eye's retina in birds and human beings) reacted to environmental changes (e.g. change in the light). What they discovered led them to suggest a theory to explain how human beings have become what we are.

According to them, any change in a living being is pre-determined by its biological structure; the external environment only triggers it. Both system and environment 'couple', which means that their structures change in a congruent manner through time (Maturana and Varela, 1987). These can be seen in Figure 3.3 (Maturana and Varela, 1987: 74) in which a system reproduces its own structure whilst coupling with its environment (internal, external).

In Maturana and Varela's work autopoiesis means that our own biological structures (including our nervous system) condition us to react to certain stimuli, whilst we are also conditioned to ignore others. Maturana and Varela put this claim forward as follows: "… we only see what we see and what we do not see does not exist" (1987: 242). This means that we are prone to see and respond to things we have been accustomed to see, whilst we ignore others.

However, as individuals, we are capable to *learn* as we have done through our biological development. We have learned to speak and to co-ordinate our actions via language, and even to create distinctions of distinctions. Language and co-ordination are vital pillars of being a human being. Autopoiesis at this individual level highlights these pillars as constituents of our nature and essential elements for our interaction with others.

As human beings, we can engage in conversations with others, in a way that our thinking and actions in language predispose us to act according to what we think is (or is not) important. Meaningful conversations and interactions can then be promoted in order to improve our future

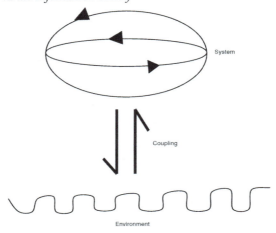

*Figure 3.3* An autopoietic system

thinking and acting about situations. This also has to do with an innate attitude to mutual respect and collaboration (e.g. love) that Maturana and Varela rescue from the history of human beings. Taken forward, this means that we could become concerned about 'other' people (with whom we are not normally) if in our conversations we talk about them or include them (Córdoba, 2002). The result of conversations might be action directed to interact with these 'other' people, as it is in conversations where we define our actions.

The possibility of learning and working together given by autopoiesis has been used in several domains from psychology to computer systems design. In the latter, the important thing is to design computers to enable us to manage conversation breakdowns so that better co-ordinated action takes place between individuals and machines. Breakdowns can also be generated intentionally in conversation in order to enable people to 'see' and talk about 'other' (issues and people) with whom there could be a beneficial connection.

### Applications of Maturana and Varela's Autopoiesis

1    Bilson (2007) uses Maturana and Varela's original ideas of the theory of autopoiesis in order to develop an intervention approach for improving services delivered to patients or those in care. The approach considers that those involved in provision have developed a 'closed' set of conversations in which actions are co-ordinated and defined in particular ways. Given that individuals are autopoietic systems, their own cognitive and emotional structures define how they respond to situations, and this can become a habit. So for instance, the way patients are treated is based on how we conceive them (weak, incapable of looking after themselves). When problems in delivery arise, the existing set of conversations often does not allow individuals (patients, health professionals, families) to see the situation in different ways, or to imagine new ways of conversing (for instance talking about the meaning of quality or how people would like to be treated). The ways in which individuals relate to each other is being pre-determined by their previous history of interactions. Bilson (2007) develops an approach that generates alternative (orthogonal) sets of conversations which challenge previous conversations and thus the ways in which people 'see' and respond to situations. The idea is to develop new emotions as dispositions to act, so that people see the human being behind existing roles (patient, doctor, nurse, etc). Such emotions

would then trigger changes in both the nervous and cognitive systems of those engaged in 'humanitarian' conversations, so they become used to responding differently. The emotion of love as a disposition to co-exist with other people is fostered so that individuals see each other as legitimate others.

2    Using the idea that we converse to produce the world around us, Winograd and Flores (1987) take forward the idea of Maturana and Varela's autopoiesis in order to argue that a new paradigm informing the design of computer systems is required. If we 'create' the world around us in conversations, and we co-ordinate our actions using language, computers should be designed to facilitate such co-ordinations; they should help us to manage 'breakdowns' in conversations when these happen, so that we keep co-ordinations going. Moreover, Winograd and Flores propose that computer software should support the continuous creation of distinctions in language to reflect new actions and areas in which conversations are being formed.

3    In information systems planning, Córdoba (2002) utilizes the idea of 'concern for the other' to facilitate sharing about common issues of concern between people being involved or affected by the definition of information systems and technologies projects. As is often the case, these projects are driven by concerns related to organizations rather than individuals. But it is individuals who are going to implement such systems. By identifying and sharing concerns in conversations, some possibilities to improve the definition or delivery of projects can also be defined. People normally have many concerns in their mind, but the ways organizations are structured force them to be concerned about specific issues (finance, marketing, IT management), forgetting their human nature and their own human concerns. The reader can see more about this application in Chapter 6 of this book.

## Implications of Maturana and Varela's Autopoiesis for Practice in the Information Society

The above ideas and examples signal a possibility for practitioners to work on generating change in society at a more detailed level of action than Luhmann is proposing. This new flavor of autopoiesis lays out a number of mechanisms to promote empathy and concern for 'other' people, which could be considered a more concrete way of provoking 'irritation' at the level of society. By knowing how we operate as individual systems (as autopoietic ones), we can design such mechanisms via conversations, taking into account the importance of emotions as dispositions for action, and the role of language in defining action. We can work by promoting concern for 'others', so that our actions become more co-ordinated with our environment, and hopefully those 'others' become part of such environment.

Thus, as practitioners concerned with the information society and its phenomena (transformations, engagements, unintended consequences), and following the ideas of autopoiesis at an individual or organizational level, we can promote ideas about mutual understanding and mutual learning about changes we experience. We can promote more conversations inside and outside organizations as a way of enabling people to define their own possibilities for the future. We can work under the assumption that we can find common issues of concern to share with other human beings in relation to how we like to live in society. In other words, we can assume more fully that we can operate as a collective, from small groups to entire societies, in which concern for the 'other' is important. These concerns can also include those we have for the role of information systems and technologies in our societies.

This could guide our work in the information society if we conceive of any initiative as being driven by particular concerns and emotions. We could contribute to these initiatives or also promote more 'orthogonal' conversations,[1] with a view to generate interest about 'other' people and other phenomena that initiatives in the information society can address. Concern for people who are being marginalized, or who could benefit from access to information and technologies could be promoted.

However, to some other researchers, concern for the other is only part of a more complex network of relationships among individuals and systems, as some experts in complexity theory have proposed. By adding complexity to the notion of system, they are detaching individuals from their ethical commitments to society as a whole. This is another development from general systems theory. We mention it here with a bias: that of leaving 'ethics' to chance.

### Complexity Theory

A recent development in systems science based on the idea of observing systems 'out there' in which we are also involved is that of complexity theory. Its advocates have seen the importance of self-producing and self-regulating systems in a slightly different way. Among other things, they argue that there are underlying 'structures' that govern the behavior of phenomena, and that such structures enable the self-organization of systems into more complicated and complex ones. As Kauffman (1996) says:

> Profound order is being discovered in large, complex, and apparently random systems … if the forms [natural selection] chooses among were generated by laws of complexity, then selection has always had a handmaiden … If all this is true, what a revision of the Darwinian worldview will lie before us! Not we the accidental, but we the expected.
>
> (p. 8)

This and other claims have led biologists and natural scientists to explain the evolution of species so that the survival of the fittest is in fact the *co-evolution* of species with others. Here the idea of open systems is followed, only the state of equilibrium for a system is continually 'challenged' by apparently abrupt and unforeseen changes in the eyes of those individuals observing the systems. Co-evolution between a system and its environment becomes selective in ways in which systems follow certain paths and not others as a way of self-organizing to survive. Systems need to adopt patterns which fit better with the dynamics of their environments (this is called *fitness landscape*). Despite the fact that these patterns can be for an external observer 'chaotic' and apparently without any order, their emergence can be an indication that systems are to change and evolve.

Complexity theory encourages us to observe things but with the caveat that we cannot see everything, even if we wanted to. Moreover, we cannot foresee the consequences of our interventions in whatever we observe. The most we could do as systems thinkers is use properties and features of complex systems to understand and possibly support change in systems. For the case of organizations, it is not necessary to carefully design or plan change, but rather to foster it when we see it emerging, and to seek 'good' rather than perfect ways of working than are close to chaos (Kauffman, 1996). An organization as a complex adaptive system will find its own ways to self-organize and respond to new or emerging challenges and opportunities. In other words, the most we can do is:

- identify existing patterns as ways of doing things, and question if they are appropriate to be followed or challenged;
- design transition to new patterns;
- stabilize new patterns.

As systems continually change, new patterns of behavior will emerge and an approach like the one just described can be used again. With minimal intervention in systems, they can then self-organize (due to their internal autopoietic structure) and find the best patterns in their own landscapes. If we decide to intervene, we should develop their capabilities to learn and adapt in the face of continuous transformations, and to encourage the incorporation of 'failure' as a way of learning.

### Implications of Complexity Theory for Practice in the Information Society

To its credit, complexity theory brings very refreshing and interesting insights to systems-thinking. Perhaps the most relevant of them is that we do not need to understand everything that happens in a system, and thus we do not need to design detailed plans (or indicators) for change. Rather, complexity can encourage us to adopt contingent strategies to foster co-evolution and fitness in a landscape of possibilities for action, and to continually learn from our mistakes. This can lead managers or those involved in change or seeking transformations to challenge those rationally oriented ways of doing things, and seek instead spaces of possibilities for action to allow systems and their constituent parts to transit to more adequate states according to what is happening in the systems' larger 'landscape' or environment. In this way, social situations and organizations could be transformed by simple but powerful rules that enable co-evolution, fitness with the landscape and other properties of a system to emerge. These rules could include for instance fostering innovation and networking, participation and minimal rules to co-ordinate action among individuals. In a way, complexity theory fosters dialogue, mutual learning and co-existence of people in situations without prescribing what needs to happen for the situation to improve.

Furthermore, complexity theory captures well the existence of unintended consequences of action. It does so by proposing 'minimal' ways of working towards a goal, without compromising other possibilities, and without even fixating those individuals involved into such a goal. Again, this would also mean that people's engagement in a situation should be flexible and not fully dictated by constraining norms of policies. We have to accept the unintended and be able to live with it, or to flow with it. Even well-intended plans can generate catastrophic effects. The information society could turn against us, or it could generate unforeseen positive effects without us planning and delivering them.

However, when it comes to deciding which possibilities, options or patterns are to be followed or fostered according to properties of systems, complexity theory does not give much insight to those people involved or affected. How do we decide what is simple and minimal? Can we live with minimal control rules? How can we manage edge of chaos situations? Should we just wait until the information society as a complex system self-organizes or adapts itself to apparently chaotic situations?

Kauffman (1996) suggests that:

> In hard-conflict laden problems [those which involve several groups of people, with different views about what needs to be done], the best solutions may be found if, in some way, different subsets of the constraints are ignored at different moments. You should not try to please all the people all the time, but you should pay attention to everyone some of the time! Hmmm, sounds familiar does not it? It sounds like real life.
>
> (p. 269, brackets added)

If literally taken forward, the above would mean that in circumstances where many people are to be affected, some 'casualties' can be allowed, as life always bring them. Although this also sounds like real life, a misinterpretation could not be allowed when managing organizations like hospitals, armies or local government with this idea. A system might self-organize most of the time, but it can also collapse or go to 'chaos' if it does not have appropriate learning capabilities. Many information society initiatives require a degree of direction so as to target individuals whose well-being is in danger of being left out in decision making. This speaks about the challenges for the information society that we laid out in the previous chapter of the book. What we have seen so far is the dominance of economic drivers for the information society. Shall we wait until this is not the case anymore, or shall we do something about it?

To some practitioners (including myself), as individuals we can do something about positive change. It is about trying our best, and although we cannot control everything in a system called society, our influence is important if we consider ourselves part of such a system. Our actions could generate some effects. In this book we will adopt a more 'proactive' and ethically driven attitude to the information society. This means that we will focus on learning from 'thinking and doing' in relation to change. We will thus prefer the word 'improvement' to change. This will also lead us to reflect on the issue of ethics in Chapter 7.

### GST: To Sum Up

General systems theory and its subsequent developments bring many insights about how systems work and how they could be analyzed and even intervened at different levels (macro, micro). Moreover, these insights should make us more aware of how our actions as practitioners can generate a number of impacts in society. Unfortunately in many of the developments that use the notion of system, there is a tendency to detach this notion from its ethical implications, in particular when it comes to talking about individuals' responsibility with ethical issues, as Figure 3.4 aims to portray. It seems that the more sophisticated the notion of system we use to enquire about situations 'out there' in the information society, the less able we become to talk about ethical issues.

This should prompt us to think continually about the consequences of our actions, and continually learn about what can be done about the systems we are observing and intervening. We are observers of but also actors in these systems.

We can explain how the information society is transforming society as a whole and how we could engage with it. This is useful, but we need to go further than this. We need more detailed ways of intervening so that we become more active in its development; *ethics as concern for*

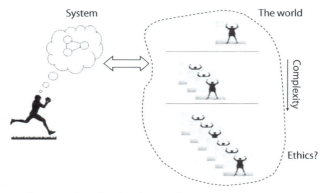

*Figure 3.4* The notion of a system 'out there' and its implications

'*others*' should be at the forefront of systems-thinking, as it was initially the motivation of general systems theorists like von Bertalanffy.

In a different line of development, other systems thinkers talk about the importance of considering our own values as observers and systems scientists in the process of enquiry. We now refer to these.

## Systems of Enquiry

As said before, the popularity of systems analysis based on the notion of a system as an entity out there that could be understood in terms of its openness and its mechanisms or properties has been high. We know of the use of systems-based methods and techniques for analysis in several areas of science and problems. Transportation, prisons, urban development and of course military operations were among others the subject of research projects and efforts. The new science was called operational research (OR).

In very basic terms, operational research uses the notion of a system to map situations in which there is a problematic issue to be solved. Models of a system to contain the issue and reflect the problematic or desired behavior are produced. The best combination of inputs, equations and outputs is suggested to deal with identified problems (Jackson, 2003).

However, for some researchers, and given their experiences of systems analysis in the 1970s and 1980s, problems arose when the system to be engineered is enlarged. Different measures of performance need to be included and accommodated. This is far from easy or free of conflict. Churchman (1968) argues that this is because what we consider to be a measure of performance has to do with what we think a system needs to do (goal). And goals are intrinsically related to human values, in other words to the decision makers and other people involved and affected by the operation of a system.

Having seen a science of 'systems out there' being developed with operational research as well as the above type of problems, Churchman (1968) argued that operational research had become so sophisticated in the use of systems models and problem solving techniques that it had stopped allowing people to ask 'silly questions', including those about what problems were being addressed according to what we think is important. Churchman provided relevant philosophical foundations to use the notion of system as an *enquiring tool*. Our assumptions and values about a system could be entered into a dialectical process of debate. If these survived, they could then guide our decisions.

The notion of a system as a *construction between individuals* was taken forward as a device which would enable them to reflect on what and who else they were considering important in decision making. A shift took place: from explaining transformations in society in terms of systems, to enquiring about/managing such transformations with the help of systems ideas. This shift also enabled interested scientists to engage with others in exploring the complexities of social problems and social designs. It constituted a cornerstone in the development of systems-thinking in some areas of the US and the UK, and we will address these developments in the next chapter.

### Example: Systems, Problems, Values, Goals

- *The policy maker*: We need to do something about the information society. There are problems of access to information and technologies. There are problems about education of people; problems of infrastructure. We also need to set up standards for the exchange and production of electronic information. Have we thought about those individuals who are being marginalized from this enquiry? We need to act now!

- *The systems thinker*: Maybe marginalization is the by-product of how the whole system operates, maybe a symptom with deep-seated causes. Have you considered relations between the so-called problems? What if we tackle access to information and technologies without properly educating people? What if we spend millions in building an infrastructure which will only provide access to certain groups of people? We need to see the connections between these problems. We need to produce 'holistic' plans to tackle all of these at the same time, with a goal of tackling marginalization. We also need to think about the overall purpose of the information society as a system composed of various subsystems (infrastructure, education, access, etc). I can help to see the 'whole' picture of the information society as a system.
- *The philosopher*: How do we know that there are these problems? It is because we can do something about them! We need to consider our own assumptions about problems and solutions. Marginalization is a problem if we decide to see it that way. But what about other problems? And we need to put ourselves as part of the system we are studying, with our own values and assumptions. Only when we subject our views about a system to debate with others we can say we are using systems-thinking.

The above example reflects the shift in thinking. In this line of enquiry with the notion of system, different people with different perspectives about a phenomenon (e.g. a system) should engage in appreciating other people's perspectives. More importantly, this engagement is necessary given that the 'problem' and its 'solutions' as we see them will bring consequences to individuals. Engagement is about inquiring about the values that drive thinking and decision making in plans. It is also about accepting the limitations and implications of our systems-based models, representations or plans.

Churchman and his followers took the idea of a system boundary as value-laden, and therefore in need of debate when it is used in social design. Not only values define what we see as a relevant system of enquiry (e.g. methodology to be used to find about problems and solutions) but also the people who are to be affected by decisions being made on the basis of such a relevant system. The shift in thinking has invited us to become more ethically responsible for our use of systems ideas.

Churchman's followers expanded the use of the concept of systems boundary in methodologies that facilitate inquiry into social design situations. We will expand on them in more detail in the next chapter. For now it suffices to say that values became prominent in systems-thinking. Methodologies using the value-laden notion of system emerged. They include (1) approaches to design a desirable and feasible future; (2) making meaningful improvements in a situation; and (3) challenging established plans or designs in relation to what or who they leave out. These methodologies will be described and used in the following chapters.

### Systems as Enquiring Devices: Implications for Practice in the Information Society

The above shift in systems-thinking brought a new avenue for development of systems research which we see emerging during the 1980s and 1990s. This avenue is still pursued, in particular in the use of methodologies for design (explained later) and the design of ways of inquiring about values, systems boundary judgments. There are a number of implications that we summarize as follows.

First, the use of a value-laden systems idea forces us to accept the impossibility of having an embracing notion of a system which would accommodate everything and everyone in our appreciations or decisions. We have moved from solving problems of a system 'out there' to becoming more aware of the value-content of our views about a system, partly because we might disagree on what the system is or should be/do. The main implication of this shift is that we can use the idea of a system to reflect on values and consequences as drivers of our decisions. Values define what we consider important as well as whom we consider important for such decisions. The adoption of values has consequences for us, decision makers and people involved and affected by such decisions; many consequences will have to be accepted after debate.

Second and in contrast to a possible 'chaotic' nature of impacts in transformations as possibly portrayed by developments in complexity theory (in which consequences are inevitable), we move towards integrating ethical decisions in our plans and designs. For the information society it means that we do not leave everything to chance or to society as a whole. We can take action, provided that such action is the result of reflection, and that it reflects values that we want to promote within the information society. We do what we can as systems thinkers. We play our part. We can still explore what we can do together with other people.

## Challenges to Systems-thinking

The above two uses of systems-thinking can inform our practice in social situations. They can yield different insights; they also yield different implications for practice as explained above. Moreover, they can entice us to take some action about change and the information society in relation to its transformations, its possibilities for engagement, and its unintended consequences. We have argued that the latter notion of a system as an enquiring device can give us a better degree of inclusion for our own values as human beings, and can support actions for those who want to do something about the information society as practitioners.

What we see in common is that these two uses of the systems idea still pose a number of challenges. Similar to the issues of concern about the information society explored in Chapter 2, we see that there is a strong tendency to focus on certain assumptions. We now draw a number of challenges for systems-thinking which we will address in the following chapters. We summarize these challenges as follows.

1   *The challenge of language.* Systems thinkers elaborate on the concepts of 'wholeness', 'relations', 'purpose', 'teleology', 'performance', 'environment', 'self-organization', 'boundaries', and 'values' among others. For audiences that are used to other concepts (i.e. 'functions', 'targets', 'work', 'markets', and others), the language of systems-thinking can be alienating. We need to be aware of the differences in language, and make efforts to present ideas in simpler ways to information systems practitioners, citizens and policy makers among other audiences.
2   *Focus on 'problem solving'.* Methodologies derived from the above two notions have been employed mostly to structure problems and solve them. However, these notions stem from a commitment to challenge mechanistic and reductionist thinking that focuses on single (e.g. economic, organizational) goals. Systems-thinking brings a commitment to act ethically and not only in the interests of a party or group. Interdependence between parts also means interdependence between groups. We should put our best effort to address groups' concerns and incorporate their values in plans.
3   *Time.* Excessive focus on problem solving has also led us to devise and privilege complex and lengthy interventions in social situations. Reality is often far from enabling practitioners and other people to engage for long periods of time and/or to secure resources and action

derived from plans. The challenge is to be part of situations whilst also inviting people to think differently considering the time available.

Together, these challenges pose difficulties but also opportunities for practice. Some of these can be addressed with the help of systems-based methodologies. We will present them in the next chapter.

## Chapter Summary

This chapter has brought a historical review of systems-thinking, leading to identification of two particular notions of 'system'. One of them can be used to look at society, and thus to study societal transformations and suggest how we can provoke them (by irritating different societal subsystems). This is a notion of a system as being 'out there'; a variation of this first notion is the use of features of systems to argue for a more proactive and individual attitude towards change in society, so that we can engage with people in designing together the type of society we want.

The second one is about using ideas of a system to enquire about situations. This is a notion that puts emphasis on values and consequences of decisions for different groups of people. It brings a possibility to be used to engage people in deciding the sort of society they want or find meaningful.

For the information society phenomena (transformations, engagements, unintended consequences) these two notions brings implications as well as challenges for practice. Implications are about opportunities to enhance practice in each of these types of phenomena. Challenges are about possibilities to develop further systems-thinking. We have detailed the former and generalized the latter. For the rest of the book, we focus on the use of the notion of system as an enquiring device to support practice in the information society. This requires working on practice when it comes to dealing with the above phenomena as Figure 3.5 suggests.

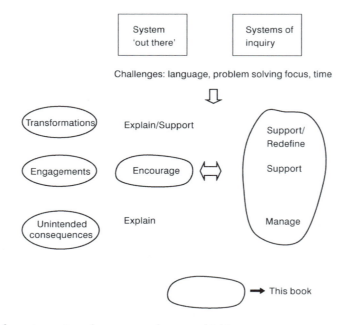

*Figure 3.5* Information society phenomena and systems-thinking

## Key Messages

- The idea of interconnectedness has been with us since the origins of Western thinking as well as in ancient Eastern thinking. Often and intuitively we think in terms of 'wholes'.
- The idea of systems has been developed in a number of ways and different areas. A common root in the twentieth century is that of general systems theory, which put forward concepts of equifinality, feedback, communication and self-organization.
- To date, we have different ways of working with 'wholes'. One type emphasizes properties of systems as existing 'out there'. The other makes uses of systems ideas to facilitate enquiry about values, plans and designs.
- These types of systems notions support dealing with phenomena of transformations, engagements and unintended consequences in the information society. We can provoke change using these notions, but in this book we focus on the use of systems as *enquiring devices* so as to enable practitioners to do something concrete in their own practice.

## Questions / Exercises

- Choose an organization or situation and try to describe it in systems terms using the features of:
  - general systems theory
  - complexity theory
  - autopoiesis (the two versions explored in this book).
- What properties of 'systems' do information systems and technologies exhibit? Use the two types of notions explored in this chapter.
- What other challenges different from the ones explicitly mentioned do you envisage when it comes to using systems-thinking ideas in your own practice?

## Further Reading

Von Bertalanffy (1968). A fully-fledged account of general systems theory, with applications in different areas including biology and psychology.

Jackson (2003). A good historical account of systems-thinking with more detail about ideas on general systems theory and complexity theory.

Maturana and Varela (1987). An ethically grounded theory of autopoiesis.

# 4 Applied Systems-thinking

## Introduction

In the last chapter, two different notions of the word 'system' were explored as potentially useful to inform practice in the information society: (1) that of a system as an 'entity out there' and (2) that of a construction to help us inquire about situations. These two notions have different implications to address phenomena of *transformations*, *engagements* and *unintended consequences*. This chapter details the development in systems-thinking in relation to the notion of a system to help us enquire about situations.

As we said before, the first notion of a system 'out there' could still be used as a way of guiding our observation of the information society with features that include self-organization. This could encourage us to work on provoking what we consider positive change in society. In practice though, we find that it is more relevant to use systems-thinking to enquire about phenomena, and do something about situations with the use of systems methodologies. This is to say, systems methodologies make use of the notion of system as an inquiring device rather than as a vision of the world to be followed or to fit in the information society. We present methodologies to help us deal with situations in which we can contribute to improving society as a whole.

Before we move on to the detail, we clarify what we mean by systems methodology. For systems thinkers, methodology is a way of guiding our *exploration* of the world, using a systems notion as a reference (Jackson, 2003; Midgley, 2000). In other words, a methodology contains principles and ideas to guide action; as described in the last chapter, this action might vary depending on the notion of system (out there, an enquiring tool) and how we use it to support our practice in the information society. The word methodology differs from a similar one: 'method' which is a sequence of steps to obtain a desired result. One can find methods or techniques in each methodology.

Although the above distinction is useful, as mentioned in the introductory chapter, we will use the word methodology for the use of a whole systems methodology or part(s) of it (methods). The reason for this is that even when we use parts of a methodology, we are still inspired by its main tenets. A methodology becomes a way of thinking about situations, something that relates well with the idea of defining patterns of thinking for our practice in the information society.

Systems thinkers have developed a wealth of methodologies to deal with the complexity of situations in social design. Rather than starting from scratch, systems practice is a rich area where people continually develop new approaches in combination with existing ones. Practice in the information society can greatly benefit from this. We aim to enrich systems-thinking with new opportunities to use methodologies in dealing with information society phenomena.

## Objectives

- To extend the use of a system as an enquiring device by offering an overview of systems methodologies in the context of information systems practice.
- To relate methodology use to address relevant phenomena of transformations, engagements and unintended consequences in the information society.

The chapter begins by presenting how transformations in the information society can be supported, re-designed or made more meaningful. This is achieved by using three different systems methodologies: (a) strategic assumptions surface testing (SAST); (b) interactive planning (IP); and (c) soft systems methodologies (SSM). The last two methodologies can also support *engagements* of people in designing improvements for the information society. We can also think of *unintended consequences* in the information society by using the ideas of systems boundary critique; this will lead us later to complement systems methodology use with notions of power and ethics.

## Transformations via Systems Methodology Use

As we said in the previous chapter, after the middle of the last century systems analysis had become popular in countries like the US and the UK. Popularity was also a by-product of using the notion of a system 'out there' in large-scale projects in several areas of social policy. However, this popularity came with a price. Significant failures were occurring in some of these projects, partly because human phenomena and human intention could not just be reduced to fit into the features of systems. In this regard, it seemed that traditional science was aiming to solve rightly the wrong problems rather than defining the right problems to be solved. Definition of the wrong problems had to do with framing them in terms of cause and effect, or functions, leaving out human values, beliefs and meanings. Leaving those out was done in order to 'average' the behavior of systems and avoid the existence of different goals for these systems to serve. Human beings as components of larger systems were being left out.

In consideration of this, the idea of a system as an enquiring device started to gain popularity among scientists' circles and with it the design of methodologies to help us use it. With this idea, practice also became concerned with the implications of human action for people. Methodologies then emphasized defining the 'right problems' to work, in other words in enabling people to discuss the ethics of their decisions.

We now present three different methodologies which can help us in dealing with transformations in the information society. These methodologies can also help us in engaging with people to define and explore possibilities for action to improve developments in the information society. The notion of a system as an enquiring device can help us to identify and talk about potential consequences of actions of our practice. The three methodologies are: (1) strategic assumption surface testing (SAST); (2) interactive planning (IP); and (3) soft systems methodology (SSM).

The first (SAST) supports an already defined (and often desired) transformation or sets of transformations which compose a vision; the second (IP) gives people the opportunity to re-define it by considering how they want to live a better future. The third (SSM) can help individuals to engage in making sense of several transformations to which they find it difficult to attribute meaning and define action to improve a current situation.

The above does not mean that methodologies are only fit for certain purposes, so that for instance only SSM can help engaging people. All these methodologies contain methods which can facilitate further engagement of people, so they can relate their own concerns to what transformations entail and can help them work in shaping up such transformations. After explaining methodologies we present some strategies for using them in relation to the information society phenomena identified in Chapter 2.

## Supporting Transformations: Strategic Assumption Surface Testing (SAST)

The degree of certainty of a proposed transformation for the information society and its related vision can be daunting for managers, decision or policy makers, or information systems professionals. We hear of cases of these people being involved in the re-design of organizations to operate virtually; in the massive incorporation of technologies in the workplace; in the purchase or expensive hardware, communication and software systems; or in the introduction of new regulations to protect electronic information. All of this takes place so that visions can become reality.

Due to the pressure of time and deliverables that is now common in information society activities, these people might not be able think of transformations in terms of systems 'out there', how they should evolve. Instead, they could be faced with lack of insight as to how they and others would react in case a transformation to achieve a vision is defined and implemented. Often, they do not 'own' the transformation; they just make it happen. The information society brings transformations that we as individuals just have to implement or adapt. This is the case for instance of pre-conditions needed to facilitate the exchange of information. This involves setting up communication infrastructures; enabling sharing of electronic information; building centralized and accessible databases; connecting existing systems, or selecting new technologies to be integrated with software applications.

From the work of Churchman in systems-thinking which we introduced in the last chapter, it became important to subject any decision in social plans to dialectical debate, so that if these decisions survived debate against 'other' perspectives, we could be more insightful about the future. The idea of a system as an enquiring device became helpful to make us aware of consequences of decisions in the midst of transformations. Based on this idea (and following Churchman), Mason and Mitroff (1981) developed an approach called strategic assumptions surface testing (SAST). As the name suggests, it is used to identify and test the assumptions that support making or withdrawing from a decision that could bring important transformations to people, so that a 'whole' system of decisions, their opposites, assumptions and consequences is considered. This is the case of new policies, plans and strategies. They are often based on decisions, assumptions and consequences that relate to the needs and intentions of an organization's stakeholders as well as possible futures for them.

SAST allows organizations to identify a variety of options and explore their underlying assumptions about their stakeholders (i.e. the assumptions that give validity to each option). It also allows participants to structure a debate about competing options, and generate new options or assumptions to support their plans.

As is often the case in the information society with transformations, the future is seen as uncertain. There is a degree of gamble and trust in information technology. The expected benefits might not be achieved or fully assessed at all. Moreover, required actions to bring transformations to place might not fall within the realm of information systems professionals, but in any case they need to be identified and managed to ensure that systems and technologies are properly and adequately implemented. Some thinking in terms of connections between different issues needs to be exerted and subjected to reflection and debate so as to help professionals make sense and gain understanding about what is to happen in a transformation.

As a methodology to help thinking about a potential decision (e.g. a proposed transformation), SAST has a number of features as well as steps to be followed by participants. Its features include (Mason and Mitroff, 1981):

- *Adversarial.* When exploring an option, the best judgment of assumptions necessary to deal with a complex problem is rendered in the context of opposition.
- *Participative.* Different groups of people, with their knowledge, need to be involved in exploring the assumptions and implications of possibilities for action in relation to a complex problem.
- *Integrative.* A unified set of assumptions is needed to support any future action plan in response to a complex problem. Such a set of assumptions can be synthesized into a unified whole from opposite options.
- *Managerial mind supporting.* Identification and exposure to assumptions would deepen participants' insight into an organization, its policies, plans and problems.

It is often the case that transformations in the information society have to do with several organizations at the same time. Policies like 'providing universal access for all', or 'increasing the number of internet users' define a new way of living and working. Governments, policy makers and technology experts among other professionals need to evaluate the implications of these and other policies. People at lower levels of management need to 'get on' with transformations that are 'required', some of which are sudden and need swift and rapid implementation. These people need to quickly come up with ways of tackling transformations to prepare to get on with them.

The case of organizations embarking into transformations with the use of information and communication technologies is not that different. Often, the issue of aligning systems and technologies to organizational strategies or *visions* (a more concrete definition of a vision will be presented in Chapter 5) needs people's participation and their commitment. However participation should first enable them to acknowledge how best they can approach transformations, and thus how they can challenge what they and other people know about what has led the transformations to be proposed. Alignment also means aligning thinking about a transformation in the best possible way, so that individuals can make the best of a transformation within the possibilities offered (or required) by it.

In short, SAST could offer people a 'breathing' space given the imminent sets of transformations they have to deal with. In such a space some strategies to deal with transformations, their assumptions and consequences could be defined, so that at least people will be better prepared to face them.

SAST involves the following steps:[1]

- *Group formation.* Groups are formed to enable consensus within as well as difference among them.
- *Assumptions surfacing and rating.* Each group is given an option (a transformation, its opposite, or an alternative) and encouraged to explore the assumptions that would support the option if it goes ahead. The assumption is an affirmation of *how organizations and their stakeholders currently behave and will behave in the future.* In order to facilitate identification of assumptions, at this stage participants are encouraged first to identify as many stakeholders in the option as possible. With an initial list of stakeholders, assumptions are drawn by asking the question: How should stakeholders react in order to make the option 'true' (or optimal)?
- *Debate.* Groups present to each other the assumptions that make their option valid. They are asked by the opposing group(s) to clarify assumptions' meanings and how they consider

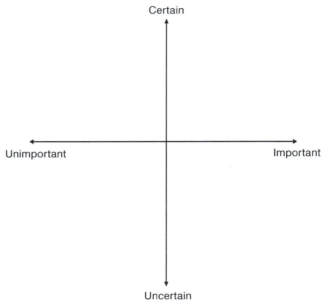

*Figure 4.1* Rating assumptions with SAST methodology

them in terms of two criteria: importance and certainty. Importance refers to how pivotal or essential an assumption is for an option. Certainty refers to how true, plausible or reasonable the assumption is. Groups plot assumptions in the map in Figure 4.1.

Figure 4.1 defines four groups of assumptions: those considered (1) certain and important; (2) important and uncertain; (3) certain and unimportant; and (4) uncertain and unimportant. Each group plots assumptions in each of the quadrants. During debate, groups are asked to justify their plotting. By asking questions the idea is to encourage the groups to review the plotting and produce a list of *certain and important* assumptions, as well as a list of those that are *important but uncertain*, which could be investigated further.

After each group presents their assumptions and receives *clarifying* questions (for instance on the meaning of each assumption), the lists of assumptions from groups is synthesized into a new and single list. The list consists of the common assumptions for all groups, as well as those being re-formulated to reach a compromise between them. Any still important but uncertain assumptions will be left for further investigation (information requirements analysis). As a result a *final synthesis* (or 'declaration') of assumptions is made to support action in the case of transformations taking place. These assumptions are called the presumptions for future plans.

In our information systems practice experience, SAST is useful to support thinking about alignment-based transformations that are to occur or that could be thought of, but need support from 'below'. It is necessary to equip people with a tool that facilitates their exploration of what leads to a proposed transformation; how it will influence their future actions; what *other areas or aspects* should be worked on that need to be included in plans; and how we can also include our own values and beliefs towards what else should be transformed to improve our quality of life. We will see an example of SAST in practice in the next chapter.

In addition and in our experience, we find that SAST works best when an *already defined* transformation is to take place (almost inevitably). When there are more than two or three alternatives to what needs to happen, or when there are a number of conflicting or unclear goals about the future, an alternative systems methodology is necessary. SAST could be used as a first step in order to help people clarify if there are two or more options, and what the assumptions supporting each option are. After that, a methodology like soft systems methodology (SSM) or interactive planning (IP) could support definition of more comprehensive options and plans of action.

## Re-designing Transformations: Interactive Planning (IP)

The breathing space for a transformation often requires a deeper degree of thinking about the 'whole' future in which people want to see themselves in order for them to be more able to play a full role in the information society. In relation to the need for an alternative way of thinking about the future (not only reacting or reducing to advances in technology), Ackoff (1981) considers that we live now in a 'systems age' as opposed to a 'machine age'. This is a new manifestation of systems-thinking in history.

According to Ackoff, the systems age means that our thinking needs to shift to consider that in any situation, we are part of a bigger 'whole' in which many people interact and hence a system's goal needs to be reviewed in a larger context. The machine type of thinking where we 'reduce' problems to their constituent parts is insufficient to deal with the variety of goals and their influence in relating people and phenomena together. With different and often conflicting goals that people have about their own future, it is more advisable to focus on a future in which there is a desired state of affairs for everyone, where problems are dissolved rather than simply solved or resolved.

Ackoff (1981) proposes an approach to help organizations to 'put things together', in other words to re-design their future by considering that they can affect their environment and with it fulfill the purpose(s) of a bigger system (e.g. society). This approach is called *interactive planning* (IP). It is interactive because it proposes a continuous process of learning about the future by continually thinking about and redesigning it, with organizations being conceived (temporarily) as systems. The design of the future requires that stakeholders to be served by the system participate in such redesign, being guided by the idea that organizations will help people to improve their standard of living and quality of life. This is what Ackoff calls development.

The methodology itself proposes a change in our mentality about the future. Rather than just simply following transformations, we can design new ones to benefit us more fully than those transformations which are simply imported or adopted under a 'foreign' vision. In a way, the methodology suggests replacing these foreign elements with our own. This requires, most of all, having the courage to do so and to venture in exploring our own future.

In relation to information systems and technologies in the information society, IP can enable people to define or re-define a desired a transformation, so that such systems and technologies contribute to the *development* of people in the wider community, and their use is conceived of as contributing at present and in the future. This transformation could be part of a bigger whole or system, meaning that the transformation would need a set of preparatory activities or even that it will be transformed into a new one to fit what is expected in the wider community. Planning transformations is about deciding where and what action can be made more significant, valuable and technologically feasible.

To arrive at such an action, IP involves the following steps (Ackoff, 1981: 74–75):

1 *Formulating the mess.* This consists of putting things in perspective in terms of carrying on in the same way and facing a far-from-desirable future. The formulation is about defining a

system of threats and opportunities that an organization and its stakeholders face if things do not change.

2   *Ends planning.* Specifying the ends to be pursued in relation to a better and desirable future. An idealized design of the 'system' is developed, considering what will be technologically feasible to support the system so that the designed ends have a greater chance of being met.

3   *Means planning.* This consists of selecting or creating the means by which the specified ends are to be pursued and the areas that need attention to close the gap between the current state of affairs and the desired one.

4   *Resource planning.* This is about determining what resources will be required, when they will be required, and how to obtain those that would not otherwise be available.

5   *Design of implementation and control.* This consists of determining who is to do what, when and where, and how the implementation is to be kept on track and monitored. Participation of people is essential to facilitate learning about the implementation of plans and to make decisions to keep the process of learning alive and useful in relation to changing conditions.

In the ends planning stage (stage 2), the *idealized design activity* is about designing a 'system' of activity which offers a number of properties to meet the desired ends for the organization and its stakeholders. The design is continually modified as new needs emerge, plans to bring it to reality are implemented, new technologies are made available and new initiatives and projects are put in place. In this regard, an idealized design is not an end stage but becomes 'the most effective ideal-seeking system' that helps the organization meet its desired ends, with a view that ends can change. To be continually modified implies that people are taking active part in the design process.

In information systems practice it is often the case that information technologies are available for implementation or use. Technologies themselves appear to solve many problems. However, organizations have certain and ingrained ways of thinking about themselves and their future that make it difficult for any technology implementation to make a good impact. The use of technologies is seen as ancillary or inevitable but not as part of a significant or integrated change process. 'Silo' and pessimistic mentality could prevail at the expense of better and more creative ways of living. Such type of mentality can be reinforced by a perceived degree of impossibility to 'catch up' with more developed regions or countries that have adopted initiatives for the information society earlier.

To this type of situation, silo and negative types of mentality need to be challenged, and technology needs to be seen as an enabling rather than a constraining element. As we said before, Ackoff puts faith in people having the courage to seek better ways of living for themselves, their organizations and the community in general. These ways of life help people develop rather than simply grow, because they take into account needs, capabilities and aspirations. As a methodology, IP can facilitate their exploration of a better and more appropriate (not copied) future in which the satisfaction of needs is helped by adequate use of systems and technologies.

### Idealized Design: Start from 'Scratch'

Ackoff is famous for challenging managers to 'start from scratch'. An idealized design exercise would first consist of an announcement: *The organization (or the situation) you were involved in until yesterday has been 'destroyed' overnight. Now take a blank piece of paper and start redesigning it from scratch.*

The idea is to imagine a system (set of interrelated parts whose behavior is the result of the interactions between parts) with a number of properties to satisfy the needs of different groups of individuals. This system embraces a vision and a mission, and ends to be pursued. Together, these reflect a number of human values that we want anyone being served by the system to have.

The resulting design should be (Ackoff, 1981: 105–106):

- *Technologically feasible.* The design must not incorporate any technology that is not currently known to be usable.
- *Operationally viable.* The designed system must be capable of surviving if it were brought into existence.
- *Capable of rapid learning and adaptation.* Stakeholders should be able to modify the design whenever they care to; experimental processes to modify the design must be incorporated; decisions made within the designed system should be subject to control.

This design should lead people to define feasible action and to continually monitor plans, to participate in definitions and focus on their needs.

### An Example: A Telephone System

Imagining that we venture to design a telephone system from 'scratch', we could think of it as serving different needs. We could even think of this system as existing in a different type of society. For instance, one in which we could easily communicate and exchange ideas freely and instantaneously. The telephone system would be part of a bigger system. It could offer the following properties to contribute to the purpose of enabling free and instantaneous communication in the information society. People can give properties similar to the ones below when thinking about how a system would serve their needs and meet their ends:

- a system that is easily accessible, so that in any public place one could get free access to it; and get connected to anyone and anywhere;
- a system where there would be no wrong numbers, and where dialing is directed by thinking;
- a system in which we could know who is calling before answering the call;
- a system that could be used without hands;
- a system with instant video;
- a system that records conversations and extracts relevant messages.

The result of an idealized design would be an idea (technologically feasible, operationally viable, and capable of learning and adaptation) that contributes to generate an ideal common future. With an idealized design we can get closer making all the above properties a reality, and one could argue that it is a matter of time. However, it is also a question of learning how we can best grasp these properties so that they support people in their desire to satisfy their needs. A comparison of this design with the current situation might lead those involved to identify a number of gaps or areas in which activity could transform the current situation into one closer to the ideal.

At later stages, IP requires stakeholders to select appropriate means, resources and monitoring activities for the system's implementation plan; participation should involve them at different levels. All this is to ensure that transformations develop in the best possible ways and that people continually review and adjust the resulting plans to changing circumstances.

Whilst IP can be very helpful to organizations, it requires courage and an open mentality as we said before. Some people might take more time to gain these two elements, and would prefer to make sense of their future in their own terms and according to what they think is currently meaningful to them. We now explain another methodology that helps in re-defining transformations as well as *engaging* people to collectively explore meaningful ways of improving their situation. By facilitating meaning creation the methodology also facilitates finding meaning and use for information systems and technologies as supporting human activity. Meaning becomes a key element for developing the information society at different levels of activity. Meaning exploration requires time, something that often is a challenge when it comes to catching up with the possibilities and demands of the information society.

## Engaging with Transformations: Soft Systems Methodology (SSM)

In the UK in the 1980s, Peter Checkland (1981) and colleagues had been exposed to the popularity of systems analysis and its focus on studying and engineering systems *out there*. This could include for instance the national health system, the defense system, or the prison system. Systems models could be built to represent these and used to find the best ways of improving performance. The goals of these systems were *pre-defined* (for instance by a government policy). The task of the systems analyst was to find the best ways to meet these goals. Little was said in systems analysis about how people contributed to the definition of such goals, and whether they could do something to change them if necessary.

This and other issues led to an increasing degree of failure in projects which used systems analysis. Failures gave an indication of science's focus on solving the wrong problems; a different focus was needed to combat more 'humane' problems of poverty, inequality, communication and understanding in societies. This also required a shift in the thinking behind the use of systems ideas.[2] It became more important to include people's perceptions and meanings so that systems-based analysis would serve them.

Today, we can still see how science has helped us address problems but has also failed to provide answers to others. The information society brings issues of access and digital divides. Rather than becoming more sophisticated in our approach to implement technologies, we should ask ourselves if we are solving the wrong problems rightly (for instance throwing money to automate activities, buy computers or the latest software packages) or if we take time to define the right problems to solve (and ask people what happens in their lives).

Checkland (1981) is one of the first researchers to take up the challenge of using traditional systems methodologies (systems engineering) to explore more *socially oriented* problems, with the aim of learning how systems-thinking could be better put to practice. After using these methodologies for a while, Checkland realized that systems ideas could be better used to explore the complexity of these problems rather than represent it. Checkland proposed to move the focus of systems analysis from finding and optimizing systems to engaging people to learn about the world in their own terms using systems models (Figure 4.2). This led him to define soft systems methodology.

### Soft Systems Methodology (SSM) in Brief

Soft systems methodology (SSM) (Checkland, 1981) is an approach in which those involved or affected by a situation attribute different *meanings* to what is happening. One person's meaning of what happens in a situation (e.g. fight for freedom) is different from another's (terrorism). We continually attribute meaning to our actions, and we also change those meanings; these meanings have to do with our activities in daily life, which could be modeled temporarily as systems, so that we can gain a better appreciation of their connections, underlying values and ultimately their purposes. SSM helps people to surface these elements and to define meaningful

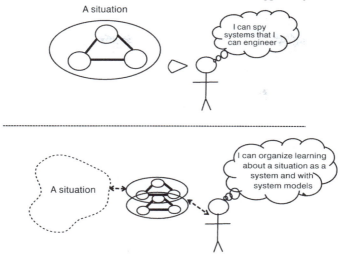

*Figure 4.2* Moving systemicity to the process of enquiry according to Checkland

actions to improve a situation. Meanings also come from our cosmology or worldviews, what we think should be valued (or undervalued). These views are formed through time and are modified as our learning of the world around us takes place.

Meanings also have to do with the use of information systems and technologies. Those using SSM in information systems practice have argued that systems are there to serve our actions. If we do not find meaning in these systems, their use becomes less than significant. It is necessary to find these underlying meanings and work with them so that systems fit in a particular context.

To arrive at meaningful action, SSM suggests using systems-thinking. People can build systems models that respond to their particular worldviews (human activity systems[3]), and compare them with what they perceive is a 'current situation', in order to gain insights as to what possibilities for positive change there could be. Models and possibilities are influenced by what people regard as relevant to tackle their particular situation. In information systems practice these models can be used as 'front-ends' of more sophisticated and technical designs, so we can continually check on the validity of designs as being aligned to human activity and supporting the creation and use of meaning in situations.

To develop this process, SSM involves the following stages (although not in a sequence) (Checkland, 1981):

1   problem situation unstructured;
2   problem situation expressed;
3   selection of relevant systems;
4   elaboration of root definitions and conceptual models;
5   comparison of models with the current situation;
6   definition of culturally feasible and systemically desirable changes;
7   implementation.

The use of systems ideas comes when systems models are developed. These are models of purposeful human activity which would bring improvements according to what is considered relevant in a situation. Within the above stages, one of them (stage 4) gains importance when

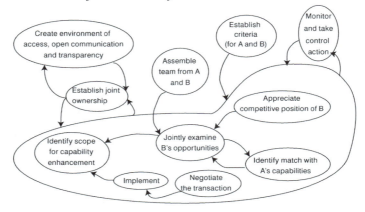

*Figure 4.3* Root definition and conceptual model of a service system. A system owned and staffed by service supplier and client – within an environment of access, open communication and transparency – which, by joint examination, seeks to match the capability of party A (supplier) with the potential for opportunities of party B (recipient) to maximize B's success, thereby simultaneously increasing the experience and income of A.

it comes to transformations. The models derive from *root definitions* (or concise descriptions of what a system would do). A root definition captures a particular worldview that makes the operation of the system meaningful. The definition specifies key elements known by the mnemonic CATWOE: the main *transformation* (T) activity of a system; the *actors* (A) involved in carrying out the transformation; the *customer*s (C) as those individuals to be served/affected by the system; the *owners* of the system (O) or those individuals able to stop the system's activity; *worldview* (W) the beliefs and values that support why we do activities defined by T; and the systems *environment* (E) or constraints from the outside that people have to live with. Models can then be built according to some properties of systems, and some activities of monitoring as well as of indicators of efficiency and efficacy can be added up (Checkland, 1981).

Models like the one shown in Figure 4.3, from Checkland and Poulter (2006), are defined and used to structure debate about changes to improve a situation. In his SSM methodology, Checkland (1981) is careful to concede that the definition of changes needs to be *culturally feasible* and *systemically desirable*. The first condition refers to the acceptance that a change will have in a particular setting given the set of norms, roles and values, as well as the balance of power among parties. The second refers to the connectedness between changes emerging from the use of systems models. Both of these should be satisfied before any change can take place in a situation.

Systems models help us to discuss both the feasibility and desirability of change. Furthermore, these models become the blueprints of computer-based systems, as the latter are embedded into larger (human activity) ones. One can decide to enquire about the information needed to accomplish each of the activities of conceptual models, as well as the information generated by them. Information categories can be built, and then their existence validated in available computer systems. Such comparison can lead to modifications in the operation of these systems, or in new systems developments. With new technologies becoming available, SSM can be used to explore the organizational context in which systems and technologies are to be used. By doing so, the methodology can become a mediating device between different groups of people with different degrees of expertise and knowledge (including those individuals with a good degree of technical knowledge).

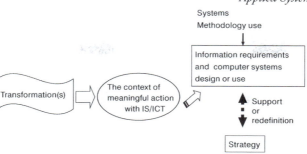

*Figure 4.4* Current uses of SSM in information systems practice

This mediating role for SSM is also being used in information systems strategy. SSM can help people make sense of several business strategies, each of them bringing a new transformation. SSM can help to develop learning cycles where the future of organizations is continually ascertained and with it the use of information and communication technologies. This will also contribute to align the use of these technologies with ICTs, with strategic plans and the achievement of 'value' in organizations. The above two uses of SSM in information systems practice are depicted in Figure 4.4.

Different from the other two methodologies, SSM focuses on understanding the context which leads to meaningful action, so that any set of transformations (including those referring to the use of information systems and technologies) can be framed in context, with the aim of defining feasible and desirable actions. SSM sits in between supporting transformations and re-defining them. It brings meaningful action to support further action, and in the process it is possible to re-define transformations to make them more meaningful. This gives SSM a particular feature that enables engaging people and working with them.

## Assumptions of Systems Methodologies

So far it could be said that the above methodologies help practitioners to deal with transformations. Each of these methodologies can also support engagement of people by suggesting ways of moving forward in relation to these transformations. Either by exploring assumptions behind transformation (SAST); by redesigning transformations in relation to a desirable future (IP), or by making transformations meaningful according to the context of meanings given by people in a situation (SSM), methodologies would help people engage in different degrees in the information society. However, the use of these methodologies needs to be informed in relation to a set of inherent assumptions that influence practice.

1   First, a degree of *accommodation* can be assumed to be reached between participants or parties involved or affected by transformations. In the search for holistic strategies, desirable futures or meaningful action, methodology use is prone to assume that agreements or accommodations can be reached. For instance, in SSM an accommodation is an explicit goal to achieve. It is different from reaching agreements, as the former are defined as situations which "parties are willing to go along with" (Checkland, 1981). Checkland uses the example of a family, where family members, although not willing to accept everything from others, are able to find accommodations to be able to interact together (visiting every period of time, celebrating Christmas together). Reaching an accommodation might not be in the best interest of all, but it could be a reasonable state of affairs, even if it is not the most ethically desirable one.

2    Because of the above possibility, the use of methodologies for information systems practice could become very instrumental and focused on problem solving. This might mean that issues related to ensuring that effective definition and implementation of systems and technology plans 'happen' can take priority at the expense of a deeper degree of reflection. Experience tells us that, as is often the case, people can hijack and use the language of systems to meet their pre-defined goals (for instance make plans happen). The aim to synthesize, re-design or accommodate views as suggested by each of the above methodologies becomes subordinated to other goals in organizations and elsewhere. Other important issues including marginalization in the information society could be left out from main decision making, because they are not easy to deal with.

3    The above assumption is thus reinforced by the use of systems methodologies to support organizational action. We have a wealth of experiences that report systems methodology use within organizational boundaries. SAST and SSM deal with decisions and issues in organizations. As some authors recognize, their methodologies are in need of being used to address societal problems. This is interesting, given that we are all part of bigger systems than organizations.

The above assumptions remind us of the challenges that systems-thinking currently has (language, problem solving and time) in order to deal with the information society phenomena as described in Chapter 3. This should make us think that it is necessary then to use systems methodologies in a more critically and ethically informed way with society in the background so that we can challenge the above assumptions. Churchman's plea to secure improvements needs to be rescued and maintained in the face of complex societal situations. Information systems practitioners should consider that systems methodologies open up possibilities for further reflection and engagement that could go beyond what they think is the domain of their practice. This can lead them to consider that their actions have consequences that need to be thought about.

We have so far explored the complexity of the information society, and we have arrived at acknowledging the importance of considering the consequences of information society initiatives. Systems-thinking also invites us to consider consequences. By reflecting on the assumptions discussed above, as well as on how methodologies can help us in our thinking, we have become more aware of the ethics of practice. It is time to be critical and consider the ethics of systems. We now present the main ideas behind critical systems-thinking to address this issue.

## Dealing with the Unintended: Critical Systems-thinking

The use of systems methodologies in several areas of social science has meant that social theory has been used to inform practice. Advocates of critical social theory have looked at unveiling the conditions of the social context under which practice is developed. These conditions are not 'neutral' or 'objective', and include ways in which people communicate (or are allowed to). Instead, such conditions privilege certain groups of people and their interests at the expense of other groups. It is necessary to identify and address these conditions, so that not only certain groups but everyone in society can have the same opportunities to interact and develop their own potential, in other words to improve their ways of living. Conditions can be reinforced by the use of information systems and technologies, which could be acting as instruments of control rather than communication.

Critical social theory has been used by systems thinkers to develop what they call critical systems-thinking (Jackson, 1985, 2003; Midgley, 2000; Mingers, 1984). The main idea is to use systems methodologies in an informed way so that they are used according to their strengths and weaknesses to tackle conditions of the context where they are used, with a view to improving a situation. This idea is fuelled by a number of commitments to guide systems practice:[4]

- *Critical awareness*, continual re-examining of taken-for-granted assumptions (including those inherent to systems methodologies) about the context where action is taking place. These assumptions have to do with the conditions for communication between people in society.
- *Pluralism* (or complementarism), using a variety of ideas and approaches (including those of systems-thinking) in a coherent manner to tackle the complexity of situations.
- *Improvement*, ensuring that people advance in developing their full potential, by freeing them of potential constraints to such development, including issues of power in a social context.

The above commitments emphasise *our thinking about action*, and how we can direct it to help people improve their current situation. In information systems practice, it has been suggested to avoid guiding our thinking by only one type of rationality (Jackson, 1992): that of considering that information systems are merely technical artifacts at the service of pre-defined goals. Social factors, and the status quo of the situation, are to be considered. Thinking about situations with the use of systems methodologies requires practitioners to look beneath the surface of a situation and think of 'other' issues and people than are normally the case. Reflection on what and whom we consider important should be continuous.

In critical systems-thinking, awareness in our ways of thinking comes from what systems methodologies can do. Awareness is developed in two particular ways: (1) one in which there is a focus on the situation at hand, with a view to employing a number of systems methodologies *most appropriate* to deal with the issues being identified as relevant in such a situation (Jackson, 2003); and (2) another in which awareness is continually supported by the use of the notion of systems boundary (Ulrich, 1983; Midgley, 2000). For the first strand of thought, there is an excellent development in information systems strategy in the work of Clarke (2001).[5] He re-thinks the nature of strategy as different from being driven by pre-defined goals which leave out considerations on information and its use in organizations. Systems methodologies can support re-definitions of information and strategy and thus the role(s) of information systems and technologies.

In this book we focus on presenting ideas on the second strand of critical systems-thinking which we have most used in our practice. It is based on the idea of systems boundary. There are two methodological approaches in this strand: critical systems heuristics (CSH) and boundary critique. These seem to be appropriate to tackle societal issues related to the information society. We now present these approaches.

## Critical Systems Heuristics (CSH)

Following Churchman (1968), Ulrich (1983) says that systems boundary is a social construction which defines what constitutes relevant knowledge in a situation, as well as the people to be involved or affected when making decisions about it. This concept is powerful because it tells us that using the idea of boundaries, we can reflect on the values and norms that guide our choice of facts as well as our choice of actions and consequences for other people. Rather than securing *all possible knowledge* derived from our identification of facts, norms and values that come to play in a situation, Ulrich suggests that we just need to acknowledge the *knowledge we use to guide our thinking* at a particular moment of time. Knowledge is bounded. It is not necessarily the result of achieving consensus among people. Rather, knowledge comes from understanding the reasons for our differences, the existence of genuine conflicts of values, the diversity of needs and worldviews from different people. Knowledge is also about allowing a reasonable degree of cooperation among parties, and securing decisions that are collectively debated (Ulrich, 2001b: 73).

To gain knowledge, Ulrich (1983) suggests a methodology called critical systems heuristics (CSH) which, through questions about systems boundaries on a situation, facilitates the continuous uncovering of values, facts and norms, as well as their debate. Hence the 'heuristic' nature of the methodology. Reflection on questions could lead us to re-think collectively what we know and what we want to know in order to guide our decisions and deal with their consequences.

In information systems practice, Ulrich (2001a) suggests that CSH can help developers secure collective understanding of the knowledge that is relevant to inform development (although he seems to be referring to information systems development in organizations). Understanding is about securing the validity of what we consider first as 'information' and later on as knowledge. Both are socially defined. We cannot aspire to provide definitions of these terms which will be 'eternally' satisfying to all parties involved or affected. However, we can aspire to review, debate and understand current definitions collectively. When we do that, our values, facts and norms can come to light. Consequences of adopting a particular subset of them can be explored and debated. New understandings can emerge which are ethically important.

The methodology is very practical and useful not only to orient information systems development but to help people conceive of what an information system is (or should be). In practice, it might be that we need to collectively develop this definition, and explore how it will affect different groups of individuals. Already built in and implemented systems or technologies can also be subjected to public scrutiny. The methodology helps lay individuals to gain knowledge about a 'system' as a social construction (which can involve computer systems as part of its definition). In dealing with social phenomena, the methodology helps people to put into place the knowledge that is considered relevant to support the system's operation. It helps them to become more aware of potential consequences that such operation will have for them and others.

One criticism of the methodology is that CSH seems to work under the assumption that people are willing to put forward their views and engage in debate, but this means that there is an appropriate democratic substratum that supports this, even at a very basic level (between individuals). Critics argue that people often act 'irrationally', given that their participation is or can be co-opted. In such situations, why would the powerful listen to the powerless (Ivanov, 1991)? Before assuming that there is a possibility of a democratic substratum, critics argue that it is necessary to explore in more depth the conditions of the context in which participation takes place. These conditions also include individuals' own conditions in being able to articulate and express their views.

Advocates of CSH (including Ulrich himself) would say that CSH aims at precisely helping individuals to become aware of such conditions by gaining knowledge of the current situation; these conditions are important when it comes to thinking about potential consequences of what we define as action for improvement. Awareness is about deciding what 'ought' to become of such a situation, given current possibilities. There is no easy answer to existing debates about CSH. For the purposes of this book, it suffices to say that the spirit of CSH (and that of its critics) is to facilitate generation of knowledge to inform ethically appropriate action. Practitioners can benefit from the use of CSH as described above. They can gain awareness of what issues

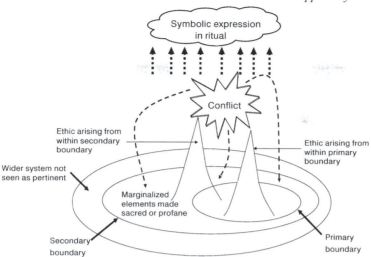

*Figure 4.5* Boundary critique

and people they should consider in improving human activity with the use of information, knowledge, systems and technologies.

To facilitate awareness of what can realistically be achieved in debate we suggest that the use of CSH can be complemented with a more in-depth exploration of how individuals are influenced to consider certain issues and people as important at the expense of others. In this way, information systems practice could look at what happens in the information society as well as how it is itself looking at it from the perspective of practitioners and other stakeholders being involved and affected. This is what could be achieved with the work of Midgley on boundary critique.

## Boundary Critique and Marginalization

Midgley (2000) follows the work of Churchman and Ulrich but in a slightly different direction, and with the possibility of *conflict* in mind. He asks: What happens when two different groups of individuals identify two different types of boundaries about knowledge and people to be considered relevant? He represents this as in Figure 4.5 above (Midgley, 2000: 144).

In Figure 4.5 there are two systems boundaries, and each of them has a set of values (or ethics) associated with them. Midgley (2000) calls the narrower boundary the primary boundary and the wider one the secondary boundary. Between the two boundaries is a *marginal* area which contains issue or people which are of concern to those operating with the wider boundary but which are excluded from the concerns of those using the narrow (primary) boundary.

It might be possible in practice to identify two different perspectives about what needs to be done in a situation. For some people it is more important to stick to old ways of working whereas for others these ways are in need of renovation or change. Each perspective would then yield different insights as to who is to be benefited and what is to be achieved. There would be people and issues which would be excluded in one perspective but included in another one. These are the marginal elements on which discussion could be encouraged as a way of enabling people to talk about their own society.

Discussion could also refer to information systems and technologies and their societal role(s); some individuals or groups prefer to keep their existing systems whereas others would like to have new or more sophisticated ones. Boundary critique helps people to visualize these preferences, to study values that support them, and relate conflicts to wider conflicts in society. It might be that conflicts about new and old systems have to do with wider struggles between managers and unions; between technology advocates and technology critics; between equality and inequality; and ultimately between different ways of living in society. Any decision in information systems practice will have consequences for these or other conflicts, and will also be influenced by them.

In boundary critique the marginal elements become the focus of *conflict between groups* as seen in Figure 4.5. This conflict can sometimes be productive, or when it is judged to be unproductive it can be resolved, but in many social situations this kind of resolution does not happen. According to Midgley (2000), situations of conflict are stabilized by the imposition of a sacred or profane status[6] to the marginal elements (see Figure 4.5). When the marginal elements are made sacred, the secondary boundary is taken as the main source of decision-making and action. Conversely, when the status of profane is attributed to the marginal elements, the primary boundary is reinforced and whatever is in the margins is ignored or devalued.

This distinction between marginalized and included elements can help people visualize how the existence of conflict leads to certain impacts (positive or negative) for groups of individuals. Conflicts are stabilized by the imposition of policies or decisions that privilege issues and people at the expense of others. In practice, this might be reflected in organizations in which despite a general attitude of willingness to adopt new information systems, there is a continuous allocation of resources to maintain old systems to the detriment of innovation. Or it might be the case that innovation becomes the norm and new systems are first implemented to be shaped then by those groups who have been marginalized from decisions about their adoption. This latter case can be appreciated in countries like Singapore. In 2005, as part of the information society initiative, it was declared that 100 percent of government services for citizens had been implemented online. The government then proceeded to work with citizens (initially marginalized from decisions) in order to modify such services.

In this and other cases, boundary critique helps us to identify issues and people which are recognized as relevant but become marginalized by decision making processes. To the potential or actual existence of marginalization, the impacts of any policy or plan could be surfaced and debated regarding its consequences for different groups in society.

With the idea of boundary critique and marginalization, Midgley also suggests that conflict is part of debate and often is resolved by the imposition of one boundary over another. How this imposition takes place can be because of the use of *power relations*. In this regard, the use of boundary critique can help people to identify better the scope of their actions, in other words it can help people become aware of who they are and what they can effectively do (Midgley, 2000). Despite this strength of boundary critique, we have to say that its use does not guarantee that we will be able to manage every unintended consequence in relation to the development of the information society. This is partly because in boundary critique little is said about how we can deal with power relations and their dynamic nature. This has been found to be an important issue in information systems practice as reported in Chapter 6, and we suggest developing new ways of thinking about the information society to deal with unintended consequences in Chapters 7 and 8.

We have now completed a review of systems approaches and methodologies that use the notion of a system as an enquiring device. The use of approaches and methodologies can help people to appreciate the complexity of situations and act on them. It is necessary to be aware of some assumptions made by the use of systems methodology. The challenges of systems-thinking presented in the previous chapter (language, problem solving focus, time), can also help us to

*Table 4.1* Concerns and challenges for the information society, systems-thinking and systems methodology use

| Issues of concern about the information society | Challenges to systems-thinking | Assumptions of systems methodology use |
|---|---|---|
| • Economic focus <br> • Thinking inside organizations <br> • Dominance of expertise <br> • Leaving out human values | • Language <br> • Problem solving focus <br> • Time | • Seeking accommodation <br> • Problem solving focus <br> • Support mostly organizational action |

be better prepared to use systems methodologies in our practice in information systems in the most adequate ways in relation to observed phenomena of transformations, engagements and unintended consequences. We summarize these challenges in Table 4.1.

The table shows that the information society and systems-thinking share issues and challenges, and that systems methodology use will have to become more critical and embrace both issues and challenges. We need to review assumptions about methodology use in order to avoid the instrumentalization of systems-thinking in the information society. Critical systems-thinking and its commitments to critical awareness, pluralism and improvement give us good insights on how we could address the challenges identified for systems-thinking. They encourage us to go beyond organizational boundaries and goals, and look at society as a whole, in particular when it comes to the information society and its claims to improving the quality of life of individuals.

As a final caveat, it is important to notice that commitments of critical systems-thinking are mainly related to systems methodology use, to what methodologies offer; moreover these commitments are about enabling people to participate, to debate and discuss issues with a goal of emancipation/improvement in mind. When it comes to the information society, it is important to consider that participation and emancipation might have different connotations to those ascribed by social theories in different contexts. If this is the case, participation and emancipation could become meaningless ideals rather than attainable goals, in particular when the information society pushes for economic focus, organizational action, dominance of expertise, and leaving out human values. And this could be problematic for people involved. It is necessary to relate systems methodology use to the ways of thinking of people, so that we can support their collective thinking about the information society.

Thus we suggest keeping the commitments of critical systems-thinking in the back of our minds (and therefore absent from Table 4.1) and focus on the information society and systems methodology use. In the following chapters we define ways to:

- Look at how we think about transformations, engagements and unintended consequences in the information society.
- Define and present ways of thinking that could help us deal with the above phenomena with systems-thinking and systems methodology use. This also involves addressing the challenges for both of these in practice whenever possible.

**Chapter Summary**

This chapter has presented a number of systems methodologies that could be used to inform information systems activities in the information society. The notion of a system as an enquiring device can help us improve our thinking in situations in which we need to:

- support transformations;
- re-define transformations;
- support people's engagements;
- deal with unintended consequences.

To tackle the above, we have suggested a number of systems methodologies and approaches. These include strategic assumption surface testing (SAST); interactive planning (IP); soft systems methodology (SSM); critical systems heuristics (CSH); and boundary critique. We have proposed that each methodology can be employed for a different type of purpose in relation to the above phenomena.

In reviewing the above systems methodologies we have also highlighted a number of assumptions that have pervaded their use. These have to do with seeking accommodations; subordinating systems methodologies to certain (organizational) goals; and working mainly within the organizational realm. These assumptions confirm our identification of previous challenges to systems-thinking (language, problem solving and time) as well as issues of concern about the information society (economic focus; thinking inside organizations; dominance of expertise and leaving out human values). Systems methodology use has been limited to the organizational realm, making such use limited and neglecting addressing these challenges more fully in our practice.

To these assumptions, critical systems-thinking suggests that we inform practice with a number of commitments (awareness, emancipation/improvement; and pluralism). We bear in mind these commitments in order to address the challenges for systems-thinking in the information society. We propose supporting the ways in which we as people think about information society phenomena so that we can tackle issues of concern about the information society 'head on' with systems methodology use.

## Key Messages

- Systems methodologies support the exploration of the *context* of practice in which information society initiatives take place. In such a context they can help deal with transformations, engagements and unintended consequences.
- Critical systems-thinking implies informed use of systems methodologies considering some key underlying assumptions.
- Use of systems methodologies in information systems practice needs to review assumptions about seeking accommodations; becoming instrumental to certain goals; and going beyond the organizational realm towards the information society as a whole.

## Questions / Exercises

- Choose one of the systems methodologies reviewed in this chapter, and discuss the advantages and disadvantages of using it as:
  - a metaphor (a reflective device, with some reference to methodological steps)
  - a full methodology (applying all the methodological steps)
  - a set of method(s) contained in it.
- What methodology would you use to support you in any of the following situations?
  - implementing a software package;
  - evaluating a computer system from the perspective of users;
  - providing internet access for underprivileged (marginalized) groups;

allowing people to use a particular technology and dealing with consequences of doing so;

challenging a policy or initiative for the information society.

- What additional assumptions or challenges for use could you identify if using a given methodology in practice?

  strategic assumption surface testing (SAST)

  interactive planning (IP)

  soft systems methodology (SSM)

  critical systems heuristics (CSH)

  boundary critique.

## Further Reading

Clarke (2007). Very clear and practical guide to incorporate systems methodologies in information systems practice with emphasis on systems to support strategic thinking in organizations.

Jackson (2003). More detailed account of philosophical underpinnings of systems methodologies (including criticisms), with some case studies to look at. Some good practical examples of methodology use.

Midgley (2000). A process philosophy account of systems-based intervention based on boundary critique and marginalization. The book offers very interesting practical examples.

Ulrich (1983). Links critical philosophy with the idea of systems boundary, and puts them together into a clear methodology to be used in different situations of social design.

# 5 The Idealist Pattern for Practice in the Information Society

> I like to think
> (it has to be!)
> of a cybernetic ecology
> where we are free of our labors
> and joined back to nature,
> returned to our mammal
> brothers and sisters,
> and all watched over
> by machines of loving grace
>
> Richard Brautingan
> (*All Watched over by Machines of Loving Grace*, 1967)

## Introduction

The information society is a complex phenomenon worldwide, but systems-thinking and systems methodologies are here to help us make sense of our practice so that we can improve our societies as 'whole systems'. We do not have only one type of information society but a variety of them. The dynamics between developments in information and communication technologies (ICTs), their adoption by groups of people, and some unexpected consequences in ICT use make us think of phenomena of transformations, engagements and unintended consequences. Each of these phenomena manifests itself in different forms, and requires us to exert critical thinking when using systems methodologies as reported in the previous chapter.

With many people being involved in making the information society happen (policy makers, ICT providers, software developers, community officers, citizens and even households among many others) it is necessary to explore how they all think. In this chapter we introduce the idea of *patterns* as a way of guiding our practice in the information society. These patterns aim to give us a view of how people (could) deal with transformations, engagements and unintended consequences. Each pattern also brings some elements to look at when using systems methodologies to guide our enquiry into these phenomena.

This chapter presents the first pattern which we will call 'idealist'. This pattern features a way of thinking that focuses on dealing with *transformations*. People deal with transformations mainly by defining and implement *visions* of society where most problems (if not all) are being solved. The role of ICT can be of supporting as well as enhancing the achievement of visions. Systems methodology use thus focuses on supporting transformations as well as re-defining them. We present experiences of using (partially or fully) methodologies like strategic assumption surface testing (SAST), soft systems methodology (SSM) and interactive planning (IP). At the end of the chapter we reflect on the usefulness of the thinking pattern to guide practice in the information society.

## Objectives

- To introduce the notion of patterns to understand how we think and act about the information society.
- To detail the main features of a way of thinking about the information society which aims to promote and implement transformations via visions.
- To present practical examples of systems methodology use to support and re-define transformations.
- To reflect on such experiences, by assessing strengths and weaknesses of methodology use so that lessons can be learned to move forward in our practice in the information society.

## Patterns

The information society brings with it different ways of living, working, talking and thinking, in other words it brings different ways of practice. The variety of its accounts and manifestations in information systems, technology and public policy domains (among others) lead us to identify some commonalities and differences. There are some common ideas regarding the use of ICTs to improve our quality of life by formulating the adoption of ICTs 'for all' together with developing market opportunities, facilitating networking and collaboration to improve countries' competitiveness. There are also common references to marginalization that emerge and the need for countries to 'catch up', or the need for governments to engage with their citizens, or the importance of considering consequences and impacts of the use of ICTs.

We have explored some of these ideas and their manifestations in the information society, and we have come to appreciate the importance of transformations, engagements and unintended consequences. These three elements have guided us in thinking about how we can improve our practice with systems-thinking and systems methodologies.

The above common ideas and ways of thinking about the information society tell us that people adopt particular 'patterns' or *recurrent* ways to organize plans and initiatives. These ways of thinking become recurrent when we see that different groups of people recognize these phenomena, and devise responses accordingly to deal with them. Our responses in practice are reflected in how we put forward new actions, initiatives, and visions; a sequence of activities or policies. This is also part of our thinking.

We apply what we know or follow a determined sequence of actions to get from one initial state of affairs to another; often we are positively surprised when we discover that there is another path we could have followed but which we ignored (De Bono, 1976). The situation can be visualized using Figure 5.1.

Figure 5.1 shows that given an initial perceived state of affairs, we devise actions to follow a particular pattern of thinking (A) in order to get to a desired situation (e.g. solve a problem). This pattern is dominant, and can represent a way we solve problems or a way we decide to adopt change. The 'dominant' route (to C via A) carves out responses to the unknown. The pattern can help if the thinking behind it is appropriate, but it will not help to consider alternative ways of developing responses. We can glide past alternative routes (B), possibilities and alternatives if we do not draw our attention to them or do not include considerations that they highlight about the situation we are dealing with.

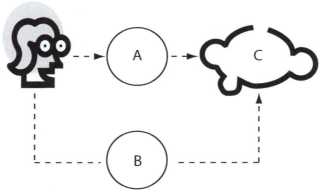

*Figure 5.1* A pattern of thinking

Recognizing the above can help us to guide our thinking about situations, to assess strengths and weaknesses, and devise ways of extending our thinking about them. For the information society, this becomes important if we consider that those individuals and groups who are being involved in or affected by transformations, engagements or unintended consequences follow certain patterns of thinking that are reflected in practice. We can support these patterns (the dominant route as described in Figure 5.1). We can also take a step back and devise new patterns to deal with emerging phenomena or new issues (for instance new routes). This will be the case for instance, of a pattern of thinking that we propose in Chapter 7 in order to deal more fully with unintended consequences of the information society (including those derived from the use of information systems and communication technologies).

At the end of this chapter and in the following two chapters, we will begin to assess each of the thinking patterns in order to highlight its strengths and weaknesses. We will do so by reviewing how the pattern has helped us to deal with a particular phenomenon in the information society. We will also assess how the use of systems methodologies in relation to this pattern has helped us to address the challenges identified for systems-thinking and the assumptions of systems methodology use as presented in Table 5.1.

*Table 5.1* Elements to assess systems methodology use in patterns

| Challenges to systems-thinking | Assumptions of systems methodology use |
| --- | --- |
| • Language | • Seeking accommodation |
| • Problem solving | • Becoming instruments of organizational goals |
| • Time | • Used mostly to address organizational problems |

## Three Recurrent Ways of Thinking About the Information Society

Based on the above introduction, we now propose the following thinking patterns which we have found useful to guide our systems-based practice in the information society:

1    An *idealist* pattern, which emphasizes our thinking about *transformations* that result from the availability of electronic information and new possible modes of interaction between people. Our thinking is guided by what we will call 'a bits-based vision', which shows how a number of *ideals* can be achieved in the information society with the use of ICTs.

2    A *strategic* pattern, which emphasizes our thinking about *engagements* in the information society. We adopt this way of thinking if we consider that the information society should be implemented in more gradual and people-centered ways, so that their social relationships help shape gradually the use of ICTs and therefore their role(s) in society.

3    A *power-based* pattern, in which our emphasis is on dealing with consequences of technology adoption and use, many of which are *unintended*. Thinking becomes focused on offering people possibilities for the use of information systems and technologies for their own purposes, within what transformations and engagements create.

In this and the following two chapters we detail the features, strengths and weaknesses of the idealist pattern. We also show how some systems methodologies and methods can be used. We illustrate our practice with some examples.

## The Idealist Pattern of Practice

This pattern aims to ensure that transformations occur. As we said in Chapter 2, revolutions come at times in the history of societies when a type of networked society (like the one in Chapter 2) is (re)envisaged. In such situations, there is a *vision* of society in which people will be able to exchange information and have more choices, leading them to improve their quality of life whatever this notion of quality could be. The use of information systems and technologies becomes subordinated to that vision, and shows that it is possible to implement it.

The idealist pattern is currently being reinforced with the popularity of electronic communication and data processing technologies. New ways of working and communicating can lead us to conceive of new ways of living. Possibilities given by technologies become endless, because every day new applications are developed. Society can see how certain ideals could become reality, for instance, the ideal of providing access to information to all citizens. Or the ideal of enabling participation in government decisions through electronically mediated voting systems.

The idealist way has the following features reflected in our thinking and thus in our practice:

1    Development of and implementing of *vision(s),* in which quality of life is enhanced through the use of electronic-based information systems and technologies, which at the same time generate opportunities for all to improve their own quality of life.

2    A 'rupture' with the current image of the society we have, and therefore defining and supporting transformations in different spheres of life. Transformations require in turn radical ruptures with existing relationships between people (customers, companies, governments, communities and even countries[1]) in societies. The rupture is paradoxical, because new visions can be implemented almost in the same way across countries, organizations and societies but they require existing relationships between people (and people themselves) to define and implement plans. Furthermore, visions require satisfying a number of *pre-conditions, and devising several projects or initiatives*[2] to be undertaken by individuals. Within this type of paradoxical situation, there is scope for systems methodology use in projects or initiatives which aim at implementing visions or setting up their conditions.

3    For developing countries, adopting a vision for the information society will enable them to 'catch up' economically and technologically (Freeman, 1997). Thus, the vision developed and/or implemented in an ideal pattern of practice carries with it the potential to address and solve many problems in society (poverty, social exclusion, illiteracy and education,

economic benefits). There is scope to re-define transformations with the help of systems methodologies.

4   Achieving visions requires first of all firming them up. Practice then consists of either creating a vision or working with a given one to support its implementation.

We now turn our attention to the notion of a 'vision', and how to firm it up via systems methodology use.

### *Origins of a Vision*

In previous chapters we have seen through the history of the information society and systems-thinking that there is an underlying theme about visualizing society as a 'system', in which different parts interact together. Since the time of the Ancient Greeks, the idea of reaching an ideal state for society has been proposed: a state of co-existence and progress, guided by an overall purpose. Those individuals advocating an organic view of society have seen this state as one of continuous evolution, in which society organizes and adapts itself as a network that serves the interests of the majority and allows them to satisfy their needs. This view reflects a vision of a society in which organization and relations are beneficial for all. In ancient times and also now, a vision requires commitment from everyone as well as the availability of governing structures in society.

A vision can help guide efforts and unlock potentially conflicting interests and as the Greeks (in particular Plato) suggested, potential conflicts in developing such vision could be addressed by explaining the vision and showing its potential and benefits to individuals. We know of Plato's cave as a notion in which those people gaining knowledge could be enlightened. From Plato we also know that a vision of society and the universe is a kind of plausible explanation, which should be told in a credible way. As reflected in his book *The Republic*, people need to be convinced of the benefits of a vision about society, in which justice prevails.

In the twentieth century the concept of a vision as a future state gained prominence with the development of approaches to strategic planning (Steiner, 1969). The vision can gather people around a common purpose. Its 'abstract' whilst at the same time concrete character has been found to be a useful way to make people think about such a common purpose, and to take co-ordinated action. The simpler the vision the easier it is to transmit. Achieving a vision requires knowing more about what it entails; it requires acting to gain such knowledge (see Figure 5.2).

In relation to the information society there are many examples of visions which aim at bringing it to reality. For instance in Sweden, the vision of the country in 2000 was that of being the "first country to be an information society for all" worldwide (Barinaga, 2008: 22). This meant that the *north* of where to go was defined; knowledge to develop such a vision was paramount, as well as the knowledge gained by being an information-based society. The vision

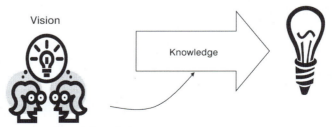

*Figure 5.2* Gaining a vision through knowledge

then had to be translated into specific actions, and specific results. For the case of a particular city, Kista, the vision became that of a 'wireless valley'. Initiatives and plans were under way. There are other cases in other parts of the globe where cities and whole countries are envisioned as becoming information-based.

In the realm of organizations it is common to see public declarations (vision, mission), by which an organization presents itself in the future as serving its customers with high standards of quality and procedures, very often supported by ICTs; knowledge of how best to serve customers and employees is to be gained and put into practice. In this regard, there is also a vision. A 'north' is defined, and the vision gains momentum thanks to the possibilities given by the power of ICTs.

A general notion of a vision that currently influences both governments and organizations in the information society worldwide is that of a 'bits-based' one. This vision has become a motivation to incorporate ICT use in different spheres of life. It also poses a number of challenges and constraints. We now explore its main features.

### A Bits-based Vision in the Information Society

The bits-based vision is derived from what can be done with electronic bits (one–zero, on–off) and for some individuals this is what the information society is about. Negroponte (1995) proposes that electronic bits are more economic to encode, transmit and decode than physical things. A bits-based representation of a physical object can be transmitted through electronic networks, offering people many possibilities. According to Negroponte, any object could represent its current state in digital form: from a car to a patient, from a supermarket to a spatial satellite, from a human embryo to a fully fledged human being.

Negroponte argues that as long as we understand how this representation takes place, we will also be able to make objects communicate with each other using their own bits-based representations. A resulting vision is that of a society as a continuous and dynamic collection of bits, whose flows will also represent our ways of life in interaction with human and non-human entities. A bits-based vision can be seen in Figure 5.3.

In Figure 5.3 any situation, object, person or group could be represented in terms of electronic bits. Negroponte (1995) suggests that we are in a bits-based era in which we can help individuals to make use of bits in order to improve their lives. A comfortable life in these terms would mean that we can tell machines what we want them to do in terms of bits. We would need the support of computer devices to help us manage the choices of what we want to do in daily life, from ordering our home appliances to cook a meal to asking our car to drive us through a less congested route than the one we normally take to get back to our house. Given that we can also represent choice in terms of electronic bits of information, we can ask devices to select the best

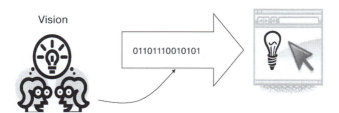

*Figure 5.3*  A bits-based vision

choices for us. Technology devices would then assess what happens in a situation (in terms of how it is represented), and will help us to make the right choices.

The vision of operating almost totally in a bits-based world according to Negroponte is feasible and desirable to almost any individual and organization. Difficulties reside mainly in our own mentality. Negroponte is hopeful that the new generation of children growing up around the world will find it easier to engage with electronic devices, to share information, and to enjoy learning with the support of technologies. They might be the ones taking this vision forward and overcoming the obstacles that older generations (among others political, cultural or organizational obstacles) find difficult to overcome.

### A Business Vision: Nervous Systems

In the case of businesses, such a type of bits-based vision can acquire the character of a 'nervous system' in which bits circulate freely as Bill Gates (2001) suggests in his book *Business @ The Speed of Thought*. The vision that he portrays is that of an electronic infrastructure in which (bits make) information flows freely. Such infrastructure allows information to be at our fingertips at any time to help us to make decisions, and ultimately to serve our customers better. To implement the vision, we have just to make sure that there is such a system in place and that its conceptual design follows what we want to give our customers (internal and external). With electronic networks being available, paper, bureaucracy and inefficiency in organizations and between them could disappear.

Gates (2001) cites some examples from Microsoft in which for instance the human resource management function has improved considerably thanks to the support of this central nervous information system. Electronic boards continually circulate information about new positions being opened at the company. 'Curriculum vitaes' (CVs) are received electronically by email (Gates, 2001). Interviews are scheduled and organized with the support of electronic agendas. Those individuals who are involved in making decisions about who is to be selected can share information and quickly communicate results or offer feedback to candidates by email. After a recruitment or promotion decision is made, the information system sends messages for requisition of office furniture, stationery, and even name badges for those individuals being recruited. Newly appointed members of staff can complete their own enrolment process by requesting additional supplies, and giving their bank details of where they want their salaries to be paid.

To firm up a vision like the one presented above it is often the case that we have to work with what is already in place than starting from scratch.[3] There could be possibilities but also constraints in the processes involved in defining or implementing a vision. We will now present several case studies to show a variety of possibilities for practice under the idealist pattern. We will show how some of the systems-thinking methodologies explained above can be used to support practice. Some of the examples bear relation to the uses of information and communication systems and technologies in different domains of human activity.

## Systems Practice in the Idealist Pattern

The use of systems methodologies is becoming more popular to support definition and implementation of visions for several reasons. First, in our societies it has become common practice to involve people in discussions about decisions[4] in order to arrive at a 'result'. Information systems (IS) activities adopt this practice given their main emphasis on working to develop a 'true' representation of a system to be developed, maintained or designed. Second, the influence of a network paradigm of society continually encourages us to consider the effects of our thinking and decisions for different groups of people; this makes us adopt visions that provide a sense of well-being for the future. Third, at the heart of systems-thinking is the consideration of people and their different perspectives and needs. This is seen by individuals in charge of transformations as a key element to ensure success, because once people are on board they can identify aspects that transformation initiatives need to address.

Given the above reasons, systems-thinking could become a cornerstone of a new type of *culture* in society in which visions are defined and modified continually. Systems methodologies can offer ways of structuring debate on situations that bring complexity when it comes to thinking seriously about the future. They can help in guiding the process of identifying issues related to the achievement of a vision, and in debating about how to take appropriate action.

We now present some experiences of supporting and/or re-defining required transformations by using systems methodologies.

### Developing Information-based Organizations

Deregulation of the economic sector in a developing country brought opportunities and challenges for profit and non-profit organizations. At the XY Financial Group[5] (where I worked as a project manager), this meant that the use of systems and technologies could help the group and its companies face imminent competition. A set of projects (called the ICT initiative) was set up to bring technologies to the forefront of core business activities and take advantage of their use. One of the corporate projects was to define and implement a technological architecture to support the exchange of information between the companies of the group. At the time, this group had companies in the businesses of savings and loans, banking, construction, leasing and insurance.

The technological initiative worked with a given *vision* that the senior management team of the group defined: to become *an information-based organization*. This meant that at any customer branch of the group of companies, integrated information about customers was to be available. This information was defined in terms of customers' existing products, demography and opportunities for cross selling of products. A working architecture was defined to support the operation of systems. Similarly to the 'nervous system' bits-based vision explained above, the architecture was to enable information to be at the fingertips of any sales person or manager in the organization.

The 'high level' information architecture shown in Figure 5.4 envisioned communication between different types of applications and the implementation of a customer information database which could be accessed from any group branch anywhere. Such a database would contain more 'static' information about customers (e.g. their demographics), and would be enriched continually with customer transactions information. In terms of information systems, applications would also include those necessary for the administration of the group (general ledger, human resource management, asset management, sales and marketing).

More important than the vision or its architecture was what the group would make of it in terms of projects. To enact the transformations required by the architecture, several projects of selecting adequate software applications were launched. One of these was the selection of a centralized human resource management application. This application was to manage the information of all employees of the group, and support processes of payroll and career development among others. A group of 'users' with a user leader was set up.

Initially, this group was to define a request for proposal (RFP) to be sent to software providers to participate in a public tendering process to provide a software solution. Out of the tendering

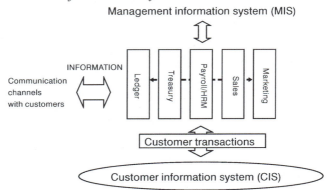

*Figure 5.4* Information architecture to support a vision

process, a recommendation was to be given about which of the providers' solutions was to be bought and later implemented.

Given the importance of this project, it was decided to run a series of activities with the aim of gathering users' views about the requirements that the software was ideally to satisfy. I used the mnemonic CATWOE (customers, actors, transformation, worldviews, owners and environment) of soft systems methodology (SSM) (explained in Chapter 4) to elaborate a root definition of the application as a human activity system. Before we proceeded to define the functional requirements of the desired application, the group of users was invited to give their views about these elements. The result of discussions is reflected in Table 5.2.

With the above elements, it became clear that the application that was sought was not merely a payroll system. It was an application to be used by all human resource departments of the group's companies, and was to offer timely information to support the development of individuals. Support required the use of systems and technologies, meaning that many companies were due to replace their existing systems. The root definition provided some clear insights as to what was expected from the application functionally and technologically.

The user group decided to divide the RFP for the application in different areas:

- CV (of employees)
- payroll
- benefits
- career plan
- reports to government bodies
- technological aspects.

The meetings that followed consisted of defining a number of requirements on each of the above areas. The technological requirements were defined by the subproject manager in conjunction with other members of the technology initiative. Once the requirements were defined, the RFP was completed and sent to a number of software providers who then presented their proposals; a short list was made within the group. A number of tests were devised and conducted with each of the short-listed candidates; in these tests several questions were put to candidates in relation to the above aspects. During the meetings, the use of the CATWOE elements helped us to convey our ideas about the system to candidates and to assess the adequacy of the applications being tested. In my view, the user group gained a

*Table 5.2* Elements of the root definition of an application as a system

| Customers | All the companies of the group |
|---|---|
| Actors | The HR departments of the companies as well as that of the group |
| Transformation | Provide the best human resource available to support the group's vision with adequate information on recruitment (including management of CVs), payroll, benefits, career development |
| Worldviews | Having centralized information will enable faster and more adequate management of human resources. Information can be better managed with the best technologies available |
| Owners | The group |
| Environment | The application has to fit with the architecture; open systems standards are to be adopted; legal requirements need to be followed for payroll and benefits |

degree of cohesiveness and purpose which enabled participants to consider different aspects of the desired application.

The project finished when one of the software providers was recommended to the senior management and an application was selected for implementation a few years later.

In this experience, the use of the CATWOE mnemonic provided insights as to the main aspects to be considered for the software to fit within the vision and architecture defined for the organization. It allowed the group of people to elicit different perspectives about what the system was supposed to do. These perspectives could be later accommodated in the RFP and the group gained the possibility of using these elements to talk to technology providers when asking questions about software packages. In short the use of CATWOE enabled a group of people to work together and to produce useful knowledge to be used in further activities.

### Working to 'Firm Up' a Research Project

The above case shows that often, information systems practitioners or policy makers have to work with *given* visions, generalizations or concerns. Existing plans need to be implemented, and some of the key issues to be considered are complementary to the use of ICTs. Systems methodology use can help people to 'firm up' visions and plans by giving them opportunities to develop strategies on several fronts to ensure that several aspects of plans (not initially considered) are addressed.

In the current climate of UK universities (from 2006 onwards), research has become an essential activity to be pursued. Research also needs to be directed to address problems in the geographical location where universities are being based. In 2007, we were approached by a work colleague at a university-based business school who was in charge of a project aimed to facilitate the transition of women to work in the logistics sector. Project funders wanted to ensure that a specific number of women were trained via a university course in logistics.

Training also included mentoring and guidance for those participants willing to enter into the logistics labor market. The project director was concerned that given this 'vision' the project would just focus on that and would leave out other aspects that would ensure not only that the vision was to be achieved, but also that the project would have a good working environment within the business school.

Using this university's previous expertise in electronically mediated mentoring initiatives, the project was to run a virtual environment in order to facilitate mentoring between women already working in the logistics sector and women enrolled in the training course. Having approved the

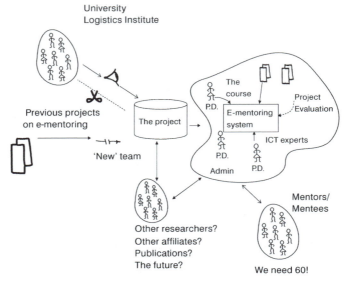

*Figure 5.5* A summarized rich picture of the project

project and the funding, our colleague (the project director) approached us (me and a colleague) to see how we could help her to improve the project definition using systems methodologies.

After an initial conversation with the project director and one of the project researchers, it was decided to use soft systems methodology (SSM) and run a workshop with the project team (consisting of the project director, an administrator, two project researchers and two moderators). The workshop would offer basic ideas on systems-thinking, SSM and would develop a number of activities based on the methodology's stages.

Prior to the workshop, I asked participants via email about any particular ideas or concerns in relation to the project which we could address in the session. Some participants expressed an interest in finding out how some of the SSM activities could be integrated into the virtual mentoring system to be used by the course students. They were interested in using the methodology to facilitate the project evaluation. To this request I replied by saying that it could be possible for students to make their own definitions about the project using systems models. I suggested we could talk in the workshop about how we could encourage students to produce their own definitions and how we could record this information electronically.

The workshop began by introducing some basic systems ideas (like interdependence between parts, the systems boundary, and the importance of people's perceptions when it comes to defining the system). The basic stages of SSM were presented, and several examples of rich pictures (including one about this particular project) were offered to encourage participants to draw their own rich picture.

Given the number of participants (six in total), the group was divided into three pairs and asked to draw their own 'rich picture' of the project as they conceived of it. The picture was to contain the main project activities, how it was related to a wider organizational structure (the university business school), and any particular perceptions about the project's current situation. Each pair was asked to present the picture to the rest of the group. Figure 5.5 contains a summary of all the pictures.

The figure shows the project as an organization whose relationships with the outside world (the university's departments, other researchers at the business school and affiliates) needed to be strengthened to ensure project visibility and project support. In addition, the use of the online mentoring system was being delegated to one of the project researchers; its use could bring challenges but also opportunities (for instance supporting the project evaluation), and it seemed that the rest of the project team did not want to have much to do with the system. This however contrasted with the views about supporting the project course with such a system and allowing project e-tutors to do their job properly. In relation to the rest of the project team, it was important to consider the future careers of team members when current funding ran out. The project needed to recruit a given number of students (mentees) as well as mentors to ensure that the e-mentoring part was to give adequate support to the course participants. This put additional pressure in some project team members.

After presentations of their pictures, I encouraged participants to identify relevant issues and made a list of them. The issues were discussed in terms of their priority to be attended by the project. The group then selected two particular issues:

1    relations between the project and the outside world (university departments);
2    use of the online mentoring system for project evaluation and administration of the course content (including an e-mentoring component).

I then presented an example of a root definition and a conceptual model of activity, and encouraged participants to define the elements of root definitions (using the mnemonic CATWOE) as well as conceptual models of systems of activity which would address each or both of the above issues. However, the discussion that followed focused on the transformation (T) sought by the project (to train people) and how this was the main concern of the project director. To achieve this, it was suggested by participants that the project should provide appropriate training in the use of the online mentoring system to both the project team and students; to provide relevant online materials for students using existing university resources (and asking colleagues at the business school to help provide such materials), and to convene another meeting to discuss how students could participate in evaluating the project. As the end of the session was approaching, I encouraged participants to define a list of activities to be integrated into the project plan. It was then agreed to do the following:

•    modify the schedule to formalize training sessions in the online mentoring system;
•    add course content to the online system;
•    organize another meeting to talk about ways in which the project could be evaluated.

In addition, it was also agreed (with some degree of consensus) that the project needed to strengthen links with various individuals and research groups of the business school so as to become more visible. This proved helpful for the project director who by the end of the session became more aware of developing key relations to ensure that the project was to be continually supported, and that project members could be considered for future posts at the business school. With these discussions, the workshop was brought to an end.

The above experience shows that creativity can also be developed by working with a particular vision in mind (that of training a number of students) and thinking about how to operate in relation to it. Outcomes of the workshop suggest that the development of a vision requires working on other activities and in relations between people so that these could support progressing towards such vision. Regarding the use of ICTs, some of the possible support activities could be integrated into information systems. In this case, IS practitioners (including one of the project researchers) benefited from exploring possibilities together with other project participants.

Later on during the project, we were invited again to facilitate a shorter session in which the project team wanted to define activities to be included in the final project evaluation. Again, the CATWOE mnemonic (clients, actors, transformation, worldview, owners, environment) was used to define an evaluation system. Complementary to satisfying the funder's requirements in the evaluation (e.g. training a given number of women in logistics), it was agreed that some key areas to consider when evaluating the project (derived from transformation – T) were the assessment of 'happiness' in participants (the project should aim to build confidence); raising the project team's profile (for future career opportunities) and the production of written research outputs of high caliber on topics like women in logistics and the role of ICT in mentoring. It was also agreed that some information stored via the online mentoring system and used in producing evaluation reports was to become available to some project clients (logistics companies, mentors, the business school, professional associations) so they could assess the effects of the project and ultimately support the incorporation of women into the logistics sector.

### Exploring the Role of 'Policeman' or 'Teacher'

In practice, we have found that people often express a general or dominant concern about the future in relation to the organization they work for and the transformations that they need to deal with in the development of a vision. Often such vision is defined or ruled from the top, and it is necessary for people to take it forward, including its consequences.

In the UK, a large part of health services are delivered through hospital trusts and primary care trusts (PCTs). These organizations are supported by regional bodies known as Strategic Health Authorities (SHAs). During 2006 a government bill was passed to restructure the SHAs. There are now a smaller number of them. A vision for the SHA was to provide leadership, ensure local (trusts) systems operate effectively, and help them to develop and improve their service delivery to patients.

During that year we (two colleagues and I) were invited to help the planning department of a UK Strategic Health Authority (SHA).[6] Under the above vision, the SHA was to be merged with another one and the planning department staff members were not sure what the future would hold for them. One staff member approached us after attending a demonstration workshop on the use of strategic assumption surface testing (SAST) (Mason and Mitroff, 1981). In his own words, he saw this methodology as useful to allow him / his colleagues / other stakeholders to unearth a number of assumptions regarding the stated vision. Assumptions could be related to how the SHA 'customers' (e.g. trusts) would perceive them once the vision was implemented.

Having agreed to help the SHA with a workshop, we[7] then proceeded to organize it. First, we discussed again with our contact the concerns that he / his colleagues had about the future vision for the SHA. We soon realized that the situation was complex, because there were many issues of concern about the future of the SHA. Having asked our contact to gather some information in the form of individual SWOT analyses[8] from his colleagues at work, it became clear that most of them were confused as to how the proposed merger was to impact upon their work, and how they could continue providing their clients with expertise and advice. Based on this, we considered it important during the workshop to give participants the opportunity to air their own concerns in relation to the proposed vision. We prepared a presentation for the workshop which contained key group issues of concern identified in the SWOT analyses. The plan for the workshop was first to explain basic ideas on systems-thinking, revisit the SWOT analysis findings and then develop an application of SAST with a key issue of concern in mind.

After discussing our interpretation of the findings obtained from the SWOT analysis, participants were encouraged to contribute their views on what issues needed to be addressed given their importance. The key issue became the new role of the SHA within the national health system. One suggested role was to conceive of the SHA as a 'policeman' organization, in charge of measuring the performance of trusts. The other suggested role was that of a 'teacher' organization, focused primarily on helping trusts to develop their capabilities and new management schemes.

As mentioned in the previous chapter, the SAST methodology suggests the following steps, and develops a dialectical process of planning between two competing options. Based on these roles, we suggested that participants explore the assumptions that were supporting them and engage in discussing how these assumptions could have implications for their future work if any of the roles was to gain prominence after the merging process. Participants agreed to this suggestion and then we proceeded to use the SAST steps as follows:

## Group formation

We formed two groups with about six people in each. One group was going to defend the option of the SHA as a 'policeman'; the other was to defend the option of the SHA as a 'teacher'.

## Assumption identification

As facilitators, each of us worked with a group. We invited each group to first consider who would be a stakeholder in the option being supported. The following were some of the stakeholders being considered by the groups:

- UK Department of Health
- UK Treasury
- primary care trusts (PCTs)
- other trusts
- universities (those delivering health education)
- other education providers
- National Health Service Institute
- SHA staff
- taxpayers
- patients
- patients forums
- local authorities.

After the above stakeholder identification, in each group we asked participants to list no more than twelve assumptions about the future behavior of stakeholders in the case that their option was to be implemented. The group that was to defend the role of 'teacher' for the SHA produced the following assumptions:

1   The Department of Health needs an intermediate tier to facilitate communication with local trusts (hospitals and other services).
2   The new SHAs have been formed to set up a regulated market and will only exist for 2–3 years.
3   Trusts need help with development in order achieve the desired 'foundation' status.
4   Trusts will look primarily to the SHA for help with development.
5   There is value in pooling the resources and expertise associated with development.

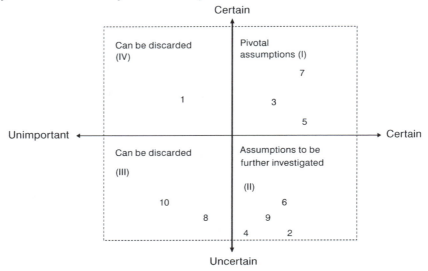

*Figure 5.6* Assumption plotting and weighting using SAST

6   Workforce planning in the trusts should be co-ordinated across the SHA area.
7   Universities and other education providers prefer to work with a small number of education commissioners (a function of the SHA) rather than directly with the trusts.
8   External standard setters (such as the NHS Institute or the Quality Assurance Agency for Higher Education) need a co-ordinating body to work with.
9   The SHA is needed to facilitate communication between trusts and to support joint development work.
10  Development is stimulated by openly comparing the progress of different trusts.

### Assumption Weighting

The groups then proceeded to weight and plot the assumptions so that different perceptions about them could be identified. As the methodology suggests, the assumptions are plotted in a grid according to their importance and their degree of certainty. The above assumptions were plotted by the group defending the 'teacher' option as shown in Figure 5.6.

Figure 5.6 shows for example that the group defending this option was fairly certain that trusts would need help to achieve foundation status, and that this activity would be as important to an SHA with a developmental function (assumptions 3 and 5) as to other stakeholders (e.g. universities, assumption 7). However, there seemed to be a high degree of uncertainty that the trusts would look primarily to the SHA for help with this development (assumption 4), given the uncertain status that SHAs would have in the future (assumption 2). The differences in location of assumptions also show the degree (certainty, importance) that participants conceded to them.

### Debate

After the other group produced their own list of assumptions and figure, we invited representatives of each group to present their lists and figures to the other in a plenary session. They were to explain each assumption, as well as the weighting given. Participants of the other group were encouraged to ask questions in order to clarify the meaning of assumptions, to find out more about the option being considered, and to suggest ways to rephrase or modify the weighting of any assumptions. As facilitators, we stressed the importance of having an atmosphere of constructive criticism and co-operation rather than one of competition to define the best option.

After each group' presentation, we proceeded to encourage participants to reflect on what was being discussed and to suggest how a *synthesis*[9] of options could be achieved. This was to be developed by focusing the discussion on the assumptions being rated as important and certain, with a view to identifying any commonalities between assumptions and building a stronger (synthesized) perception of the future of the SHA.

Throughout the discussion most participants realized the existence of potential opportunities and challenges for each of the future roles identified for the SHA. The 'teacher' role was seen as analogous to 'formative assessment' in education, and the 'policeman' role analogous to 'summative assessment'; both could help the SHA and its members improve their relationships with customers although it was preferable first to 'teach' and then to 'assess' them regarding the adoption of new service standards laid out by central government.

Because of this, the group acknowledged the possibility of moving the two approaches closer together, so that developmental efforts are focused on areas of under-performance. We decided to call this new option *developmental management*. It would consist of educating the SHA's clients (i.e. primary care trusts, hospital trusts) in how to manage themselves in order to meet performance-based measures established by the government; the SHA would provide training and continuous advice; the SHA would also establish performance indicators jointly with these clients, and then it would collaborate in assessing clients' performance based on agreed indicators. For the education activities, the SHA could use its expertise in development together with its pool of available resources. In this way, it could also satisfy the demands for performance management being made on its clients. The option was supported by a synthesis of assumptions, some of which provided adequate ground to proceed (important, certain), whilst others needed to be investigated further in order to consolidate the option as a possible strategy to follow after the SHA merged. These assumptions can be seen in Figure 5.7.

Combining the above certain and 'to be investigated' assumptions, a synthesized option proved adequate for the whole group, as it offered stronger assumptions about how the SHA could develop its future strategies. It also allowed participants to feel part of the SHA by contributing

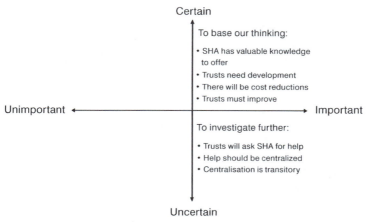

*Figure 5.7* Synthesizing assumptions from both groups

their own expertise in several areas that the SHA's clients could tap in the near future. More importantly, the exercise helped participants to gain a more grounded view of such a future, so that they could themselves engage in making sure that they would have opportunities to go for. At the end of the exercise some of them expressed their satisfaction; they had gained valuable knowledge about their situation and the use of the methodology which was to help them think about and deal with the pressures of the merging process.

### Designing an Ideal System for Students

Under an idealist pattern of practice, it is also possible to use some parts of systems methodologies to promote creative thinking and to explore ways to improve our thinking about a situation, so that we can design creatively ways of working and using information and communication technologies.

At Javeriana University we engaged in a process of institutional ICT planning that involved several stakeholder groups. One of these groups (of approximately forty individuals) was composed of students from the computer science and systems engineering degree. These students had a degree of knowledge and interest about the potential of ICT, and they were eager to see how ICT could help them during their studies. We had the possibility of teaching them a number of systems methodologies including interactive planning (IP) and critical systems heuristics (CSH). With these methodologies and based on students' issues of concern in relation to their life in society (see Chapter 6) we planned a series of activities to think about and design a system to improve the delivery of education. Students participated with their answers to some of these questions which we then used to inform the design of such a system.

In terms of an idealized future state of affairs, the system was to cater for the needs of students and staff with the aim of making education delivery more flexible. At the time of doing these exercises, issues of concern had to do with the rigidity of the timetabling process for courses and seminars. Despite the apparent effectiveness of such process in allocating rooms and times for classes and tutorials, students felt that one of its effects was to limit the availability of educational content. Staff members were also limited to delivering content in face-to-face activities. It was necessary to develop a new vision of the educational process and use the potential of ICTs to support it.

With the students we then focused on defining and designing a system to support educational delivery and detailing its ideal properties. Such a system was to make educational activities more flexible, so that both students and staff had different choices when selecting times and contents for their courses. With the help of ICT, allocation of classrooms would be done on demand and considering the number of students who would sign up for a particular session of a course. The system would then explore availability of tutors to meet the proposed schedule. Also, students would be able to take their sessions 'online' by accessing relevant material. From a range of topics, they would also be able to decide on their preferred one as well as on their preferred method of assessment.

In addition, the system would enable students to keep an electronic memory of the projects being developed during different courses. The purpose of doing this was to enable other stakeholders (e.g. companies) to access this information and get involved in the projects. This would also enable students to define projects which would respond to the needs of these and other stakeholders. A database of projects and possibilities for future work would be kept as a result. Any stakeholder would be able to consult this database and on the basis of existing information, formulate new possibilities for projects. The resulting design is shown in the Figure 5.8.

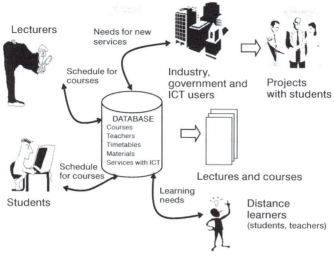

*Figure 5.8* An idealized design of an educational system at a university

With the resulting design, it was then possible to see how existing projects at the university were considering emerging needs of students and staff, and see if there was any possibility to improve project delivery. We showed this design to departmental directors who expressed an interest to take it forward to implementation. The ideas contained were taken into account for future plans. For further detail the reader can see Chapter 6, in which we show how this was part of a longer process of engagement.

## Reflections from Practice

We now have a collection of experiences in which we have followed an idealist pattern of thinking. This type of thinking emphasizes enabling transformations through the (re)definition of visions. In practice, we find that systems methodologies help people by supporting the definition of plans to take visions to reality, as well as encouraging them to 'blue sky' thinking and come up with new insights, ideas and properties of systems of activity which include technology.

Thus, it is possible to claim that overall, an idealist pattern of practice is developing in relation to the information society in different areas. This pattern aims to work with 'visions', and aims to put them into reality as a way of showing that the information society is happening. People find visions useful, because they help in the articulation of ideas. Visions compel us to act, to find solutions to existing problems, and to use our creativity when it comes to putting information systems and technologies in the picture.

With the help of systems methodologies and techniques (or methods, not necessarily full methodologies as describe in the experiences), we find we can support discussion between people. In this regard, a strong contribution of systems methodology use is that it helps *validate* existing thinking about what aspects need to be re-considered and firmed up more strongly. In the experiences of using SAST and SSM, it became clear that we were providing support for the definition of projects and policies that were bringing new ways of working and operating in organizations. We were able to validate these and to involve people in discussing better definitions and strategies to help them deal with the complexities of change. In the last experience and using IP, we could subject our creative ideas to feasibility in terms of what can be achieved with ICTs.

*Table 5.3* Challenges and the idealist pattern of practice

| Challenges to systems-thinking | Assumptions of systems methodology use |
| --- | --- |
| Language: *The language of planning* | Seeking accommodation ☑ |
| Problem solving: *The problems associated with visions* | Becoming instruments of organizational goals ☑ |
| Time: *The time to validate existing plans.* | Used mostly to address organizational problems ☑ |
| | ☑: assumed |

The above experiences show a variety of activity in which the information society can be developed, and different types of areas which could be supported (decision making, managing change, learning, etc). These not only have to do with ICT-based implementations. Once we decide to explore such areas with a wider (e.g. systems-based) perspective, a number of elements emerge to be considered as relevant. An idealist pattern of practice requires us to put effort into identifying and addressing these aspects in order to ensure that a vision has a good chance of being implemented. Among other issues, the experiences presented in this chapter lead us to consider issues of relationships, definitions of new role(s), functional and technical aspects of software applications and flexibility in what we do.

Despite this variety of issues and possibilities when it comes to thinking about visions and transformations, we find that there is a lot of work to do to prepare the ground for visions in terms of fulfilling a number of *pre-conditions*, and it seems that efforts are mostly being spent on satisfying these pre-conditions (in terms for instance of firming up a role for organizations or individuals, establishing key relations between people, or securing ICT support). This insight could give us assurance about the work to be done in preparing the ground for the implementation of a vision, but at the same time could be a sign that there are constraints we need to work with despite an intention to provoke a 'rupture' with the information society in the ways things go. In the cases presented, a common constraint is that of developing practice that resonates with what has been formulated as 'best practice'. It is often the case that visions have already been defined and we work with what has been established. Under this idealist pattern, possibilities for questioning or challenging such visions might not be available. Or they might be difficult to include in existing plans or initiatives, presumably under the assumption that it is not possible to do so!

In relation to systems-thinking and systems methodology use, Table 5.3 suggests that under an idealist pattern of practice we put emphasis on working with given elements (e.g. visions), and then subordinate methodology use to their implementation. We find that the language of systems fits well with the language of strategic planning. Once this link is made, problems of language can be overcome. Systems methodologies have helped us to solve particular problems (e.g. putting plans or policies into practice, or helping to redefine them); but in doing so we have remained within organizational boundaries. We have not gone beyond the assumptions of systems methodologies identified from previous chapters (e.g. accommodation, instrumentalization, focused on organizational problems).

It seems then that under the idealist pattern the challenges laid out for systems-thinking and systems methodology use are being partially addressed because the emphasis is on other elements (e.g. vision, strategy). This could suit many organizations or initiatives in need of ensuring vision implementation but not stepping aside of them to define what we broadly want from society.

In relation to the above reflections and in particular to subordinating methodology use to certain boundaries, it is worth asking if practitioners need to become more critical about developing the information society as based on visions. We could work under this pattern but also try to engage themselves and other people more fully in constructing these visions so that they respond to people's concerns and needs. We will explore this possibility in the next chapter.

## Chapter Summary

In this chapter a pattern of practice for the information society is presented which emphasizes the importance of formulating initiatives, policies or actions as based on visions. Currently a vision is a powerful way of gathering people's efforts and directing them towards collaborating. A vision can be strongly supported by possibilities given by ICTs. A vision can also engage people across organizations and disciplines. Practitioners can gain from helping firm up visions and addressing aspects needed for the implementation of visions.

Systems methodology use has proved effective in supporting definition of actions on different fronts to support vision implementation, as well as making practitioners more aware of other aspects that need to be tackled to ensure implementation. More needs to be said about shaping visions in the information society according to what people want and need.

## Key Messages

- An idealist pattern needs a vision of what life would look like in the information society if we use ICTs to improve the quality of life of individuals.
- A vision could also be a good way of addressing information society challenges related to marginalization.
- Different systems methodologies and techniques can be used to firm up a vision so that people involved and affected by a vision's implementation can further knowledge and ultimately firm up themselves in the future that a vision proposes.

## Questions / Exercises

Choose a project or initiative you are familiar with or one about which there is available information on the internet.
- Define and discuss possible visions associated with it.
- Suggest how a systems methodology could be employed to improve its chances of being implemented.
- Define a vision for the above project initiative.
- Based on what 'bits' could do for the above project (for instance establishing a 'nervous system' or an 'information-based organization').
- Based on other ideas about the project.
- Select one of the experiences presented in this chapter.
- Discuss how you would have undertaken it, considering that it was possible to foster a higher degree of creativity.
- What possibilities for use of ICT would you consider adding to the work done? Why?

## Further Reading

Checkland and Poulter (2006). A short and well-written account of soft systems methodology with some examples of the full methodology use.

# 6 The Strategic Pattern for Practice in the Information Society

## Introduction

So far in our practice the information society can be developed by supporting or re-defining transformations required by visions; this can become a creative process and can help us to think of different aspects of a vision. Visions gain importance thanks to the power of information and communication technologies (ICTs) which gives us opportunities to think of them in terms of 'bits'. Systems methodology use has showed us how practitioners can help firm up visions by looking at particular issues or problems related to putting plans into practice.

Whilst this can often be the case because there is very little time or space to think outside visions, in some other types of situations we find it is better to focus on *engaging people*. This is because the information society development requires people's participation not only to solve particular problems but also to go beyond them. This could lead us to reconsider the purpose, scope and impacts of a vision or a creative exercise. In the experiences presented in the previous chapter a key element we had to overlook was the engagement of different stakeholders whose involvement would have been desirable. These and other people could have helped to shape up visions, and clarify a bit more what was possible with the help of information and communication technologies; and to help us learn from putting ideas into practice. In processes of engagement in the information society, it is often the case that ICTs need to be adapted to a context of use.

The idealist pattern of thinking about the information society (presented in the last chapter) can be somehow victim of its own success. Alignment between people, organizations and technology is at the same time *assumed and pursued* through visions. We assume alignment between people and organizations because we commit people to implement new ways of working with the help of ICTs. We pursue alignment between people and technology because individuals take forward possibilities of technology use. What the idealist pattern of thinking does not fully assume though, is the possibility to align both technology and organizations to people, to their values, beliefs and ways of life, as Figure 6.1 shows.

This chapter considers that the engagement of people constitutes a pattern of thinking to develop the information society. Through engagement, strategies and action plans for the information society can be further developed in practice. Systems methodologies can help us in doing so.

The pattern of thinking is called *strategic*. In it, different interests, values and concerns of people are taken into account to shape the definition and future incorporations and uses of information systems and technologies in a variety of realms of life. People define their own strategies to adopt and use information and communication technologies. As Figure 6.1 suggests, the pattern of thinking aims to complement the idealist pattern of thinking (explored in the last

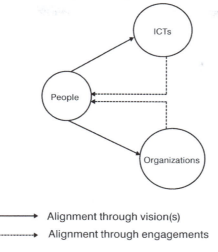

> → Alignment through vision(s)
> ┈┈┈┈┈▶ Alignment through engagements

*Figure 6.1* Aligning people to ICTs/organizations and vice versa

chapter), because it might be that engagement is driven by the need to shape visions to people's own values and interests, and this might require us as practitioners to go beyond organizational boundaries. In this way we would be addressing more fully the challenges laid out in previous chapters for the information society, systems-thinking and systems methodology use (see Table 4.1).

Systems methodologies can be used to facilitate engagement. They help us include people's perceptions and ideas about a situation, even of those who are not directly involved but could be affected. Methodologies can also promote more interactive processes of planning with a view of considering a variety of values and concerns of stakeholder groups. By doing so, they could contribute to longer and more meaningful engagements, in which organizational and technological possibilities could be aligned to people.

## Objectives

- To present the main tenets of another pattern of thinking and acting for practice in the information society, called 'strategic'.
- To describe how it can be developed by using systems methodologies and /or methods.
- To reflect on strengths and weaknesses of the strategic pattern of thinking for the information society.

## The Strategic Pattern

Some people in the information society would like to see it developed step-by-step rather than in radical ways. They argue that any change due to the incorporation of a new 'paradigm', 'vision', or 'transformation' is to be digested first, and gradually defined by considering what is important for individuals and groups in society. People's existing social relations, values and beliefs become the background or medium in which any change or transformation in the information society can be defined, discussed and re-shaped.

There could be many reasons for people to prefer gradual rather than radical transformations. It might be that their societies value participation and consensus in decision making rather than quick or blunt imposition. Or it might be that they also want to use their people's creative thinking. Or adopting change gradually might also be suitable in economic and cultural terms. Information systems practitioners and managers could also feel that gradual change is more sensible because it gives them possibilities to try ICTs and learn from their use rather than simply adopting them. This would give opportunities to shape and re-shape technology use with people.

Considering the above and the importance of engagements in the information society already highlighted (see Chapter 2), we now suggest a pattern of thinking to guide information and systems practice with the following features:

- It considers that engagements aim at *shaping up* the design and uses of ICTs by people who are to be involved and affected by them.
- It bases the shaping up of ICT design and use on people's concerns, values and interests about their societies.
- It uses systems methodologies with explicit attention to people's engagement to shape up technology use. Methodologies can also help to structure debate around improving the current situation of individuals in society. In debate, the roles of ICT can be discussed and integrated in agendas for improving situations according to what is appropriate.

We begin by presenting how the information society has been shaped up by processes of engagement of individuals and groups, and how it can be further facilitated.

## Revisiting Engagement(s) in the Information Society

Turner (2006) argues that the perspective of a network (information) society (as described in Chapter 2) originated in the first part of the twentieth century. He identifies key circumstances during and after the Second World War that facilitated collaborative work between scientists from different disciplines. Thanks to these circumstances, scientists developed a number of concepts which would then be used to foster research on technologies for the processing and exchange of electronic information.

For instance, the emergence of cybernetics as a discipline brought with it a particular language which scientists then could use to communicate with each other. Concepts in cybernetics included feedback and information. With these concepts also came the idea of humans and society as self-regulating systems in which parts could exchange information through feedback mechanisms (see Chapter 2 for a description of other concepts of general systems theory, autopoiesis and complexity). Human and non-human phenomena could also be modeled as information processing systems. This insight enabled scientists to model behavior and devise artifacts to enhance, manage or improve communication processes.

In addition, inter-disciplinary work among scientists was facilitated by the existence of 'trade zones', or spaces in which collaboration was mediated and fostered through the exchange of ideas. In these zones, there were people with particular personality traits which enabled them to bring together multiple and often segregated scientific communities. These people were driven by the idea that society could live up to ideals of egalitarianism and democracy.

The importance of such spaces and key individuals is also recalled by Castells (2001). He describes the evolution of the internet, and shows how different and disparate communities were brought together and exchanged knowledge towards enabling the internet to become a public commodity to be accessible to all (government, businesses, technology suppliers and community groups). Through conversations, trial and error, forums and even key figures or political movements, the internet has been shaped up by people with different interests and perspectives about what to do with it.

This historical reminder shows how initiatives that have played a key role in developing the information society require people to become engaged: people conversing and interacting have given shape to initiatives which bring close to reality the vision of information pervading almost every aspect of daily life. The idea of engagement is used to foster practice under a pattern that considers it a key element for information society developments.

## Shaping up the Information Society: Groups and Their Concerns

The above historical reminder shows the importance of development of the information society as being shaped by conversations between people leading to gradual or radical transformations. Regarding gradual transformations, advocates consider that any change takes place within a particular social context of *relationships* between people. These relationships have made possible the emergence of technical artifacts (e.g. ICT), and could also make possible their widespread use.

This becomes more evident in societies where construction or manufacturing of ICTs is important and where people's inventions generate many possibilities and tangible products. However, only a few 'see the light' of being patented, accepted, marketed and finally used by 'lay' people (consumers). Selection of technology has to do with making it 'fit' within a particular set of circumstances including cultural, economic and political.

Thus, it can be inferred that it is people, their values and social networks which have facilitated technology adoption. Bijker *et al.* (1987) for instance talk about the bicycle as a technology. When ideas about it became popular, many designs were proposed by inventors and the like.

Figure 6.2 signals that out of a number of possibilities only a few technology designs 'made it' to the market. Through processes of social interaction, negotiation and 'stabilization', only one of these possibilities was then accepted as a 'true' one (others might have survived for some time and then been abandoned). Socio-technical experts like Bijker attribute this evolution to

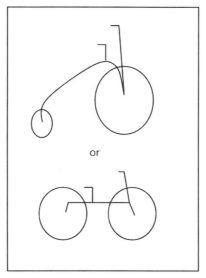

*Figure 6.2* Why is one technology adopted rather than a similar one?

people's decisions about technology according to their own preferences, values and interests. Not only people who are consumers, but also those building and marketing technology will make decisions which will privilege certain artifacts at the expense of others. Decisions would also fit within broader agendas of other individuals and groups, so as to make artifacts relevant, necessary, valid, marketable, and ultimately 'valid'.

Similarly to the issue of technology invention being shaped by different groups of people, there have been studies about the incorporation of information technologies at work. This includes for instance Wanda Orlikowski's (1992) work on the duality of technology. She looks at how the introduction of information systems and technologies generates a number of routines (positive, negative) in people which would also affect their further (future) adoption and use of existing and new technologies. What she shows is that information technologies become 'institutionalized' (adapted, stabilized), and influence the ways organizations operate. It also generates ways of working for people, in which they might decide to adapt technology use to their own needs and aspirations.

But the story does not end there. People make ICT their own and use their experience to make sense of future technology adoption and use. In other words, they help shape technology use (Orlikowski, 1992). This means that technologies like ICT become 'embedded' and 'dependent on' in the fabric of people's organizational relations. As an embedded element, technology becomes a medium and an outcome of change, as Figure 6.3 shows.

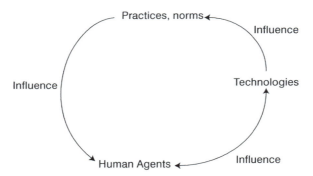

*Figure 6.3* Mutual influence between practices, technologies and people

The above examples show us people's engagement with technologies, and how they transform them. Different groups of individuals are driven by different interests and this also makes adoption and use very heterogeneous. We could guess, interpret or make assumptions about what drives individuals to engage with each other, to design and market products or services, and ultimately to accept or reject them. But rather than guessing, we had better attempt to explicitly articulate people's views, values and interests in relation to change and technology use. In order to engage people in action for the information society, it becomes important to be able to tap into the set of relationships, meanings, values and interests of individuals, with the aim of trying to make sense of them.

In practice, it could be argued that none of this is new. Some information systems and technology practitioners could claim that they have already started tapping into some of these elements when they use traditional methodologies (e.g. waterfall development cycle), in order to appreciate their client's needs – what they want IS or ICT to provide them with. This could be a form of engagement, which will also ensure that there is engagement between technology and people in organizations. Other practitioners would claim that any form of engagement will not produce a full picture of how technology use will unfold. The problem with these answers is that engagement is not focused on what people are concerned about in their lives as a whole.

In our view, engagement in the information society is about *continual re-thinking* of relations between values, interests and technologies, as well as exploration of other relations which might affect ICT adoption and use. Some of these relations can already embed particular uses of ICT and therefore will influence future adoptions. These relations can take us beyond organizational boundaries and allow us to see 'whole' lives in the information society.

## Boundaries

The continual re-thinking of values and technologies to be used or adopted mentioned above is also about considering the *boundaries* adopted to explore how ICT use is defined and shaped up by people. Even if we become aware of the need to articulate different values and perspectives from people, we might include only those whom we think can play an active role in technology design, adoption and use. Those individuals being passive, disinterested or not directly involved could be left behind or be *marginalized* from discussion or possible interpretation of what a technological change would mean for them.

It is necessary to be critical about the boundaries of *what* is to be considered a process of socio-technical change, as well as *who* is to be involved or affected in the process. In engagements, we should ask ourselves questions about the impacts of decisions as a way to understand how any information society initiative is to be shaped. Here the ideas of systems boundary critique explored in Chapter 4 can help us greatly. With critical systems heuristics (CSH) and boundary critique, we can enquire about purposes, clients, measures of performance and other elements of a plan or initiative. We can ask about other issues and people that are included or marginalized, the underlying values supporting decisions and their consequences for different stakeholder groups. The knowledge that we build in this type of inquiry can inform further decisions and the shaping of future uses of systems and technologies in a particular situation.

One additional clarification needs to be made at this point. The above does not mean that our information systems and technologies are to be entirely shaped by one particular group of people (e.g. the users). In particular, systems and technologies can bring their own embedded values and routines which might be different from what is the case in a particular context of future ICT use. There can be a variety of *contexts* as sets of values and rationales which are necessary to identify, understand, review and gradually 'accommodate' in order to mitigate potential mismatches or tensions between them (Heeks, 2005). This would mean shaping up technology use by considering people's perspectives and technology's possibilities in a given situation (see Figure 6.4).

Considering the existence of diverse contexts, it becomes important to engage a diverse group of stakeholders in inquiry when talking about concerns about society and how we could address these concerns with the help of information systems and technologies. Engagement would also involve continual conversation with people throughout implementation and use of systems and technologies.

In translating ideas and designs from one context to another, Figure 6.4 also suggests that there could be some elements that, whilst being important in the previous context (e.g. invention), are being marginalized in subsequent decision making processes in the next context(s) (e.g. design, deployment). It is necessary to ask how and why marginalization happens, and if it is inevitable. Practitioners and other stakeholders need to be sensitive to potential differences between groups and their own contexts in which they could be inventing, designing or deploying ICT. They could employ systems methodologies in the ways described before to support engagement. For instance,

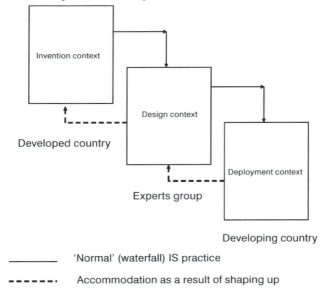

*Figure 6.4* Contexts of invention, design and deployment of electronic government systems

they could use the ideas of critical systems heuristics (CSH) and/or boundary critique to ask about elements which appear marginalized. They could then promote participative design and gradual implementation of systems and technologies by using methodologies like strategic assumption surface testing (SAST), soft systems methodology (SSM) or interactive planning (IP).

To sum up, if we consider that participation or engagement in shaping up the information society initiatives is important, a pattern of thinking that emerges should consider that people shape ICT use according to their own values, perspectives and relationships. We call this pattern strategic. Thinking for this pattern can be guided by systems methodology use to enable participation, debate and reflection.

We now propose a number of elements to develop the above pattern. These elements would enable us to link people's concerns and values with systems methodology use and with definition of actions to improve the current situation, some of which would involve systems and technologies.

## Developing a Strategic Pattern

To develop the strategic pattern the following elements are supported:

- *Concerns.* Identifying what people are concerned about in society so as to improve their current situation.
- *Sweeping generalizations.* Identifying and challenging ideas that might negatively inhibit definition of new ideas or proposals for action.
- *Systems methodologies.* Used to support engagement via the identification of concerns and participative debate or design of any initiatives.
- *Boundary critique.* Ensuring that questions of inclusion, exclusion and marginalization of people and issues are dealt with.

These elements are related in Figure 6.5.

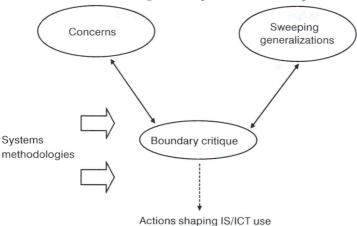

*Figure 6.5* Elements of the strategic pattern of practice

By identifying concerns and sweeping generalizations, we could develop a good start in engaging people in thinking about improving their lives in the information society. We can use systems methodologies to support any participative reflection and design about possibilities for improvement. Boundary critique could help us to further reflect on how any decision through engagements is having potential consequences for improvement.

Before we explore how these elements work in practice, we briefly define what we mean by (1) concerns and (2) sweeping generalizations.

### Concerns

A bits-based vision for the information society – like the one identified in the previous chapter – could engage policy makers and other stakeholders in thinking *how* to bring technologies and systems to society. What we are talking about here is the possibility of allowing these systems and technologies to serve people's concerns and interests. In management thinking, this is often and unfortunately obscured because visions are being developed by organizations and for organizations, and individuals do not count much. If we are not careful with people's own concerns and values, we as practitioners could end up importing such types of vision to the whole of society, and we will then produce a foreign type of society. Or our vision will not have much to do with the world around us, confining us to isolation. In either case, conflicts of values might ensue, as has been the case in societies where the information society has been used to exploit the power of technologies with little regard for people's own values (Wickham, 1997) – those values being about the present and the future.

To avoid the above, it is thus important to ensure that a vision addresses and is built up by including the concerns of people. We are to focus on improving the quality of life of individuals (possibly via a bits-based vision) and we are doing it in a way that should respond to what they want to improve. The possibility of firming up possible visions for society requires practitioners to listen to what people have to say about their ways of living, their issues, their perspectives, beliefs and values. It would also require us to review the meaning of 'quality of life', as it might mean different things to different individuals.

From the systems theory of autopoiesis as defined by Maturana and Varela (see Chapter 4) what we live our concerns with others in conversations as a prelude to action, and that the emotion of love as a willingness to co-exist and accept each other influences strongly what we decide to do. Achieving mutual collaboration and listening to each other requires us to challenge generalizations that inhibit our creative thinking or our conversation. In other words, we need to 'irritate' ourselves and others by challenging such generalizations. We call them 'sweeping' ones.

### Sweeping Generalizations

A generalization is an assumption made about what we as individuals can (not) do and why. Generalizations are part of our cultures and our ways of thinking. The nature of 'sweeping' means that often we do not reflect on their content or their implications for people who might be involved or affected by it. According to de Bono (1976), such a type of generalization carries with it a value-laden abstraction that separates human work from a desired reality, and in this case a desired type of society; it also leaves us almost without anything to do after we implement a vision!

There could be many sweeping generalizations that influence the definitions of action to bring the information society to reality. This type of generalization should be reviewed and challenged *whenever possible*, given that human beings can explore possibilities and alternatives to firm visions and actions up more effectively and meaningfully. It is important to try some creative dialogue as to why we believe this might be the case, and to imagine new possibilities. Those practitioners facilitating a process of engagement with different people should encourage a more proactive attitude in terms of 'what can we do then?' so as to start firming up thinking for improvement.

The types of generalizations about societal change given in Table 6.1 are derived from my own experience and classified according to the type of dimension they emphasize.

Table 6.1 gives a few hints about some generalizations that are often made in processes of planning change in society, some of which could affect initiatives for the information society development. Ideally, engaging people would work if we relate to values that are desirable to keep in the information society (Wickham, 1997). This would mean reviewing our common beliefs, and avoiding generalizations that portray the extremes of situations (we will do it, or we will not do it). These should be challenged equally, or put to the test of looking at how much they could affect positive change in society. Generalizations (and visions) that have worked well

*Table 6.1* Some sweeping generalizations about change

| Dimension | Sweeping generalizations | Examples |
|---|---|---|
| Cultural | "We can (not) do it in our culture"; "We will lose our identity" | "This nation is a nation of innovators"; "The country will be developed in less than 20 years"; "We are the best in being positive towards ICT"; "We will never be fully developed as a country"; "The most important problem of society is education" |
| Collective | "This is the only way of solving problems"; "We do not need a new way to guide our thinking" | "It has worked in the past, it will work in the future"; "We know all there is to know"; "This is our only market"; "This is our vision; we already have plans for the next few years, so there is no need to introduce any changes" |
| Individual | "It does (not) fit with my values or my worldview"; "I am too old for this"; "I cannot learn new ways of solving problems" | "I will fail like I always do"; "It is always everyone else's fault" |

in a different country should be reviewed in the light of what could (not) help in a particular context.

So we should challenge the sort of generalizations we find in organizations or groups, where previously successful ways of doing business or solving problems might not be entirely appropriate when it comes to integrate uses of ICTs. Mentalities of group thinking that can be seen in 'the way we do things here', or in 'the already laid out plans' might enable but also inhibit the exploration of alternatives when it comes to reviewing visions and the generalizations that support them. Complacency with the ways in which things are going can often be encountered. These complacencies not only arise in having developed for instance successful business or institutional practices. They also arise when people think that they do not need to adopt 'foreign' practices, because they consider them less than practical or applicable to their own organization or setting. There could be many missed opportunities derived from this attitude, and possibly in the long term some problems related to organizational learning.

Finally, we see generalizations at the individual level derived from our own ways of thinking which influence how we receive information and solve problems, and ultimately how we imagine our life. These generalizations can be derived from the way we conceive of learning. We could conceive of learning as a process of desiring and arriving at a comfortable state of knowledge. For Zuleta (2005) our idea of a motionless state of *comfort* is a generalization which undermines life itself. Zuleta suggests that life should be better conceived of as continuous work – striving, enquiring, asking and pursuing; in other words, life should be continually defining, achieving and defining again.

A generalization which suggests a state of life in which we as human beings "return to the state of the egg" needs further refinement if not upfront challenging (Zuleta, 2005). Our engagement is the journey leading us to generalize what we really want and what is adequate for us. This requires continual work, curiosity in exploring possibilities, research into putting ideas into practice, and ultimately having an open and enduringly courageous mentality to define actions we want to see implemented (Mendoza, 2006).

As individuals, it is very tempting to live for ideals of comfort so that systems, technologies but not people will do the job (some of Negroponte's ideas about a bits-based vision presented in the previous chapter could be interpreted in this way if we are not careful). This state of affairs has been portrayed by some as the 'big brother society', in which control has been delegated to machines; this lends itself to the overuse of machines' powers by some people at the expense of others. Such generalizations, if possible, should be challenged.

With concerns and generalizations as elements to be identified, it is then possible to use systems methodologies to help in the process. Systems methodologies can help us express views of a situation (SSM); identify potential options for action (SAST); define systems models to help us in exploring feasible and desirable possibilities for improvement (SSM); or design a desirable future for all (IP).

We now look at a case of developing a strategic pattern of thinking in the information society. In our experience, it takes time to engage with people in their own time as time is a challenge we need to consider in our practice (see Table 4.1). Moreover, it also takes time to reflect and report back in a meaningful way on what has happened. This is why we talk about only one experience here. The experience is presented in detail to show how the different elements were addressed. Afterwards, we present our reflections on how the strategic pattern of thinking has helped us to improve the information society.

## Engaging People: Information Systems Planning at Javeriana University

In 1999, we (a research team from the Universities of Hull and Javeriana) were invited to conduct a planning exercise at Javeriana University in Colombia (Córdoba, 2002). The main idea was to explore how information systems and technologies could help improve the delivery of education at the institution. This was clearly an opportunity to engage with groups of individuals in exploring how the information society could be shaped within Javeriana, and how information systems and technologies could help.

We (a research team composed of me, another researcher and an assistant[1]) proposed to use systems-thinking and systems methodologies to guide our intervention. In the proposal presented to senior management, we defined a methodology with the following stages:

1   *Distinction of concerns.* Initially, we would raise with a number of stakeholders a variety of concerns about education in Colombian society, with a view to gaining an appreciation of what people thought about society and how education could help improve ways of living.

2   *Dialogue for design.* Once concerns were identified, we would facilitate a number of 'design' exercises in which we would help participants define a number of suggestions to improve their current situation (which included the delivery of education). We proposed to use systems methodologies to help us in the facilitation process.

This methodology reflected different elements of a strategic pattern of thinking. The first stage was about working with people, and constructively challenging their own sweeping generalizations when we saw fit. We were to use some methods of systems methodologies to reflect the identification of concerns. Our idea was also to use boundary critique to illustrate existing tensions between different value systems and ways of doing things. Throughout the project, our task as facilitators was to continually encourage critical reflection about issues and people 'lying' between boundaries adopted by participants to guide their decisions through the process. We also offered our expertise in systems methodology use.

Initially we suggested a list of people to be interviewed in the first round. The list included administrators, directors of departments and research units, lecturers and some students. By following the ideas of boundary critique, later on we were going to 'roll out' the boundaries of participation by asking each interviewee if there was someone else who they thought should be included in the process. In this way we would include some people who had initially being marginalized due to our own boundary of who was to participate in the project. From an initial list of twenty people we rolled it out to forty by the end of the stage of identification of concerns (stage (1) above).

### Distinction of Concerns and Boundary Critique

To identify people's concerns, we used photographs and pictures as suggested by the work of Susan Weil on reflective action research (Weil, 1998). A picture shows a 'whole' of things; it shows a particular moment in time; it also evokes memories, ideas, values, and possibilities. At Javeriana we initially collated a number of pictures that in our view reflected the Colombian society's current situation. From an initial list of ten individuals, we rolled out the process and conducted several other individual interviews. We also organized four group workshops with other people.

In both the interviews and workshops, we invited people (individually or in groups of three) to choose two to three pictures which reflected their interests, concerns and values about themselves and their society. We then invited them to talk about their impressions. We asked the following questions individually and in groups:

- What do the pictures represent to you? What values do you want to highlight?
- What concerns about yourself and others in society does it make you think about?
- What other concerns you would like to talk about which are not necessarily related to the pictures? This question intended to identify elements lying between relevant systems boundaries for people, and to challenge people's thinking about potential sweeping generalizations they were making.

A picture is often a good vehicle to encourage people to break the ice and talk about society as a whole. By talking about a picture, two or more individuals can converse about situations in which they could have some common concerns, or ideas. It can also be a way of working with groups, and inviting them to share their concerns as a way of encouraging some creative and grounded thinking later on. In the case at Javeriana, the selection of and talking about pictures proved useful for some people to air their concerns.

Moreover, during each interview or group exercise, we made sure that we did not marginalize any ideas or issues raised by participants. At the end of each participant's intervention one person (either one of us or another participant) would be encouraged to ask alternative questions to the interviewees, or raise other concerns which could be considered important. We would point out if we saw a type of sweeping generalization which we could further explore and discuss.

Whilst for some people the use of pictures proved useful, for others they did not play a significant role. They suggested that we should make the use of pictures optional; they could talk more freely about their concerns without using them. This made us realize that up to that point, we had been marginalizing other issues of identifying concerns (for instance speaking about concerns). We were also ignoring other methodologies or techniques to identify concerns and ideas for improving the situation at Javeriana. Using the ideas of boundary critique we made it possible to represent these issues, and acted upon what we saw happening, as in Figure 6.6.

As Figure 6.6 suggests, we were privileging a more graphic way of identifying concerns, leaving other elements (e.g. plain speaking) within the margins (not paying attention to them). As a result of this reflection, in the project we decided to keep the identification of concerns by pictures as an optional activity, so people could speak plainly if they wanted to. The new

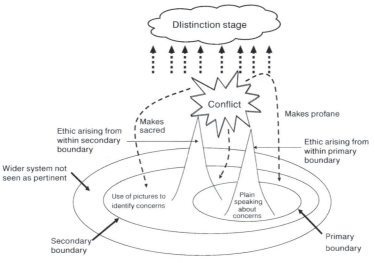

*Figure 6.6* Boundaries related to the identification of concerns

- Marginalization in development
- Isolation of some groups from education
- Our identity in educational processes
- Education to create social consciousness
- Looking at the context of education
- Values promoted in education:
  - Religion
  - Solidarity versus indifference
  - Tradition
  - Community
  - Discourage the value of money

- Resources available for education
- How to help in the current situation?
- There has to be leadership in the Colombian community to promote and sustain change
- What is the purpose of providing IS to education?
- Who will benefit?
- We have double standards in our values
- Society needs a collective memory
- Not everybody has the same perception of reality

- Students should take educational opportunities to manage globalization
- What is the model of society to follow ?
- Human resources should be a priority in society
- How to conduct change in society ?
- We should rescue the countryside and see the impact of technology on it
- Harmonize IT with living in society and in this country
- One lives the values learned at home
- Tradition in universities influences education
- Why does everybody have to be a doctor ?

- IT is affecting the natural environment
- IT can help to improve quality of life
- IT needs infrastructure
- IT education should generate information about the situation of the country
- IS should allow flexibility in lecturing and learning
- Everyone should benefit from IT education

- Education should be 'integrel'
- Need of more research
- IT and education should  benefit society through projects and services
- There should be links with industry and community
- Students should participate in decision taking in education
- Students should help anyone in any region of the country
- What is the profile of IT students?

- Education and IS to live with nature in mutual respect
- The IS guide the search of information but do not replace people
- Images already provide an interpretation of reality
- Media creates ideal images of man

- There could be differences but a common project
- Individual talents and creativity should be fostered in society
- People should be commited to change
- Different views can coexist

*Figure 6.7* An enriched picture of concerns, ideas, values and interests at Javeriana University

boundary included both of these elements. This also made us realize that as a research team we needed to be more self-conscious whenever possible. This was to become a key issue for reflection, as will be presented later in the chapter.

Throughout the stage of distinction and in order to keep a record of concerns being raised, we collated the information into an 'enriched picture'. This is a slightly modified version of soft systems methodology's (SSM) rich picture. It not only portrays the situation 'as it is', but also contains ideas, concerns, values, interests, and possibilities for action in society. Figure 6.7 is a summarized and 'enriched' picture of what we identified as being relevant to people (Córdoba, 2002). Some of the elements of the picture refer specifically to the roles of ICTs.

This picture was also used during further interviews and workshops, and participants were shown it in order to encourage them to share their own concerns about society. It was a good way of awakening some emotions which people could connect to, with a view of doing something together about such concerns.

### *Dealing with Other Sweeping Generalizations*

By asking people about their concerns in society, we were gaining a variety of responses, which included some sweeping generalizations and which, in our view, were inhibiting any attempt to improve the situation. These generalizations included (but were not limited to):

- Nobody cares about each other in our society.
- I just want to leave this country.
- We are the most inventive people in the world.
- Information technology is not for me, I belong to another generation.
- You are the experts, you should tell us how to use systems and technologies in education!

These generalizations showed us that there were elements (issues, people) which could be considered by participants but which were not yet seen as relevant because there were more pressing concerns or ingrained assumptions they wanted to deal with. We took some of these generalizations to debate in order to encourage reflection about them. In group exercises, we asked people about why they privileged the 'negative', and challenged it by putting forward more 'positive' or more 'useful' ideas (including the opposite ones, and exploration of what would happen if alternative ideas were followed). We were challenging their current emotions about change.

To continue being engaged with people, the idea of 'shaping up' plans became useful and necessary as participants could then be encouraged to assume some degree of ownership and action about any improvements. We then encouraged participants to take responsibility to shape change in society if we all wanted to see other things happening. Between the 'negative' and the 'positive' generalizations being identified, with further encouragement to shape up things, some ideas were found 'lying' and in need of further exploration. For instance:

- We feel this way (e.g. hopeless, depressed) because of the situation of continual armed conflict in the country. But we can still change things.
- We need dedication and respect for each other if we want to succeed individually and as a society.
- We should encourage certain values for living (respect, peaceful coexistence).
- Only if we promote the use of ICT to support cultural diversity and other issues, can we lose the fear of ICT.

The encouragement proved in general useful for participants, and most of them were willing to continue with the project. We even organized a couple of workshops with people not working at Javeriana but who were interested in talking about the role of IS/ICT in Colombian society. Their concerns and interests were included in the enriched picture presented in Figure 6.7.

Based on the participants' willingness to continue, we planned the activities of stage (b) of our project (dialogue for improvement). We were going to use systems methodologies to support the definition of improvements, some of which were to include the support of information systems and communication technologies.

People were reluctant to challenge only the generalization 'You are the experts!' In one of the workshops where this generalization emerged, we declared our interest in facilitating discussions rather than in providing expertise about what should be done with information systems and technologies. We encouraged people to own their plans and initiatives. However, some participants decided to withdraw from the project, on the grounds that we were not providing useful knowledge or advice. Some of them also withdrew in the following activities. We now describe the next stage of our project.

### Use of Systems Methodologies and Boundary Critique

For the next stage of our project, we designed two types of activities: (1) design exercises and (2) critical engagements.

1   The first type was a series of workshops in which participants, with the help of systems methodologies, were to address identified concerns. This was going to be done with two main strategies:

One in which insights for improvement were to be defined using root definition, conceptual models and comparison with the real situation. This was based on Checkland's soft systems methodology (SSM) (Checkland, 1981).

Another in which people designed a *system of human activity* with a number of ideal properties to engage people in a number of desired transformations which would emerge from debate about issues of concern. With a systems definition, we would then encourage participants to design changes in existing processes and structures at the institution so that the transformation would take place. Design was to be based on comparing the systems definition with the current situation. Based on that comparison, a number of areas of intervention were to be defined, and actions to address existing gaps (between the desired activities and the existing ones) planned. Throughout the exercise, support was offered using Ulrich's critical systems heuristics (CSH) to define the system, and Ackoff's interactive planning to design it (Ackoff, 1981).

As a result of these activities, it was expected that participants would define a number of insights to improve their current situation, some of which would explicitly require the support of information systems and technologies. Insights would then be presented to the senior management of Javeriana to gain their approval and support to define (or redefine) projects at the institution. It was also expected that some of the insights would be useful in defining future roles for the use of systems and technologies in corporate plans.

To complement the above activities, the ideas of boundary critique were to be used to continually encourage participants to identify issues and people who could be considered in the definition of such insights for improvement.

2   The second type of activities was labeled *critical engagements*. These consisted of a number of meetings with people at Javeriana who were in charge of initiatives or projects related to information systems and technology use. We (the research team) aimed at getting to know better the scope of these initiatives, and to bring different issues of concern raised in the previous stage of the project to the attention of managers. This meant that if considered appropriate, we would then raise a number of issues in relation to the aims and objectives of projects, so that we could share our ideas on elements that could be marginalized from the projects, and we would promote reflection on consequences of this marginalization or, on the contrary, on potential inclusion of these elements. The aim was also to call the attention of project managers to other boundaries which could potentially and in a better way guide decision making and action in their projects.

We now present the insights obtained in each type of engagement activity.

### Design Exercises

We invited participants to a series of two-hour sessions called design exercises with no more than ten participants each. As we said before, the purpose of these sessions was to work on defining suggestions to improve the current situation at Javeriana as a whole. Some of these suggestions would contain recommendations for the design and use of information systems and technologies.

In each of these sessions we started by introducing the 'enriched' picture of the situation (Figure 6.7) according to people's perceptions. The idea was to get any additional views of participants. People could raise new concerns, ideas and interests, or they could challenge what they saw in the picture. We would also declare our own concerns and values, and would invite people to share or challenge them.

The process was not straightforward as the identification of new issues could lead us *back* to the stage of distinction of concerns, in which we would then identify different boundaries being privileged or marginalized. Based on the boundaries identified, we would ask for some marginalized elements (concerns, people) that had not been directly considered in previous projects or plans. In so doing, our purpose was to find issues of concern which we could share, so that any decisions about improvements could be shared by participants and us. With new concerns being identified, the picture could then continue being enriched, facilitating a continuous relationship between activities of distinction (previously mentioned) and design. We (the research team) would then invite people to select two or three issues from the picture which they considered most relevant, and present two ways in which these issues could be addressed.

In one particular case in an exercise, we could not advance further from this point. A couple of participants complained that they were expecting us to be 'experts', and to tell them exactly how they should be using IS/ICT in education. They conceived of us (the research team) as very knowledgeable individuals who, having studied abroad, could suggest ways of using systems and technologies to benefit the institution. We objected to this because we wanted to work with people, not at them. We also said that our approach was systemic, and even if we could suggest particular areas for information systems and technology use, it was important to shape any suggestion by participants who knew the context in which suggestions were to be implemented.

In the other exercises we could move forward and together with participants we defined relevant systems to address these issues, and then produce root definitions and conceptual models of such systems. Using Checkland's ideas of soft systems methodology (SSM) (Checkland, 1981), we aimed at defining a system of human activity which would be perceived as meaningful to improve the current situation. In one of the design exercise workshops, participants developed a root definition of a culture system for Javeriana as:

> A system within Javeriana which promotes in all the faculties reflection on how to contribute to creating and maintaining awareness of and sensitivity to the different concerns that surround the lives of teachers, students and other members, in such a way that this culture sets an example for the rest of the Colombian community.
>
> (Córdoba, 2002)

The root definition was built using the following elements of the mnemonic CATWOE from soft systems methodology as follows:

- *Customers*: Members of the Colombian community, including members of Javeriana.
- *Actors*: Members of Javeriana interacting with each other.
- *Transformation process*: The system develops awareness and sensitivity in any member to a variety of concerns that people raise.
- *Worldview*: There is concern for people and their concerns at Javeriana, because its members are human beings. Javeriana has always set examples of social awareness in Colombia.

- *Owners*: Javeriana University, any member of the institution.
- *Environment:* Awareness can be promoted within the philosophy and principles at Javeriana, and within the possibilities of action about concerns we could have at the institution.

The above definition showed that some participants considered it important to have an institutional environment in which they could express their concerns, be listened to, and get support if they decided to take any action to address such concerns. One of the effects that was foreseen from this system was that any graduate from Javeriana University, by having become 'aware' of the different concerns of people, could him/herself become a useful and valuable member of the different types of communities they were participating in (family, work, professional associations, etc) with his/her actions directed to address such concerns. This system was to act as a sensitizing device for people about other people and their concerns.

It was considered that the best way to start 'operating' this system (by putting in practice awareness and sensitivity) was to set clear examples. Participants committed themselves to be 'agents of reflection' in their jobs, so that they could contribute to maintaining an environment (inside, outside the institution) of sensitivity to concerns. In such an environment, there were activities to support them so that such sensitivity could be fostered and maintained. Activities within the system would enable people to reflect with other individuals on their roles and actions regarding sensitivity. In addition, it was expected that these activities would produce an impact on education. This is illustrated by the conceptual model shown in Figure 6.8.

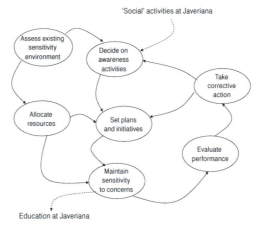

*Figure 6.8* Conceptual model of a system to nurture sensitivity to social concerns

The idea of having an environment in which sensitivity to 'other people' could be maintained was reinforced through another exercise of design. A group of computer science students engaged in defining a plan to improve what they saw as the 'delivery' of education. The issue became that of preparing individuals to be useful professionals in their jobs. Using the ideas of critical systems heuristics (CSH), participants defined a 'system' to provide students with facilities, resources and knowledge so they could design and implement projects of interest to the industry. A summary of students' answers to some of the CSH questions is presented in Table 6.2.

From the above two exercises it became clear that an area in which information systems and technologies could be used was in the facilitation of knowledge creation and sharing to address social problems in society. Some participants in the exercises could see how information systems and technologies could be used in activities like:

- inclusion of groups into education (for instance low-income sectors);
- linking educational activities with industry and businesses initiatives through a shared knowledge repository or database;
- promoting conversations about social problems among people concerned, using electronic forums.

These ideas were to be aired later on with individuals in charge of existing projects to bring systems and technology into use within the institution as the following section reports.

*Table 6.2* Critical systems heuristics questions for a system to improve delivery of education with ICT at Javeriana's computer science engineering department

1. Who ought to be the client (beneficiary) of the system S to be designed or improved?
- Students from the department
- Students from other faculties
- Society in general.

2. What ought to be the purpose of S; i.e. what goals/states ought S be able to achieve so as to serve the client?
- Prepare students to deal with changing circumstances of the environment of organizations and society
- Providing a broad knowledge of their discipline but also of general education.

3. What ought to be S's measure of success (or improvement)?
- Number of people successfully addressing current problems in society with the help of information technology
- Number of research projects involving students, members of staff, businesses or other organizations in the country.

4. Who ought to be the decision taker, that is, have the power to change S's measure of improvement?
- Students and people from the business sector could intervene in decisions
- Other groups in society (i.e. government) should be considered as having a voice.

5. What components (resources and constraints) of S ought to be controlled by the decision taker?
- The content of projects could be developed with the help of students or people from businesses
- The content of educational courses, so that once a project is started, students could decide on which courses will provide them with relevant knowledge to successfully complete the project.

6. What resources and conditions ought to be part of S's environment, i.e. should not be controlled by S's decision taker?
- Changing circumstances in the environment of businesses, organizations, the country and abroad
- The philosophy of the university contains some (Jesuit) principles that should be honored as much as possible.

7. Who ought to belong to the witnesses representing the concerns of the citizens that will or might be affected by the design of S? That is to say, who among the affected ought to be involved?
- Citizens who need information services from the graduates working in different organizations
- Community organizations need to be involved to raise the concerns of marginalized groups in society, for example the elderly or the illiterate.

8. To what degree and in what way ought the 'affected' be given the chance of emancipation from the premises and promises of those involved?
- Students could have authority to change the curriculum of the courses if they see possibilities of improving their own education and responding to possibilities and challenges sets in projects
- They could also include material that they consider important to be shared with other students.

### Critical Engagements

Tapping into people's concerns and values could also be achieved – in our view and following the ideas of the strategic pattern of thinking – by engaging in conversation with people who are concerned in similar ways to improve the delivery of education at Javeriana. We knew that there was a set of projects already taking place at the institution in which a number of information systems and technologies were being planned, designed and implemented. To us this was an opportunity to contribute to shape the future roles and uses of systems at the institution.

To engage with people involved in projects, the research team contacted them and organized a series of meetings. Meetings were planned with participants of the following projects:

1   a project to digitalize educational material and make it accessible to students through an intelligent database;
2   a project to set up and deliver an internet-based library catalogue;
3   a project to incorporate the use of information and communication technologies in architectural design education.

In each of the meetings, the research team adopted an attitude of listening and then constructively challenging what was in place in the projects. Let me explain. After getting to know what the project aimed to achieve, and some challenges and opportunities for the future (we asked them about this), we briefly brought into discussion the set of concerns being identified and represented in the enriched picture. Facilitators then played the role of advocates of our project's participants by raising these concerns and asking questions about the projects:

•   Why hasn't this element (issue of concern, group of people) being included or taken into account (in other words, been marginalized)?
•   What could be the implications of including, excluding or marginalizing certain elements? For whom?

These questions were informed by the ideas of boundary critique. We were encouraging project participants to identify which elements could impact different groups of stakeholders by their potential inclusion or marginalization. With these questions in mind, the research team could then raise a number of issues, which in our view had been identified inside our project and learn from the discussions with the other project's members.

Overall, it can be said that in our critical engagements project managers and team members received our input and participation with enthusiasm. Some of them explained why what we called potential marginalization of elements was occurring. Discussions were fruitful, and they considered for future activities some of the issues that we had raised. In one case, the manager of the catalogue project invited us to deliver a workshop with staff members on accessing information on the internet, so that we could continue exploring how people could use such information for a variety of purposes.

Furthermore, the manager of the architectural project expressed the view that the institution was very 'selective' in terms of the areas to be supported in their use of information systems and technologies. Institutional plans had already defined a number of projects. There were a set of values and practices which reinforced the idea that "we must stick to the institutional plans, they are the right thing to do",[2] and this idea was undermining any effort to bring new insights to support practice.

We were about to confirm and deepen our insights when we decided to present a report containing the findings from our project to senior managers.

### Some Insights

Once we finished our design exercises and critical engagements, the research team considered it appropriate to summarize a number of insights obtained through these activities. The aim was also to represent the people who had been engaged throughout the project before the senior management with the hope that the insights being obtained could be taken forward as potential projects or included in the agendas of existing ones.

The summary of the insights included the following:

- Javeriana had successfully started adopting a number of systems and technologies, and it was clear that they were supporting the development of institutional plans.
- The variety of projects made it necessary to improve co-ordination and communication among them, so that different groups of stakeholders could be benefited by and involved in them.
- Javeriana could take forward its social orientation and put in place systems and technologies to support social inclusion, flexible delivery of education and the use of knowledge to benefit businesses and society in general.
- The culture of 'care for each other' in the institution could be made more explicit and developed, so that staff members, students and other people involved in the delivery of education could set good examples of care for the rest of Colombian society.
- Students could use information systems and technologies to make their learning experiences more personal, flexible and sustainable in the long term.

Out of these insights, the following suggestions were proposed to be taken forward in new or existing projects:

- Improve the co-ordination between IS projects and the evaluation of the social impacts that information systems were to have.
- Develop an information system to provide flexibility and support in the delivery of lectures and in the definition of research projects in conjunction with the industry.
- Encourage members of the institution to develop a culture of solidarity in which there could be tolerance and respect for diversity.
- Establish mechanisms for the evaluation of impacts of information systems projects, including their consequences for different groups of stakeholders.

These insights and suggestions for action were presented to senior management together with a presentation of the process followed by our project's research team. Managers received these with enthusiasm, and said they were very relevant to the current situation at the institution. It seemed as if engaging with people had become meaningful to them and to other decision makers.

The implementation of suggestions for action derived from these insights would prove difficult to accept, as will be seen later in the chapter. We now move to reflect on the use of this pattern of thinking for information systems practice.

## Reflections from Practice

In presenting our insights and reflections about the strategic pattern, we emphasise how it has helped us to develop initiatives on the information society, and what we can learn from the use of systems methodologies.

Overall, it is reasonable to claim that in practice, the use of this pattern enabled a better degree of engagement from people in exploring, designing and deciding different types of actions to improve their situation. Although it cannot be said that these actions were only about the use of IS/ICTs, a better appreciation of how they can help people in society *as a whole* was gained. The example of Javeriana shows that people were able to identify a variety of concerns and possible uses of systems and technologies to support doing something about such concerns. In relation to information systems and technologies, very interestingly, we could see that people were aware of their potential to include different groups of individuals, and how systems and technologies could facilitate flexibility and efficiency, gaining and a more 'outward' looking attitude in education which could benefit, among others, students, staff members, community groups and businesses.

A number of ideas were gained, which also led us to think that under this pattern, any action that is being shaped concerns how people like to live in society, in other words, which values they like to preserve and promote (e.g. peace, solidarity, co-existence, quality). Suggestions for action that were defined covered a very interesting set of issues, which could well be supported in the future or with existing initiatives (see Figure 6.9). In particular for the case at Javeriana, a good number of suggestions referred to the culture of the institution, and more specifically how existing ways of doing things could facilitate developing awareness and sensitivity to different groups of people, or alternatively, could inhibit the definition of new initiatives.

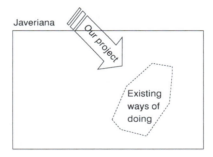

*Figure 6.9* The strategic pattern and the 'ways of doing things'

Thus, it seemed that our project and the use of a pattern of thinking that promoted engagement, collective definition and debate, resonated on the one hand with some values and ways of doing things at the institution: those which promoted inclusion, social awareness and 'care'. On the other hand, the project seemed to clash with the existing project initiatives and practices which had their own ways of doing things (which also included labeling us as 'experts'). These elements seemed to interact together to privilege certain projects whose aim was to promote Javeriana as an international institution and therefore use systems and technologies to help the institution become recognized as such (therefore privileging the achievements of efficiency). Other existing practices (for instance the way in which financial resources were allocated to projects, and as will be seen in the next chapter, 'ways' to approve projects) were reinforcing these types of initiative. The situation can be best illustrated in terms of boundaries in Figure 6.10 (Córdoba, 2002).

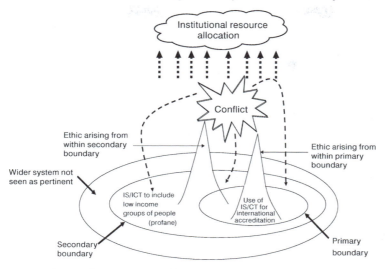

*Figure 6.10* Boundaries influencing action plans

Figure 6.10 also shows how when we (the research team) presented insights and suggestions for action, they were taken on board in a very positive way as reasonable and well thought out. However, we were told that there were already plans in place which needed to be followed; these also had to do with ways of doing things which could not easily be challenged. In the discussions at the presentation of findings meeting, we were encouraged by the senior team to be in charge of the implementation of the portfolio of suggestions. We became aware of the potential difficulties lying ahead (in relation to implementing something that could possibly go against established plans, with no resources available).

Furthermore, it seemed that our own ethics, which were based on empowering people to own their own initiatives for change, were clashing with existing ways of taking action, mainly based on the (external) provision of expertise feeding into the institution. These ways of taking action were manifested in certain generalizations (e.g. our institutional plans) which proved difficult to challenge. The ethics that accompanied these ways were aligned to the aims and strategy of Javeriana, which had a key focal point: achieving international accreditation. To this particular tension, we found there were no easy answers.

We realized that our approach to engagement in the information society via systems methodology use, although enabling participation and facilitating reflection prior to and through any definition of improvement (including those related to information systems and technology use), provided little guidance on dealing with *existing tensions* in relation to what was considered ethically sound. Tensions also led to the identification of opposing roles: that of an 'expert' versus that of what we considered a 'facilitator'. This proved a generalization which was not possible to challenge under our pattern of thinking.

Considering that we would not be happy to follow what was seen as an institutional 'way of doing things', we thanked senior managers for their offer to continue overseeing the implementation of insights and suggestions for action, but we declined and brought the project to a close. We now summarize some insights obtained.

### Summary of Insights

Following a strategic pattern to guide systems practice in the information society has brought us a number of benefits. First, it has allowed us to define ways in which the process of engagement can be developed. This resulted in strategies to shape the definition and use of information systems and communication technologies with people's concerns and values in mind.

Second, we were able to arrive at a number of suggestions for improvement which, together, can constitute a 'whole' plan. The processes being followed can help us to justify the nature of such suggestions and, to a certain extent, their validity as deriving from the identification of concerns, and addressing them with the help of some systems methods.

Third, it seems that we need to enrich our understanding of what happens in the context of information systems and technology design and use, in particular what happens with how people 'do things', and what is expected of them to 'be'. These ways surface when it comes to defining potential action and it is there where proposed action meets existing action on the grounds of a terrain that we can call 'ethics'. This terrain needs to be explored in situations where tensions could arise, in other words where there could be many ways of doing the 'right things' in society.

### Revisiting the Challenges for Systems-thinking

In comparison with the idealist pattern of thinking, the strategic pattern of thinking has enabled us to address challenges for systems-thinking in the ways summarized in Table 6.3.

Developing a strategic pattern of thinking about the information society was useful in engaging people with a common language (e.g. concerns) and devising strategies to work together considering people's own time and commitments (including existing projects); workshops and interviews worked well with most people, although not with everyone (this is also why they preferred us to be 'experts' and tell them what to do!). By using ideas of systems methodologies and boundary critique we were able to extend the scope of enquiry into societal issues. We were able to talk about society as a whole, and we came up with suggestions to shape technology use according to the type of society we were able to envisage.

As with the idealist pattern, the strategic pattern of thinking became a victim of its own success. Engaging with people in their own terms and promoting participation in ways adequate to their own setting also meant we had to deal with their own ways of doing things. When these ways had ethical implications for us as practitioners, tensions arose. For practice, this would mean that engagement should consider how people's ways of doing things bring implications which need to be identified and debated upon whenever possible in relation to their ethics.

Given the importance that we gave to ethics after this engagement, the next chapter aims to clarify this issue by proposing a new pattern of thinking about the information society which could complement the existing patterns.

*Table 6.3* Challenges and the strategic pattern of practice

| Challenges to systems-thinking | Assumptions of systems methodology use |
| --- | --- |
| Language: *The language of concerns* | Seeking accommodation ☒ |
| Problem solving: *We did not limit problems to those of organizations but to society* | Becoming instruments of organizational goals ☒ |
| Time: *We engaged according to their own possibilities.* | Used mostly to address organizational problems ☒ |
| | ☒: challenged |

## Chapter Summary

In this chapter a strategic pattern to guide systems practice has been defined. It emphasizes the process of engaging with groups of people, identifying their concerns and values, and collectively addressing them with the help of systems ideas and methodologies.

Engagement under this pattern also means being able to challenge some generalizations made by participants, and to promote an attitude of improvement of their current situation. By putting the ideas of the strategic pattern into practice, in the case studied, a number of interesting insights were obtained. Systems methods were combined in various ways to offer people opportunities to engage in shaping up improvements and use of information systems and communication technologies to support such improvements.

This way of thinking helps to open up debate, discussion and reflection, and to find alternative ways of systems and technology use to those commonly 'envisioned' in policy making, plans and initiatives. However, more needs to be said about how these ways can be used together with existing ways of doing and justifying things.

The ethical dimension of practice has come to the fore and needs to be addressed. That will be done in the next chapter when we define the power-based pattern for practice.

## Key Messages

- The information society can be developed through a participative dialogue which signals engagement and shaping of information systems and technology design or use in a particular context.
- Systems methodologies and methods can be combined and used to address concerns that people have and support participative debate and definition of insights to improve a situation.
- In practice and using parts of systems methodologies, together with systems boundary critique, it is possible to identify a number of concerns, and link them with suggestions for improvement. Roles of information systems and technologies can be defined to support addressing and ultimately 'living' of these concerns.
- Existing ways of doing things in the context might be in favor or against suggestions for improvement.

## Questions / Exercises

- Use the insights and reflections from this chapter to design your own approach to practice. Suppose you are allowed to conduct a participative process to look for uses of IS/ICTs across organizations.
    - How would you start?
    - How would you look for common concerns, interests and values?
    - Which systems methodologies/methods would you employ? Why?
    - What would you do in relation to some generalizations like:
        "We do not like technology, we are an 'older' generation"
        "Tell us what to do, you are the expert!"
        "We do things differently"
        "We do not need to change"
    - How would you explain that your intervention might generate suggestions for action that are not explicitly related to IS/ICT use?

- A new software package is to be implemented, but it is unclear how it will be adopted/accepted by different groups. Apply the above questions to guide your reflection.
- Will there be any difference in the pattern of thinking if we work across organizations?

## Further Reading

Córdoba (2002), and Córdoba and Migley (2006). They show more detailed accounts of the case at Javeriana.

# 7 The Power-based Pattern for Practice in the Information Society

> I feel regret for the anxiety caused to thousands of customers … It was a good business model, but it could not cope with the unforeseeable circumstances of the global economy.
> (Former Chairman of the UK Northern Rock Bank, when resigning in October 2008 after the collapse of the bank)

## Introduction

The journey so far into practice in the information society has moved on from working to support the implementation of visions (idealist pattern of practice) to enabling the definition and discussion of issues based on people's concerns to shape the use of information systems and technologies (strategic pattern of practice). The last chapter showed how systems methodologies enabled us to engage with people in planning and defining ways to improve the quality of their lives. It was possible to use systems-thinking and systems methodologies to open up and structure debate about people's concerns, and the impacts of any possible action.

An interesting aspect of bringing the context of the information society to inform practice is that a number of meanings (quality of life, 'right thing to do', 'expertise', etc) surface and thus need revision in the light of what is *accepted* but also *made possible within existing relations* between people. At the end of the previous chapter these two aspects led us to explicitly consider the ethical dimension of practice. The issue of *ethics* has surfaced and manifested itself in a variety of ways. Systems-thinking was found to be enlightening and facilitating for debate, but can do little to help us understand how ethics emerges in people's relations.

Although this does not mean that practice is only about ethics (in fact, the two previous chapters show a variety of uses of systems-thinking to support different types of practice[1]), it is important to continue investigating what it means to suggest improvements in situations in the information society (with the use of information systems and communication technologies) taking ethics into explicit consideration. This means becoming more aware of how ethical reflection, in practice, takes place in contexts in which the information society is deployed via people's relations – what they consider is 'appropriate' to do or to be.

This chapter aims to address some of the issues related to ethics by proposing a new thinking pattern for the information society which is based on *ethics and power*. For practitioners this means that what we believe is ethical to do or to be, relates to what is acceptable in a particular context of relations between people; this has to do with power. Conversely, within such relations it might be possible to develop new ways of being ethical or acting ethically in improving situations.

This chapter has a more practical message for practitioners. Those that consider that they live and work in an information society should also consider themselves as *inevitably taking part in power relations* that contribute to the design, use and implementation of information and communication technologies (ICTs) as well as information systems (IS). Therefore, they should become aware of how they can improve their practice with both power and ethics in mind.

## Objectives

- To define a pattern for practice in the information society that is based on the concept of power as an aid to help practitioners become more aware of the nature of change in society.
- To reinterpret some of the key issues encountered previously in the light of power relations.
- To propose ways in which ethical reflection can be developed in practice with power in mind.

The chapter starts by revisiting some key issues encountered in previous chapters about our practice and relating them to how we are involved or affected by it. This leads us to define a power-based pattern to guide practice. We present Michel Foucault's key ideas on power and ethics and one example of practice based on the ideas of power and ethics. We then reflect on what we have achieved by following this pattern.

## From Practice to 'Who We Are'

If we look again at what the information society is (Chapter 2), the sort of visions it brings (Chapter 5) and how we have fully engaged with it (Chapter 6), we can say that there are proposed ways of living embedded in the concept. Living with more autonomy, having more choices, improving opportunities in life, all these seem to affect how we conduct ourselves, and also how we relate to other people.

Within different discourses about the information society already explored, IS and ICTs are said to help us to make possibilities a reality. With more electronically based networking and communication, new issues appear that could affect how we use IS and ICTs. Information is now a valuable and protected asset, in particular when it comes to personal information about ourselves or other people. Issues of privacy, confidentiality and security start putting 'us' as individuals into the picture of the information society. This is most evident when we share and trade personal information in banks, supermarkets, holidays and when we pay our taxes.[2]

When it comes to individuals (not groups) using IS and ICTs, what we are witnessing is a shift in our understanding. This shift indicates that different people can use the same systems and technologies with different purposes, even if they develop a single vision (idealist pattern) or engage in re-defining new ones (strategic pattern). The shift also suggests that we need to embrace a variety of different consequences of systems and technologies for people (Robey and Boudreau, 1999). Whereas for some groups of individuals technology can generate benefits, for others it can generate sometimes disastrous consequences. A system that helps in computer-piloted airplane navigation can be a welcome relief for pilots, but it can be a worry for passengers. A system that makes a procedure for paying taxes more efficient can become a nightmare for citizens who use it. How can we then proceed in the light of the fact that any action might have unintended consequences that we cannot fully foresee? What can be said about those individuals who become part of such systems and somehow see their lives changed by them?

In the last chapter, our experience of developing a strategic pattern for practice shows how different groups of people are willing to engage in exploring possibilities for developing and improving the information society. By doing so, we can all recognize aspects that could be in

*Table 7.1* The information society and some ethical issues worldwide

| Regions of the information society (broadly speaking) | 'Emerging' ethical issues |
| --- | --- |
| 'Developed' countries | *Information*: piracy; confidentiality; property rights of content; sharing between countries<br>*Processes*: offshoring computer operations; global construction and delivery of ICT products and services |
| 'Developing' countries | *Processes*: global delivery; access to internet<br>*Other*: education and ICT literacy |

principle 'outside' our own boundary of interest, profession or concern. However, when it comes to defining agendas for action, or making sure that plans become reality, there seem to be ways of *acting and behaving* which, if followed, guarantee effective action, and if not, could inhibit it.

Practitioners could then venture to identify and explore these ways. Doing so can lead them to reflect on our own values and our own ethics. In other words, exploring how change in the information society is 'deployed' can lead us to ask ourselves the question of who 'we' are.

But asking this question of who we are becomes related to that of what we can do in relation to ethical issues. In practice, it becomes necessary then, not only to be able to embrace different views and perspectives and foresee different consequences from any decision to different groups of people, but also to understand how things work in a context, in other words to understand how an 'idea' becomes accepted on ethical grounds. This goes *beyond* including and articulating perspectives and concerns in defining change, supporting it through actions for improvement (including those related to IS/ICT) or debating about foreseeable consequences of actions as previous patterns of practice have suggested.

We need to be able to grasp the dynamics between groups of people whose activities have to do with finding 'true and good solutions'. The roles of IS and ICT would depend on the changing nature of what is considered 'good' and 'true'. This might be different for different countries, and Table 7.1 offers a (possibly too) brief statement of ethical issues related to different contexts.

Table 7.1 also suggests that understandings of 'ethical issues' themselves might be different, and therefore it is necessary to look at ethics from a perspective that could provide general insights to practice. This perspective is *practice itself*. This means that ethics will be looked at when it 'emerges' as such in practice of planning, developing or maintaining initiatives in different spheres of the information society. In practice, it is also important to consider (again) its 'unintended' consequences as will be seen in the next section.

## The Unintended Consequences in the Information Society Revisited

In Chapters 1 and 2, phenomena of unintended consequences were brought to light as key phenomena in the information society. We are continually surprised about how people make their own use not only of information systems but also of technologies. For instance (and positively speaking), mobile technology has taken off in a way never expected by those designing or selling it. In regions like Africa this technology has enabled people to communicate across geographically distant areas, leading individuals to use it more and more. The integration of mobile phones with mobile computing has paved the way for new and more sophisticated technology devices which have helped people to become more productive and to focus on maintaining a work–life balance. Many individuals accomplish their own daily plan with the use of laptop computers, mobile phones, personal digital assistants, etc. There are as many products as different types of uses.

Furthermore, in different parts of the globe we are now witnessing the emergence of a 'new generation' of children for whom personal computer is part of their enjoyment and play. Parallel to this we increasingly see new forms of cybercrime (some of which also affects our children); criminal organizations have made full use of electronically mediated communication and have created their own 'networks' of operation. This is something we did not expect, at least not in the ideals proposed by the information society.

This speaks about the nature of changes and effects in the information society. The unintended has also appeared and is difficult to identify or to grasp. Many of the 'predictions' made by futurists of the 1990s are being left on paper, whilst more interconnected ways of working are emerging. For many individuals, their working time has increased with ICT use despite promises during the early 1990s (some of which have been reported in Chapter 2) that ICT would replace human beings or given them more 'free' time. Efficiency has been gained, but possibly in ways which do not correspond to initial ICT plans in organizations. These unintended effects must be managed by individuals themselves (for instance in relation to work–life balance issues). Not only for employees but also for customers, more ICT has improved communication and response but has also increased demands for them to become more knowledgeable and skilful when dealing with technologies and systems.

Some of these effects are on a global scale. The use of computer technologies, which are becoming widespread and cheaper in some regions of the world, has become a concern because of the disposal and recycling of electronic equipment. It becomes a challenge for countries to fully comply with related environmental regulations. This can generate opportunities for business and educational establishments if they help localities and businesses to recycle equipment.

Unintended effects speak about the complex and dynamic nature of changes in the information society. Change is part of our daily agendas, but it is becoming more multifarious, and difficult to fully predict or manage (even if we use boundary critique to talk about impacts of inclusion, exclusion or marginalization). However, in our practice and by looking at how we have been developing the information society in relation to transformations (idealist pattern) and engagements (strategic pattern), we could acknowledge that we have some *power* to define what we want to use IS and ICTs for, but we cannot entirely control how such use will unfold. Even if 'desirable' effects are being designed and generated with IS/ICT, we also have to make use or live with the 'undesirable' ones. It would be better if we as practitioners were more prepared to accept and manage the unintended, which could be desirable or undesirable.

## A Power-based Pattern

Does the above mean that we need to be more ethically aware in our practice and for instance think about the consequences of our actions before proceeding?

This could lead us to consider some theories of ethics to support our thinking and guide our decision making. But then again we could run into difficulties of having to clearly define ethical issues and their consequences, and moreover we do not know what practice could bring in relation to consequences. These considerations together with the 'unintended' dynamics of the information society will require us to pay more attention to the dynamics of practice and how people define ethical issues within such dynamics.

When the Javeriana project that we reported in the last chapter finished in 1999 (Córdoba, 2002), there were many unanswered questions related to the ethics of the process of planning (Table 7.2). In particular, there were questions about how systems practitioners could proceed in interventions, in the light of different perceptions about the 'right thing to do'.

*Table 7.2* An initial exploration of ethics

| Key questions | Strategies followed and their result |
| --- | --- |
| What principles should guide ethical practice? How to live a 'good life'? | Study different ethical theories: deontologism, consequentialism, relativism, etc. Find the 'appropriate' one to explain issues and actions to take.<br>Study different ethical codes relevant to the IS profession and principles to guide action.<br>*Result:* Is it the case that we need to adopt a 'single' set of principles, theories, or codes? |
| How can IS practitioners deal with tensions or conflicts about the 'right thing to do'? | Follow the idea that decisions on systems will have consequences, and take responsibility for such consequences.<br>*Result:* Who are 'we' to just stand apart from or engage with what happens? |

These and other questions point out to the practitioner him/herself, his/her own ethical principles and how s/he deals with apparently conflicting views on what to do. This 'individualization' of ethics became more apparent at the Javeriana project in 1999, when the research team (including myself) decided not to continue with the project on the grounds of personal ethical values. As part of the research team, I decided to explore ethical theories to see how I could explain the situation of people arguing that it was the right thing to do not to accept any improvements on existing plans.

This required us to go beyond the study of systems methodologies and/or methods. Before the Javeriana project, methodologies had been helpful in providing guidance on how to make sense of situations, and how to identify issue and debate in order for people to arrive at collectively and ethically secured decisions. But it was left to individuals themselves, with apparently competing views about the 'right thing to do', to discern and face situations where agreements could not be reached. Systems methodologies could not help us with this unforeseen and possibly unintended situation.

The above questions prompted me to address the issue of engagement by individuals with moral and ethical issues in practice (Walsham, 1993). Like Walsham I also wanted to encourage myself and other practitioners to become more interested and committed to ethical aspects, so that we could be aware of the importance of decisions. My questions became ones in which I wanted to explore ethics in practice: how can individuals engage with ethical issues in the light of dynamic (and often conflicting) situations, which often require them to reflect on ethics whilst still acting 'in the present'?

At Javeriana in 1999 there was a degree of interdependence between ethical claims and their emergence in practice when dealing with initiatives or projects. It seemed that notions of ethics were related to people's actions. This was taking place in the *relationships* between them – relationships within projects, relationships between projects and relationships with corporate plans, and ultimately between people in their daily conversations, some of which we encouraged when conducting our intervention.

From that experience, and after spending sometime researching and thinking about ethics, key ideas on another pattern to guide practice emerged. This is defined as a *power-based* pattern, with the following features:

- It enables reflection on ethical aspects, using power as an analytic concept to help deal with existing tensions in relations between people and to help us define appropriately ethical action in the light of such tensions.

- It considers that information systems and technology design or use have both intended and unintended consequences due to power relations.
- In relation to 'unintended' or 'unforeseen' effects, this pattern allows people to act in order to make the best use of these effects *for their own purposes*, so that they can imagine new possibilities for action according to what they think is ethical in relation to power. This means using power relations to our own advantage and according to what we think is ethical.

In order to show these feature of the power-based pattern, we now explore the concept of power by using key ideas of the work of Michel Foucault on power and ethics (Foucault, 1977, 1984a, 1984c).

## Foucault's Work

Although the work of Michel Foucault (1926–84) was mainly in the area of history, he cannot be declared only to be a historian; nor entirely can he be declared to be a philosopher or politician. His work on the history of Western civilization has provided an interesting insight on the subject. Although he explored history and phenomena through it, his work was focused on providing a view of how human beings are made subjects. For Foucault (1982), the meaning of 'subject' is twofold: "someone subject to someone else by control and dependence, and tied to his own identity by a conscience or self-knowledge" (p. 212). Both meanings in the above definition suggest a form of power, something which, in principle, subjugates people and makes them subject to someone else's actions.

What Foucault is interested is in exploring how 'subjects' (individually or collectively) became who they are, and how analyzing this can offer people choices for their future. Given the history of Western thinking, Foucault argues that what we consider 'true' knowledge, how we obtain it, and how we behave are the by-product of relations between people. Conversely, it is those relations which have made it possible for certain knowledge to be considered 'true' as well as 'ethically acceptable' by individuals. For Foucault, relations are relations of *power*, and he uses the concept of power to explain how people become subjects, as well as what they can *ethically* do about it.

It is these aspects of power and ethics that Foucault blends together in his work. These aspects can help us to explore how we could address ethical issues in practice. Some practitioners might argue that their work does not involve dealing with 'power' (commonly seen as politics by many). But Foucault would put them back into the picture of change, arguing that we cannot avoid power, but we can learn how to work within it.

### *What is Power?*

To support the above claim about power, Foucault challenges the idea that power only resides in formal or 'juridical', authority, use of certain resources (financial, material, etc) to advance one's own interests, or any influence exerted by persuasion, charisma or leadership. These manifestations are common nowadays in our societies and they relate to how a society is 'governed'. They can be considered as power, but for Foucault power is present in every relation between individuals. Relations influence actions whilst at the same time are influenced by them.

For Foucault, power is "a total structure of actions brought to bear upon possible actions; it incites, it induces, it seduces, it makes easier or difficult" (Foucault, 1982: 220). In a simpler way, power is "a general matrix of force relations at a given time, in a given society" (Dreyfus and

Rabinow, 1982: 186). This means that power is not an abstract concept, but manifests itself in action in the whole of society and in how some actions influence (or are influenced by) other actions. Analysis of power is thus a way of looking at society and understanding how societal action is conducted.

According to Foucault, science and what we conceive of as knowledge has been shaped by power. Foucault studies different 'discourses', as they are ways of studying the human subject in different areas. He shows how these discourses have emerged and become accepted through history. Continually, new discourses cancel, resist or modify existing ones as they try to produce more or less homogeneous accounts in their search for universal explanations about phenomena (Foucault, 1977).

Moreover, the operation of power is manifested at different levels: either targeting individuals in their possibilities of being 'subjects' (selves) or guiding the conduct of groups (Foucault, 1977). The operation of *inducing action* is very prominent, because it means that power is very influential in determining the conduct of individuals in society. If this is the case, then relations in society have to do with individuals' freedom and how they are able to conduct themselves. Power then needs to be analyzed to determine how actions of individuals are to be 'governed' adequately.

In our societies and following Foucault, it can be said that power operates at different levels. We are part of groups, networks or associations in which we are required to perform certain actions (as family members, employees or citizens). Failure to do so would lead us to be considered 'abnormal' or 'asocial'. As practitioners, we are required to do things in certain ways. Either as systems thinkers or otherwise, there are ways to do things. The case of Javeriana indicates that we all were required (but not explicitly forced) to adopt certain ideas and standards and to reject others. With this type of awareness, Foucault invites us to consider some conditions and possibilities of doing something about power relations.

To complement this 'social' awareness Foucault offers another dimension which is not entirely formal or residing in institutions: that of the individual exerting power upon him/herself. These relations entail issues of observance; ways of subordinating oneself to norms or codes; means by which one develops as an ethical subject; and a 'telos' or views about what type of subject one wants to become (Foucault, 1984b). These types of relations also need to be studied, and their potential effects analyzed. Analysis of power would then allow people to become aware of the type of 'subjects' they have become, and what they can do about it.

But even if individuals become aware of the operation of power at different levels (individual, collective), its nature makes it very dynamic and difficult to ascertain. What can be a resistance to power could become a dominating power later on. For this reason, Foucault also attributes another feature to power: its effect cannot be fully foreseen (Foucault, 1982). There is only so much that individuals can plan for when using power. It can help some people whilst generating negative effects for others, but this situation can change with time. This sits well with the idea that in the information society there are unintended consequences from well-intentioned actions; that for instance, there is marginalization when we provide technology access opportunities for individuals, as reported in Chapter 2. As will be discussed later in this chapter, we can decide to use our freedom to address this type of situation, considering the operation of power relations.

For now, it suffices to say that Foucault's notion of power could help us account for the possibility of embracing both intended and unintended consequences of action in society. On the one hand, it would allow practitioners to become aware of how power operates across society and how its effects through our actions can influence institutions, groups or individuals themselves. On the other hand, it challenges any attempt to fully control the effects of such actions. This is a kind of paradox that we as individuals in the information society have to live with.

In the practice of information systems we see Foucault's ideas being used to explain how systems become instruments of managerial power and how they can produce effects on individuals' freedom. More needs to be said about his work on ethics and how his interest in the human subject can be taken forward to explore the implications of operating ethically in relation to power. Within the constraints and apparent limiting power of information systems, there is the possibility for individuals to design their own uses and reactions to managerial practices through the same systems that control them. People can always do other than expected and this confirms our idea that there are unintended consequences in the use of systems and technologies. This is ethical action. Practitioners could then take into account how people really make sense of systems and technologies (not how they should), and provide spaces for them to make better and more meaningful use.

Some practitioners though could claim that this is no different from engaging with people and shaping up systems and technology use as suggested in the previous chapter (strategic pattern). However there is a difference according to Foucault. Awareness on power means that we cannot avoid it but we can act in relation to it, as will be seen in the next section.

### Why is Power Important?

For Foucault, power is a necessary element in the conduct of society's affairs (Foucault, 1984a). Power is needed to regulate the conduct of individuals. This means that we cannot ignore power in society, but we can use it. Foucault offers a view on power which indicates that it is possible to operate within it. In other words, we cannot operate in an external way to power. Any action (for instance to improve society via use of systems and technologies) is influenced by power, and will also influence its operation. We need to avoid becoming 'normalized', in other words to avoid becoming powerless, without any freedom. To analyze power, the following aspects thus need to be considered:

1   People cannot operate within a position of exteriority to power (Foucault, 1977). This means that even resistance to power is part of power relations and *power development*. Awareness of this condition can make us more conscious of and responsible about our participation in relations, and of the effects that such participation generate on our freedom as a condition we continually have to re-define.

2   Having considered our inevitable participation in power relations, we need to analyze power (its development), so that we can portray a landscape of *constraints and possibilities for action* in relation to it. Foucault offers some methods of analysis of power which would enable people to 'map' how knowledge gets deployed through relations. Such relations generate asymmetry and inequality between people, but also some spaces in which individual freedom can be exerted. Analysis can start in situations where ethical issues are highlighted, or where individual freedom might be at stake (even in situations where 'autonomy' or choice is being offered).

3   With an analysis of power relations, and without knowing fully how power will unfold, it might be possible to act whilst being in the present (Foucault, 1984c). This is what *ethical behavior* entails for Foucault. He indicates how through history it has been possible for people to operate within what is established, whilst still imagining new possibilities of acting and being. He invites us to do the same in our present situation although in different forms from the past. An attitude of continuous vigilance about ethics is then required so as to encourage people to decide what type of subjects they want to *become*.

With these ideas, it is then possible to provide an alternative understanding of ethical issues in the practice of developing the information society: one which could provide key insights as to how people consider something as a 'right thing to do' and what can be done about it. These ideas then encourage us to consider who we are in practice as an invitation to develop new ways of being and acting in practice. We now provide an example of how ethical issues can be dealt with using Foucault's ideas on power and ethics.

### An Example

*Confidentiality* of electronic information has become a key ethical issue to deal with, in particular with a view that this type of information in organizations is the 'blood' of activities. Codes of ethics and conducts issued by professional IS associations (for instance the British Computer Society or the Association of Computing Machinery) regard the protection of information as an ethical goal to achieve.

1   It seems that once established as an ethical issue, we cannot escape either recognizing or ignoring confidentiality. Any action in practice will inevitably influence or be influenced by it. We cannot operate in a position of exteriority to confidentiality, given that at some point we will have to deal with it in our practice.

2   A brief analysis of confidentiality using a Foucaultvian lens would require us as practitioners to try to ascertain how this 'ethical' issue became deployed. In particular, to study the *development of certain relations* between people at different levels (associations, organizations, interest groups) which were used to define and promote the idea that confidentiality was ethical. It might have been the case that organizations saw confidentiality as a way of advancing their own economic interests, so they promoted this idea elsewhere. Or that confidentiality became an issue that arose when organizations became more able and interested in sharing information with other entities. Or it could be that confidentiality became related to personal issues (privacy). Organizational strategies could contribute to make confidentiality important in their business plans.

3   At a personal level, bringing confidentiality to the fore would require individuals to focus on it; to subordinate their behavior to norms related to preserving confidentiality; to be 'trained' so they could become 'confidentiality aware' individuals; and ultimately to become 'good' individuals by honoring confidentiality in their actions. By reflecting on what is possible or allowed to do would provide individuals with a 'terrain' in which confidentiality arises and offers *possibilities and constraints* for action. With these in mind, it might be possible to promote action for other purposes. People might decide to 'honor' confidentiality with a view of acting about other issues (for instance freedom of information).

In short and by analyzing power, practitioners could then become more aware of the *inevitability* of power, as it is power relations that help deploy certain issues as 'ethical'. Even if we do not want to do anything about the issue at hand (e.g. confidentiality), its importance might continue and affect how we design and deploy change (including information systems and technologies). Analysis should also show *how power operates*, so as to render confidentiality (individually and collectively) as an 'ethical' issue. Such analysis should also serve to identify *possibilities and constraints* for action. These possibilities and constraints can illuminate ways of acting for practitioners so they can become the *ethical people* they want to be.

## The Power-based Pattern in Practice

With the above elements for analysis, we now present a case in which the power-based pattern was reflected upon. In 2003, an opportunity was offered to visit Javeriana University again and find out what had happened to the project reported in the previous chapter. During the period between bringing that project to a close and visiting the institution again, more awareness had been gained on our (my) part about issues of power and ethics in the use of systems methodologies and methods. Foucault's ideas were becoming influential to inform awareness, reflection and action in practice.

With the opportunity for a visit to Javeriana for a two-week period, the purpose was to explore the dynamics of power and their potential relationships with ethical issues in practice. A small-scale project was devised to conduct an evaluation of the suggestions for improvement generated in the previous project. The evaluation exercise was proposed to some of Javeriana's computer science and systems engineering staff. In the exercise definition, it was suggested that a review of the previous project was necessary with a view to improving the chances of some of the suggestions for action to become better implemented or refined.

Whilst there had been some personnel changes at Javeriana since 1999, some people who took part in the initial project were still available and interested in talking to me and I considered it important to include their views in my review. Two types of activities were proposed for the evaluation. Some were *review* activities, in which interviews were to be conducted with former project participants about how and why changes had been implemented. These would be complemented with *engagement* activities, in which I would take part in any additional activity if I considered it important to do so. In a way, these activities reflected a personal desire to use (again) an idealist pattern of thinking by looking at transformations and possibly supporting them, as well as a strategic pattern of thinking to promote shaping up of evaluation activities.[3]

For this particular case and in relation to the above discussion, three different aspects were considered in relation to Foucault's work on power and ethics:

1   *Power development.* This was about understanding how power relations influenced practice, in other words how certain relations between people contributed to 'deploy' IS activities.
2   *Possibilities and constraints for action within power.* From the above analysis, the aim was to identify certain points in which the influence of power could inhibit certain activities whilst favoring others.
3   *Ethical awareness.* To complement the above analysis and to inspire future action, analysis would also consider ways of behaving and acting which were considered (un)ethical in the context being studied, so that 'new' forms of being ethical could be developed in relation to power (within).

### Understanding Power Development

From a perspective on power, it could be said that these two types of activities (review, engagement) could help identify two different manifestations of power. The first one would allow the researcher to get involved with more 'formal' relations at the institution (including the ways in which they approached 'foreign researchers', as will be explained), as well as to gain access to information. The second was important in enabling a more subtle engagement with people, their own thinking about uses of information systems and technologies in the institution and ways of relating to other people 'outside' formal communication channels. To support my reflection about the evaluator's role and decisions I kept a diary of all these activities.

Prior to my arrival to Javeriana, I was able gain access to five of the participants (there were initially around forty), and I sent them a semi-structured questionnaire with the purpose of finding out how far the suggestions from 1999 had been taken forward. In my contacts with the institution, I was also allowed access to an office in the computer science and systems engineering department where the 1999 project was based, and this helped me to gain access to more informal conversations with people who had participated previously.

The 1999 project had generated a number of suggestions which stakeholders (mainly within the institution) were encouraged to take forward and implement. The main suggestions for action included (see also Chapter 6):

- improve the co-ordination between IS projects and the evaluation of the social impacts of information systems;
- develop an information system to provide flexibility and support in the delivery of lectures and in the definition of research projects in conjunction with the industry;
- encourage members of the institution to develop a culture of solidarity in which there could be tolerance and respect for diversity;
- establish mechanisms for the evaluation of impacts of information systems projects, including their consequences for different groups of stakeholders.

### Power Development: Relations and Mechanisms

Considering the time that had elapsed between the original project and this evaluation exercise, an effective strategy to help establish contact again was for me to introduce myself as a UK-based researcher who was actively conducting research. This generated a degree of positive acceptance by people at the institution. One senior manager in particular was very pleased with the visit and offered support regarding any information I could collect. Other people at the computer science and systems engineering department expressed the view that my visit was a good opportunity to get acquainted with possibilities for researching and studying abroad. After these and other conversations, I realized that I could continue engaging with people as I could contribute knowledge and views about research. Besides, I wanted to share my ideas about research on power and ethics in evaluating information systems practice!

The role of being a 'foreign expert' soon became accepted within existing relations as it brought valuable knowledge. Moreover, it set the scene for key conversations about research-related topics. Regarding the evaluation exercise I was conducting, I could get access to people and be able to tap into their knowledge.

Other possibilities were explored with different people. For instance, I offered to support any planning activity at the computer science and systems engineering department, as they were preparing for an incoming accreditation process. I also offered to give a research talk to staff members, and made myself available to conduct a workshop with staff members at the library (more on this later). This shows that a number of possibilities could have widened the scope of the evaluation exercise, given that a particular role was being used to tap into relations.

Some of these possibilities offered valuable knowledge about how practice was being influenced by relations. An example was given in an interview I had with the senior research manager of the university. When presented with the recommendations of the 1999 plan, he praised them because he considered that they still had valuable insights to offer. However, I noticed in a rather constraining way that according to this manager, these recommendations *did not* consider the *current* institution's pre-existing project *approval* scheme. This assessment and approval scheme stated the following sequence:

- recommendations should be justified by departments;
- then taken to the corresponding research committees and approved by faculty directors;
- after this, senior management would allocate resources for their implementation (which in some cases required further analysis);
- monitoring of the progress of projects should be made by those responsible for their development.

The senior manager's judgment was that any proposal for change needed to be framed within a particular discourse about what constituted a good research methodology. The institution was about to apply for international accreditation, which meant that they had to show that they were following standards for definition and approval of initiatives and projects.

The above shows that there was a mechanism by which things were approved, in other words they were made acceptable. This mechanism related different groups of people at the institution: researchers or planners and decision makers, and possibly outsiders (e.g. accredited agencies). Moreover, by this mechanism resources were being allocated so that any 'approved' initiative could run and be assessed in the near future.

This mechanism is clearly a manifestation of the operation of power; although not formally recognized in its totality, it was influencing the definition of actions for improvement. A discourse of approval overtakes others (research ideas) and makes them (in)valid. Through this discourse, other actions follow (standardization, financial allocation, project definition and project management). People then have to adapt their actions to this 'mechanism' if they want to have their ideas approved. Moreover, through this mechanism, some people's ideas for specific departmental projects become 'institutional initiatives', so that their scope, impact and expectations are raised.

In parallel to the approval mechanism described above, it seemed that a related one was to prevail over any other, including that of facilitating 'foreign' research activities. For the senior manager in question, the suggestions made in 1999 also lacked *credibility*, as they had been the result of using a qualitative (not quantitative) methodology. Not enough people had been included for their definition (although in total forty people were either interviewed or took part in the project). For this manager, to properly justify any recommendation, a quantitative survey should be done, using a 'representative' sample of the population at the university. Recommendations should then be passed to higher levels for further review (and then linked to the approval mechanism described before). As this senior manager acknowledged the fact that the 1999 project as well as the current evaluation were based on people's perceptions (they are not only about information systems and technologies), his interest in and support of the project seemed to have diminished.

This shows that at the time of engaging with evaluation activities there was a set of ways of relating between people who were very influential in the definition of action. These ways (mechanisms) determined what was to be considered valid or acceptable knowledge. Moreover, they also determined the type of behavior that people needed to fulfill in order to be seen as professional. This type of behavior required first to focus on getting ideas approved; to submit any idea to the approval mechanism; to work on being able to justify ideas by learning the approval mechanism; and to incorporate this learning in any future behavior or way of acting, so that one's image could continue being seen as professional[4] and 'committed' to the institutional plans.

## Possibilities and Constraints for Power

Despite the apparently constraining behavior that could be inferred from the operation of the above two mechanisms (approval and credibility based), I noticed that people at Javeriana could get things done in their own particular ways. At another interview with a staff member of the computer science and systems engineering department, I shared my perceptions about these mechanisms which defined 'good' projects to be implemented at the institution. Although he partly agreed with this insight, he also described to me *another* mechanism by which departments could get approval and funding for their projects. It was a local approval scheme.

This scheme enabled researchers to present their ideas to departmental deans, and if approved, to get funding for subsequent projects. It was not necessary to go to a higher level, also partly because of the risk of getting an idea 'institutionalized', in other words becoming an institutional project that needed to deliver a wider set of impacts. Rather than becoming an institutional project, if an idea was regarded as having an impact beyond a departmental level, two or three departments could be invited to join the idea and collaborate in its implementation.

An example of the operation of this local mechanism was a software product being conceived of at the computer science and systems engineering department. The product could help track the academic progress of students throughout their degree and the support received by staff members. From previous experiences with the institutional level of approval, it was agreed that those leading the project needed to be careful about their role to avoid being stripped of the project ownership. Together with staff members of other two departments of the faculty of engineering, a group of individuals (academics) undertook this project to respond to their own needs. Expectations outside the project were kept at a low level so they could carry on with this project without any potential disturbance (e.g. being unveiled as a potentially useful project to other departments and the university as a whole).

The operation of this local (inter-departmental) level of power was confirmed in another two interviews with a member of the 'virtual university project' and the university library director. The former expressed a view that certain projects, once being 'unveiled' as having a potentially institutional impact, could be put under scrutiny and in many cases were delayed or cancelled. This was the case of a project to use virtual technology to support education. For several years, the project had continually been re-started. One of its main activities is the gathering of information about the existing use of this technology in departments and faculties. The articulated reasoning behind this is that with this identification, a 'best practice' could be selected and implemented across different areas. At the time, the project had not been implemented and despite having being 'approved', it did not have enough resources and support, given that the main project idea is good but still needs to 'gather' relevant requirements from many more departments.

In contrast to the above project the library director had been very successful with the implementation of internet-based services, resulting in continual institutional support (and trust). The library had also been implementing software packages to support cataloguing services to users. There was no need for close scrutiny at a more institutional level. Although the library provides a different type of service than an academic department, it was clear that they enjoyed a degree of autonomy, possibly partly due to successes being achieved, but also to the director's own ideas about their work:

> Our goal is to facilitate users' access to resources. Technology is just a component that
> helps support this goal. More importantly, one (as a staff member) needs to have the right

attitude to service. It is like having a five-star hotel which offers good service. Our main service is information.

(quote from interview)

This discourse seemed to resonate with the idea that only good projects were approved. Furthermore, awareness of the existence of this discourse was to prove very important in facilitating my further engagement during activities at Javeriana.

When interviewed, the library director also raised an issue of concern about the apparent 'lack of professionalism' with which we did not follow up the 1999 project activities; it seemed that my evaluation activities could be constrained by my previous project activities and what seemed to be another mechanism to be 'approved'. This prompted me to prepare a response, as she also was of the view that any evaluation should lead to action (improvement). I decided to propose to support an evaluation workshop in which together with library staff members we could assess the development of information services and find ways to improve them. I considered that it was *ethical* for me to provide support. That could also become a way for me to show commitment and a good professional attitude towards the library director, who up to that point regarded my activities as lacking any follow up.

## Ethical Awareness: Acting 'Ethically'

By this time, it was clear that there were different forms of power operating at Javeriana. Through exhibiting a particular role (that of foreign expert), I had become involved in them, given that this role offered initial access to understandings about how things got done at the institution. My reflections are summarized in Figure 7.1 which will now be explained.

At the time of conducting the evaluation exercise at Javeriana, it can be said that there were two layers of power: one operating at an institutional level, the other at a more local level, both of them with different manifestations. The first one required any potential idea (including those emerging from IS plans or projects) to be justifiable, defensible and ultimately approved and supported. It established procedures to be 'deployed' so that the chances of success of a project (once it was justified and defended) could increase. Moreover, it required those individuals presenting ideas to become competent and professional, in other words to behave in ways

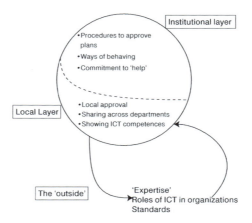

*Figure 7.1* A map of power relations

according to what the institution required, and more importantly to exhibit a commitment to help the institution.

In my analysis of power at that time, the institutional layer was being reinforced by and reinforcing other practices 'outside' Javeriana. One of these was 'traditional' project management which requires 'good' projects to be justifiable on financial and managerial grounds and *expertise* in dealing with ICT for the case of technology projects. Adoption of standards was also an increasingly important factor for the institution (as demonstrated by pressures at Javeriana to get international accreditation for their educational courses). These influences also showed that relations of power could target individuals across organizations whilst at the same time being reinforced by individuals' practices. Power analysis could also help to explain why I was allowed to enter into the set of relations as a 'foreign' or 'international' person.

The operation of the apparently overwhelming influence of the institutional layer of power was producing some *unintended* consequences. Those projects that were not 'good enough' for the institution as a whole were delayed, cancelled or resisted by different means (including personnel replacement). Those which were supported were provided with resources and a degree of autonomy. Projects were then influencing the ways in which people were working. The library projects (e.g. internet-based services and electronic library catalogues) were influencing the ways in which people were to access information.

On a more 'positive' slant about the operation of this layer of power, the institutional practices of project definition and approval were generating (also in an unintended way) a different layer of power, which can be called 'local'. Within this level, there were also successful projects, but their rationale and supporting discourse were different. Although their influence could be perceived across departments, it was not perceived by every department. The way people assessed the relevance and progress of these projects was embedded into each department's style and did not echo the institutional approval schemes, methodologies or discourses.

The behavior of those individuals involved in projects of this local layer was not explicitly 'seen' as a threat to institutional activities, but required (in the case of some projects) exhibiting a competent behavior and expertise in the use of ICT for the projects to be developed 'in house'. People operating at this 'layer' of power were competent but prudent in their actions, in order to avoid tensions with institutional practices which also included definitions about technology platforms and projects.

Again, this layer of relations had to be aware of what was happening 'outside' the institution, so that relevant knowledge and expertise in the use of ICT and in project management could be taken into account (assimilated or ignored). The influence though was not generating constraints (for adopting standards) but innovative possibilities to adopt and use systems and technologies.

By reflecting on the operation of these layers, as a visiting evaluator and researcher at Javeriana, I realized that I could not escape from any of these layers. My evaluation activities were to be 'framed' within them; these layers had given me access to activities and relations and by doing so, they required me to perform certain activities according to certain ways of doing things and behaving. The institutional layer was exhibiting a certain type of 'logic' for projects to be defined, justified, approved and implemented and its discourses were about good performance according to standards. The local layer exhibited a different logic driven by a motivation to help students and staff members in certain areas or departments and to try new systems and technologies to support education.

Within the institutional layer I perceived an implicit *ethical commitment* for me to fulfill: that of supporting evaluation activities as an 'expert' with what they considered to be 'expert knowledge' in technology to help the institution.[5] As said before, this became clearer in further conversations with the library director; she remarked on our lack of follow-up activities after the previous project finished. This made me define an ethical issue: that of conducting more practical and useful evaluation activities. It became clear that I had to operate within the possibilities of action given within this layer.

Taking this into consideration, I organized a workshop with the purpose of discussing ways of improving the delivery of library services. I took on board the director's goals for the workshop. She wanted to make sure that action was taken in relation to service statistics being collected periodically by the library staff. The suggested format consisted of two activities: first to identify the type of services that could be improved; second, people could define indicators that could be used to monitor the improvements of services, and we could then compare the type of information items they had been gathering, to see if they could tell us more about such services.

## Acting 'Ethically': The Workshop

We start the workshop by introducing evaluation and discussing the importance of it being continuous in order to improve daily activities. For evaluation to be useful, it needs to be focused on exploring the 'value' that people attribute to services being provided. A staff member mentions that evaluation needs to consider the impact of evaluation activities in the workload (hinting possibly that she does not want to be 'drained' in the process of collecting and preparing information for evaluation activities). We then move to divide the group into two, to choose a service they want to talk about, and consider both requirements and expectations from users. The director influences the decision of which service to choose by proposing looking at internet-based services. I make the suggestion of considering the service as a 'system' which converts some requirements and expectations into specific features. Still using the role of an 'expert', I ask the groups to define more specific features or attributes that users might like to see in each service being evaluated.

Tensions rise when one of the groups suggests that a key feature of some services should be that of being offered for 'free'. The director intervenes and reminds people about the importance of having a five-star philosophy service, which should not come cheap. We move on to define some questions that could be asked to service users, in order to get information about how well the features of the service have been provided. I ask whether they collect data that could be used to produce information about features of the service.

Despite the initial silence, the director then takes the floor and hints that some of my 'questions and suggestions' have already been addressed. She says that people have a weekly meeting in which they define goals to be achieved in terms of service being provided. She shows me the list of service indicators that they produce, and a magazine which contains customer perceptions. I also hear again her remarks about service and how well they think they provide it. I 'hit back' and show them some indicators that libraries throughout the world collect to assess their service deliveries, and continue asking questions about how they know what users need. I now feel I am raising my own concerns about users in evaluation and challenge the apparent 'service satisfaction' set of practices that is being promoted within the institution. *To me, it is ethical to do so, and I have taken the opportunity in this workshop to be myself as I want to be.*

The workshop comes to an end. I am invited to continue supporting the improvement of services by reviewing a service survey that the library is to send to users. I give my email address and thank them for their participation. I think that there is still the possibility that some of these 'unintended' effects of my ethically driven action (e.g. to serve customers better with evaluation) could be influencing people at Javeriana.

On reflection, a further issue became apparent after the workshop. My role as a 'foreign expert' was seen by some (e.g. research senior manager, library director) as a threat to what had been established. Whilst they and other individuals provided me with support for evaluation activities, these activities had to be directed to what they considered was appropriate. Some possibilities for the evaluation were closed, possibly because my role had generated questions about the meaning of 'valid' projects and 'true' research. But some other possibilities became more relevant and meaningful for me as a practitioner. *I personally felt that I had made my own ethical commitment prevail* within what was possible at the time of the evaluation exercise.

There were intended and unintended consequences derived from my intervention and the uses of systems and technologies were related to the operation of power within which I operated. The nature and outcome of the evaluation activities were definitely influenced by power relations and the ethics that one was (dis)allowed to have as an individual within such relations.

With this reflection I brought the evaluation to a close. I presented my final report to the computer science and systems engineering department director. Since then, there has been little degree of further engagement. Next time, I would try to become even more aware of how I became a subject of the existing power relations and what I could ethically achieve in relation to my own purposes.

## Reflections from Practice

This chapter has presented a pattern to guide practice in the information society. As a pattern, it brings some assumptions that practitioners could follow. A power-based pattern was suggested, and its main ideas followed in a practical experience. No systems methodologies were used and therefore no assessment of our meeting the challenges of Table 5.1 will be made. The pattern emphasized the following:

- inevitability on the participation in power relations as influencing and being influenced by action (power development);
- assessment of constraints and possibilities for action in relation to analysis of power relations;
- acting ethically within these possibilities and constraints.

In practice, it was found that power relations decided what type of action was allowed. Moreover, a certain type of *role* enabled the practitioner to 'get into' a set of relations that played in favour or against projects. Later it was found that these relations were of two types: institutional and local. In each of these, it became apparent that there was a particular logic in operation which allowed or disallowed further action. This logic speaks about activities that need to be performed for any idea for action to become accepted and valid.

Furthermore, this logic defines ways of acting and behaving for practitioners which, with some 'outside' influence also at play, define to a good extent possibilities and constraints for action as well as ways of behaving and acting 'ethically'. For the information society, the use of this pattern can help identify mechanisms which influence practice and determine what is allowed to propose and do. Issues of expertise, standardization and professional knowledge influence ideas and projects to bring the information society to reality.

By getting a basic grasp on power relations and their underlying 'logic' in the case studied, it was possible to assess better possibilities and constraints for action, and it was possible to be within the institutional layer and develop 'new action'. With the practical experience at Javeriana, it was shown that it was still possible to operate within the constraints imposed by

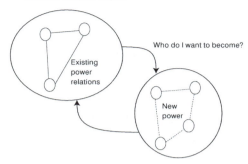

*Figure 7.2* Ethical reflection with power in mind

'power' (in this case the constraints of making practice useful for people), whilst raising ethical concerns and questions as the person I wanted to become: someone who likes to improve service to users, and not only someone with expertise to help those in power. By doing so, it became possible to develop a new type of *ethical subject*.

With time (and by maintaining an attitude of awareness), it became essential to let new ways of being ethical flourish, and this could be said about my 'new' role at the workshop (critical enquirer). Combined with an ethical commitment of 'helping', the practitioner became a subject of existing power relations which were influencing further action. However, such relations opened up opportunities to design 'new' ways of being and acting, and led to further reflection about what sort of person the practitioner wanted to be. S/he could continue being 'an expert' whilst trying to raise ethical concerns; or s/he could decide not to engage in certain relations.

As represented in Figure 7.2, analysis of power and ethics (power–ethics) constitutes a *twofold* process: (1) analysis of how one has become an accepted ethical subject, and (2) definition to become different according to certain ethical purposes and existing power relations. The figure portrays practitioners as subjects as inevitably immersed in power relations. Power (or what we are allowed to do and to be) determines our actions but we can also operate in relation to power.

In the course of our actions within existing power relations, we can determine how we can use power to our advantage. Reflection on power and ethics should be continuous because power is dynamic and things might change. We continually need to reflect on how power defines what is accepted to do and to be, and within possibilities given, decide how to act according to what we think is ethical.

### What Does This Pattern Tell Us About the Information Society?

First, it tells us that society can be looked at as complex grid of power relations, which define and regulate how we act, and the types of initiatives and actions which are allowed according to other actions. Any initiative to develop the information society is immersed in such a grid and influences our actions and those of other people. This grid is different from what we regard as the network society because it is dynamic, asymmetric and unpredictable.

Second, we can influence action if we decide to do so according to our own ethics. There might be consequences which could or could not be foreseen but we should learn to live with them as we exert our freedom in relations with ourselves and other people in practice. In short, we should become aware of power and ethics in analysis. We suggest this can be called power–ethics formation analysis.

## What About Systems Practice?

In Chapter 4 we advocated the possibility of using the ideas on boundary critique to identify and debate unintended consequences of initiatives or plans in the information society. In this chapter we have focused on issues of power and ethics; we have deliberately left systems-thinking aside. However we can review the elements of power analysis when it comes to reflect on boundaries adopted for decision making.

We said at the beginning of this chapter that systems methodology use provides little guidance on how to deal with tensions and unforeseen consequences. Power analysis could help us to address these issues. We can complement systems methodology use with power–ethics formations analysis as presented in this chapter. Elsewhere (Córdoba, 2002, 2006) I have argued that the setting up of boundaries is influenced by power relations, and that these contribute to the definition of improvements in a situation. This idea echoes our findings in this and the previous chapters, in which we have said that people have particular ways of doing things and frame (or bind) actions according to what is seen as ethically appropriate. At the same time, any definition of improvements in a situation will have an impact in existing power relations. When it comes to providing access to knowledge and benefits to marginalized people, for example, the balance of power as action influencing action will change.

The mutual influence between systems-thinking and power–ethics formations analysis also means that when we are defining improvements via use of systems methodologies, there are forms of individual ethics that we put forward to which it is also necessary to be critical (Córdoba, 2006). I have taken this argument further to suggest that the use of systems methodologies helps to make some forms of being ethical more prominent, for instance by promoting participation, inclusion and facilitation. These forms enter into the context of relations in which systems methodologies are used. In the experiences presented in the last two chapters, it became apparent that there were *forms* of defining improvements in a situation which had their own and accepted mechanisms to produce valid knowledge. One of these forms was systems methodology use.

What this means for our practice is that we also contribute to the operation of power when we develop the information society by using systems methodologies; that these influence what we come to define as possibilities and constraints for action; and that our pattern of thinking (systems based) also brings forms of being ethical which we need to reflect upon. In a power-based pattern of practice for the information society, systems methodology use will then contribute to:

1   develop power relations (helping to reinforce, resist or change existing ones);
2   help people to define, in principle, possibilities and constraints for action (improvement);
3   enable people to reflect on ethical issues.

These aspects can lead us to become more cautious when using systems methodologies, because their use plays a role in power relations. To become more fully aware about this role, it is necessary to extend our power–ethics formations analysis to include an exploration of the conditions in which systems methodology use has been 'allowed' to be considered interesting or important; how such use reinforces or challenges existing relations; and how it has implications for what is considered ethical. In other words, systems methodology could also help action if its use is continually complemented with power–ethics formations analysis in a particular context of the information society.

## Chapter Summary

This chapter has proposed another pattern to better understand and manage our information systems practice activities. Within this pattern a concept of power has been introduced to help us become more aware of possibilities of action in the information society. Using this pattern, it might be possible to become more aware of ethical issues in practice, how they come about, and what we can do about them. More importantly, it is possible to reflect on the type of ethical individuals IS practitioners become in practice.

With this type of reflection practitioners are encouraged to continue deciding on who they want to become in the information society through their practice. Their ethical practice becomes a power–ethics practice.

## Key Messages

- Action in the information society is influenced by as well as influencing other actions. We need to become aware of how this influence is being developed.
- Power is a concept to help us as practitioners to gain awareness on the influence of actions, and gives us insights on what we can do about such influence.
- There are intended and unintended consequences of actions, so we can decide what actions we take and what power we can use to our advantage.
- Ethics is at the core of our practice, as it inevitably defines what we accept to do in it. We should become more aware of the consequences of our actions for ourselves and others in the information society.
- Systems methodology use should be complemented with a deeper degree of analysis of power relations and ethics.

## Questions / Exercises

Pick out a contentious ethical issue arising in your practice. Try to assess the following:

- How did it come to be a contentious issue?
- What mechanisms have facilitated its emergence?
- What other mechanisms are required to follow in order to do something about the issue?
- What type of ethical subject is this issue related to? What norms, activities, practices and goals are involved with this subject?

In your organization, try to assess how power operates, with the following elements:

- Any particular mechanisms that the organization follows as 'the way we do things here' or 'the ways in which we approve of ideas'
- Any rituals, procedures, values, or key people that are used to 'approve' things (ideas, initiatives, projects)
- What sort of 'person' do these mechanisms portray so as to become accepted and seen as 'ethical'?

Using the figure of ethical reflection, assess what type of 'ethical' practitioner you have become, and what type you want to be.

- How do you think a systems methodology could (or could not) help you to do it?

**Further Reading**

Willcocks (2004). A thorough review of Foucault's work and its applications in information systems. Practitioners might draw on some good insights from this review.

# 8   A Dynamic Practice Framework for Living and Working in the Information Society

## Introduction

The previous chapters have helped us to understand and manage the complexities of practice in the information society. We now know that the information society can be developed by (1) envisioning transformations; (2) by engaging people; and (3) by using the power we have available to act according to what we think is ethical and will lead us to improve our society as a whole. In all these possibilities we can use information and communication systems and technologies.

In the last chapter we saw how helpful the notions of power and ethics can aid practitioners to act ethically. We have briefly proposed complementing systems methodologies with power–ethics analysis and vice versa. Let us first summarize how systems methodologies can help us. Methodologies help practitioners to *enquire* about concerns, perceptions, values, beliefs and aspirations in relation to situations and the use of information systems (IS) and communication technologies (ICTs) in the information society. They also help in promoting reflection about consequences of action so that we know what we can do about the information society. Whilst this phenomenon can be still considered foreign to us or our practice, we can make it our own. With systems methodologies, we can support transformations, redefine desirable futures, and accommodate views. We can also be critical about issues and people who could be marginalized from initiatives or projects. We can also become critical of ourselves and what we think is ethical to do towards improving a situation.

Power–ethics analysis helps us to frame any possibility of action within relations which extend beyond an organization and influence the ways we are as ethical individuals. Analysis helps to identify constraints and possibilities for action. It also helps us to address challenges for the information society and systems-thinking; in particular a predominant focus on problem solving which gains force if we decide to operate within existing organizational boundaries. The information society development could change little if we are not careful and forget key issues of concern and challenges for systems practice (see Table 4.1).

Despite our achievements in proposing patterns to guide our practice in the information society and deal with transformations, engagements and unintended consequences, we are still left with one more challenge to consider more explicitly in our practice in the information society: the challenge of temporality. So far we have assumed that we can orient our thinking and support it with systems methodologies. We have also assumed that we can operate with some timeframes in mind. Our practice could improve if we can have *time* to think and act appropriately when we face the identified phenomena. In relation to temporality the different patterns presented offer us possibilities and implications:

- *Idealist pattern*. Adopting, supporting or redefining a vision means changing, venturing and imagining, often in sustained efforts. For many people and organizations this is an opportunity which includes new uses of information systems and technologies. However we might not see results in a short span of time, or we are constrained to operate within existing project schedules. Flexibility of practice is required if survival is to be guaranteed, and before we know it we get onto implementing another vision. Often there is not time to assess whether adopting a particular vision has been worth the effort.[1] Practitioners can find themselves going from one initiative or project to another without seeing the results of any of them.

- *Strategic pattern*. Engaging with people means that although we are open to any of their (and our) ideas, suggestion or issue to be considered, in practice not all of these are seen to be desirable (as seen in Chapter 6); we have said that *courage* is needed by practitioners to challenge or stay with them in the best of cases, and give themselves and other people 'time' to work. This also relates to the ways in which people interact; what they consider important to do, and the procedures to be followed to get ideas 'approved' (as we saw in the last chapter with the evaluation exercise at Javeriana). The time taken to approval or action is dependent on the situation at hand. Again, it might be difficult to have time and see a change going through.

- *Power* helps us to become more aware of what we can do and hence to inform our practice. However, the operation of power also means that we will never be able to grasp fully its effects and operation. What we see of power through analysis is only a snapshot in time. Our practice is only part of the overall operation of power in society. We need to take stock and see how best to direct our efforts as professionals living and working in a society which changes by the day.

The above (somewhat negative) issues lead us to consider how temporary and transient our practice in the information society could be. Although we have gained ideas on what to do to deal with transformations, engagements and unintended consequences, often we need to be more dynamic and continually 'think on our feet' in a given situation; we might not have another chance with participants. This gets more complicated, as we not only need to deal with the physical world. The virtual world also leads us to consider as practitioners the ethical issues arising and the encounter of different ethical views across geographically dispersed regions (Poster, 2003). We need to be able to quickly grasp what happens in a situation and act accordingly. This means that our roles and participation in any initiative need to unfold dynamically (through time) when new issues of concern, new visions, new engagements and new unintended impacts appear in our society and in our lives.

In relation to the issue of time, the above also means that systems methodology use might need to consider the possibility of becoming 'minimal' so that we are able to deal with all these aspects within the dynamics of life in the information society. Methodologies need to be adapted to a situation and how people are better able to interact; combinations of methodologies need to be simple, straightforward and in many cases adopted to guide our thinking rather than being used explicitly (Checkland and Winter, 2006). From our practice as presented in the previous chapters, we seem increasingly to have more opportunities to practice when we engage in short interventions.

With new forms of interaction (e.g. electronically mediated) across organizations and societies, how can we still be ethical and systemic to deal within such temporal and transient dynamics in the information society?

A possible answer to this question uses what we have done so far in this book. We have tackled specific phenomena (transformations, engagements, unintended consequences) with particular ways of thinking (patterns) to guide our practice. If we now consider that one of this phenomena changes dynamically, we can then consider that we could use different thinking patterns *almost at the same time*.

The above means that whatever could have begun as a vision for the information society, could then become a series of engagements with intended and unintended consequences in relation to people, information systems and technologies. We could then combine our thinking patterns to facilitate our work and to still give us possibilities to think about and act in relation to ethics. We need to be aware at the same time of transformations, engagements and unintended consequences as if all these phenomena could happen in a single event or a series of events. There would be questions to ask which are more relevant to others if we decide to 'think on our feet' in our practice.

This also means that systems methodologies could still be used to facilitate work under one or several of the patterns being identified, and that we would be using them for different purposes considering also the strengths and weaknesses each systems methodology offers (Jackson, 2003). As said previously, systems methodology use could be combined with analysis of power to give us more clarity on what we can ethically do according to the way things are in a particular context. Both of these areas of practice need to come together within these dynamics.

And finally, at any point in time we need to *let it go*, given that we will never be able to 'stay put' in the information society; there are unintended consequences which we can neither foresee nor manage. We need to let things go their own course, and be prepared for what comes next. As practitioners living and working in the information society we need to start again and see new things happening, and get involved in them. There will be new possibilities for supporting or redefining transformations; designing and taking part in new forms of engagement; and acting within constraints and possibilities for action by analyzing power–ethics formations. As information systems and technologies change, we adapt to change.

Does the above mean that we as individuals need to live our lives (including our practice) more intensively without knowing what is coming from one day to another? Perhaps some individuals might interpret the temporary nature of practice in this way. What we are also saying is that our thinking needs to become more flexible and give us possibilities to adapt ourselves to the dynamics of what we have to do in our practice.

Following the above ideas, we now present a framework to allow us to guide our practice in the information society. The framework considers that at any point in time there could be an information society scenario in which some types of questions become more prominent than others, and therefore our response in practice needs to be tailored to a particular scenario. There could be different types of scenarios to which we need to respond with two elements: systems-thinking and methodologies and power analysis.

In Figure 8.1 we define a scenario as a way of looking at a temporary situation which can have characteristics of one of the phenomena of the information society (transformations, engagements, unintended consequences). In such a scenario, and considering that we need to 'think on our feet', our way of thinking would adapt to the phenomena by following an idealist pattern, a strategic pattern or a power-based pattern of practice. Just before we know it, a new scenario would unfold which would require us to change our way of thinking and therefore adopt a different pattern. Systems methodologies would be employed according to what we think suits a situation.

To guide our 'thinking on our feet' and in relation to what could come 'next', we propose the following types of scenarios:

- *Society as a network.* Following the idealist pattern, this scenario suggests that a central concern is that of enabling a network of communication to be developed, and the definition

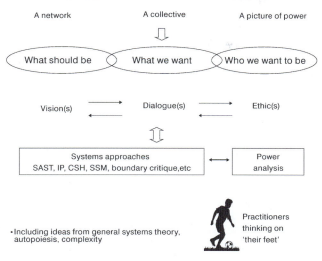

*Figure 8.1*  A framework for practice

of visions within such network. The key question to guide practice is: what types of (network-based) society should we have? This type of question should lead us to work on the (re)definition of vision(s). Within this particular scenario, we would be able to use ideas from systems-thinking theories (for instance with autopoiesis or general systems theory as presented in Chapter 3), in order to explain the nature of such a network and refine our vision(s). We would also be able to use systems methodologies or methods to support such refinement and redefinition by allowing us to look at other aspects that need to be taken into account to continue with our practice. We can do this until we think we need to move to another type of scenario.

- *Society as a collective.* Based on the strategic pattern, the scenario considers that whatever is to be defined as information society will be the result of dialogue, participation and shaping up of systems and technologies. The key question is what do we want (as a collective)? Therefore we would focus our thinking in engaging people (strategic pattern). Systems methodologies could be used to engage people on defining what 'we' want and shaping up the definition of actions for improvement of a situation. Reflection and debate can be part of this scenario, and it might be possible (but not necessary) to arrive at insights for action. It might not be possible given the operation of power and the unintended consequences of our processes of engagement.

- *Society as a picture of power.* In this scenario, society is considered as a dynamic set of relations between people at different levels and hence our power-based pattern of thinking can help us; we are able to grasp how the operation of power is influencing the definition of actions. Thinking on our feet in this scenario means that we need to quickly assess what power–ethics formations allow (or do not allow) individuals to do. Thus the possibility of defining action might be improved by considering such formations. The question that practitioners should ask in this scenario is: what type of ethical subject do we (individually, collectively) want to be? From the power-based pattern of thinking, we as practitioners can use some power (including that offered by systems methodologies), whilst we continually reflect on how power makes us 'subjects', and what we can do about it.

With these scenarios, the hope is that as practitioners we become more flexible to switch between modes of thinking (idealist, strategic, power-based) so as to be able to cope with the temporality of situations we are immersed in. We now present an experience in which we have tried to become flexible whilst still reflective about our thinking in practice. The experience provides a context in which we (me and my colleague Dr. Amanda Gregory from Hull University) found ourselves when helping an organization define its feasible future. The narrative aims to show the unfolding of events and our thinking and acting about them. We divide the narrative in a context, followed by several scenarios of practice.

## Dealing with Temporality in the Information Society

### The Context

The Hull Council of Voluntary Services (CVS) is an umbrella organization that currently supports and represents the interests of voluntary organizations in its region of influence (Humberside and East Yorkshire in the UK). The majority of their activities are focused on supporting the establishment of voluntary organizations and acting as an approving body for funding to be allocated. There are many of these organizations which are continually created or terminated due to funding.

In 2007 voluntary organizations became more aware of emerging pressures in the UK. The UK government issued new regulations which required voluntary organizations to become more accountable with the funding being allocated to them. In addition, new forms of public-private partnership were being fostered at the level of local and regional councils, which meant that new organizations (private) could participate in tendering processes to deliver public services, an area normally within the domain of voluntary organizations.

Processes of public tendering were also being automated in order to ensure transparency and agility in the decisions being made and in the allocation of public contracts. In this regard, voluntary organizations found themselves lagging behind others, as they felt that they did not have capabilities, knowledge or expertise to properly compete for funding. Moreover, some of these organizations and representatives felt that competition could be against their core principles of serving the public in a disinterested manner.

In order to facilitate the airing of these and other concerns, members of the CVS approached us to help them set up and run a debate about the future of the organization and its associates. The chairman and information manager of the CVS (our main contacts) felt that there was a need to air a number of concerns and ideas. They also felt that it was important to be proactive and not only 'mourn' about the current situation, but move forward with possibilities and ideas for the future.

The information manager was responsible for running the CVS website; at the time when they approached us, the information provided through this website was mainly directed at helping voluntary organizations to use the CVS services. Within these services, the main one was that of applying for funding. As this manager suggested, there could be possibilities to modify the website and give further information about resources or opportunities which voluntary organizations could use to increase their chances of success in getting funding.

### Preparing the Workshop

After an initial discussion with the information manager and the chairman of a network of voluntary organizations (which the CVS was using to disseminate information), we agreed to run a half-day workshop. The purpose of the workshop was to collectively imagine and design the future of CVS as well as to define a number of possibilities for improving the CVS's situation. We suggested using a combination of the ideas of two systems methodologies: interactive planning (IP) (Ackoff, 1981) and soft systems methodology (SSM) (Checkland, 1981). The CVS information manager knew about SSM and welcomed the suggestion. She was also knowledgeable of the work developed at the Centre for Systems Studies of Hull University, and was keen to receive support in the application of methodologies during the workshop. The co-ordinator of the network of voluntary organizations was to contact organizations' representatives. The cohort of representatives included voluntary and non-voluntary ones (from Hull City Council and other relevant government bodies).

Using the ideas of the above methodologies, we devised a workshop format which consisted of a welcome by the CVS chairman (who would also briefly present his own view about the current situation of the voluntary sector), followed by an introduction to systems-thinking. After these introductions we would split participant groups into subgroups, who would then be encouraged to elaborate a rich picture of the situation by addressing the following two questions:

- What is the future we are locked into if we do not do anything about it?
- What is the future we desire for CVS and ourselves as representatives of voluntary organizations?

In IP (Ackoff, 1981), these two questions aim to encourage participants to acknowledge the existence of a number of barriers to their own development and to move beyond them to idealize a better future.

With the above questions in mind and in small groups, participants would proceed to define a number of relevant issues which would be considered by the whole group. Following SSM (Checkland, 1981), the idea was to select two or three of the most relevant issues and define conceptual models of systems of human activity which would address these issues. Comparing these models with the current situation would give participants insights into what could be done to improve this situation, and formulate a number of changes. As facilitators of the workshop, we envisaged that if necessary we would provide support to guide the group through these activities.

## The Workshop: A 'Network Scenario'

As planned, the workshop started with the introduction given by the CVS director. He spoke about new complexities in the relationships between government and voluntary organizations. He also highlighted issues of funding and accountability. This meant that voluntary organizations were being required to show more clearly how funding received led to achievement of a number of goals, and how these goals were being achieved. This challenge however presented voluntary organizations with an opportunity to raise their profile, address their administrative problems and get support. For the CVS director, this also meant that it was about time for voluntary organizations to partner each other in the search for funding opportunities.

For the CVS as an umbrella organization in the voluntary sector this introduction clearly resembled a vision of the CVS as a *network* with interactions on the outside and on the inside. Within this network there was to be a continuous flow of information across the CVS, voluntary institutions, profit organizations and government agencies in terms of government policies and standards, funding opportunities and accountability. Within this 'space of flows' (using Castells' terminology as presented in Chapter 2), voluntary institutions needed to make a collective stance to better participate in it. They could have new opportunities for funding; however the government and other partner organizations (e.g. voluntary and profit) would require them in turn to become more efficient.

Within this *network* scenario, information systems and communication technologies could make the flow of information more transparent and efficient. Voluntary organizations could make their information available to other (e.g. funding or profit) ones whilst at the same time accessing funding opportunities. The CVS could then use its own website to provide information to voluntary organizations about how best to use existing funding sources and electronic resources. In turn, voluntary organizations would need to review their own information resources and make them more accessible to the outside world.

After the CVS director's introduction, we (Amanda and I) briefly introduced systems-thinking with the idea of a system and how things are interconnected. From that moment onwards we encouraged participants to use this idea to think about themselves and the CVS as being parts of a whole system. We also gave participants a quick introduction to both IP and SSM approaches. We proceeded to divide the whole group into smaller groups (four or five people) and ask them to draw a rich picture of the situation at CVS. We used the questions mentioned above to guide the discussion in smaller groups.

With the introduction to systems-thinking and how we need to consider the 'context' of voluntary organizations, we were initially adopting an idealist pattern of thinking to operate within this type of 'network' scenario. Following the director's introduction, we were encouraging participants to work in defining a vision and incorporating elements of the expressed context in it, so that we would define ways of transforming the current situation into a desired one. With the drawing and sharing of rich pictures we aimed at fostering creativity and brainstorming. We were engaging people to some extent, but we were not (yet) considering their own values, concerns and beliefs to shape the definition of plans and potential uses of systems and technologies. This was about to change as the sharing of the pictures took place.

### *The Collective and Power Scenarios: 'Us and Them'*

When the time came for each small group to present their picture and insights about the future of voluntary organizations and the CVS, differences in perceptions indicated to us (the facilitators) that the group of participants was taking a particular stance. There were concerns about their organizations becoming like profit-making ones, given that they now had to collaborate and compete for government funding. Some participants expressed the view that they did not want to be shaped by the government's agenda. To them, it was not possible to become accountable because voluntary organizations were the ones 'cleaning up the mess' left by government policy and action. Voluntary organizations were there to help, with or without appropriate administration or funding arrangements.

The expression of these views reflected the concern of some participants for keeping certain values and ways of working as core elements in the design of any new plan or initiative. This clearly indicated to us that people were interesting in shaping their future and including their own perspectives. To this situation we as facilitators kept asking questions about which issues would need attention in relation to participants' concerns. We also shared our own experiences as members of another public service organization (i.e. the university) and shared their concerns for issues like funding and accountability. For us (the facilitators), there were opportunities and challenges in the adoption of goal-oriented practices for the delivery of public services.

Throughout the debate these and other views were expressed. Participants aired their own concerns in order to shape the agenda for future action. Our aim as facilitators was to finish the first part of the workshop (the morning session) with a list of issues which we could work on in the second part (the afternoon). However, we encountered a key challenge.

### A Picture of Power: Being 'Local'

Discussions about key issues for voluntary organizations took an unexpected turn. A couple of participants challenged the nature of the exercise. According to them, other people's perspectives (which favored the adoption of efficiency-related practices and systems by voluntary organizations) were in their view misleading. These participants challenged these views by saying that any individual interested in the future of CVS and its member organizations should be 'local', in other words s/he should be born in the region. Otherwise, his/her views would lack credibility, and this seemed to apply to other individuals who were present (including me as a facilitator).

We all got confused. The challenging participants argued that none of the government initiatives for voluntary organizations had considered the realities of the locality in which they were to be implemented. This was generating in the participants' group a feeling of despair. In this situation, it was clear that we were entering into another scenario: that of a picture of power. Participants were using their own expertise, their participation in local relations and their condition to influence other people's actions and acceptance of views. With the view that the rest of us would be constrained to act, they were getting the upper hand by creating an atmosphere of pessimism, something that the CVS staff members who initially approached us warned us about. A quick analysis of power–ethics formations (using the power-based pattern) led me to articulate[2] the analysis summarized in Table 8.1.

As seen in Table 8.1, there were some relations that could influence the workshop outcomes by privileging local knowledge and expertise; these relations seemed to be in conflict with relations that we as facilitators wanted to develop (based on participation, sharing of ideas and different types of expertise). The discussions that followed showed more clearly a 'battle' terrain. Participants and facilitators were being constrained by the meaning of being local. However, there were still opportunities to express our views. One of the other participants claimed that she had worked for over ten years in helping people in the city of Hull, and although she was not born in the area she felt she had the same right to work in the voluntary sector as anyone else. We (Amanda and I) followed her. Amanda reminded the challenging participants that she was born in Hull and that she had worked previously with the voluntary sector. I said I had spent more than ten years in the area and that I was concerned about helping people in the city of Hull. To me this was part of being a good academic: I wanted to provide expertise in problem solving and the CVS workshop was an opportunity to learn how to do it in the region of influence of the university where I was working.

*Table 8.1* Power-based pattern at the Hull CVS workshop

| Power development | Possibilities and constraints within power | Ethical action |
| --- | --- | --- |
| 'Local' relations were defining what constituted appropriate knowledge | It was *not* possible to engage actively for non-local people, but some kind of 'local' expertise could be claimed | Use existing conversations to re-address this balance. As a facilitator, claim a desire to help regardless of where we came from. As an ethical subject, claim that we wanted to be 'helpful' facilitators for the CVS |

The above conversations and claims made by other participants (better use of existing financial resources, and follow central government advice) contributed to generate a more 'positive' type of atmosphere. Conversations turned to collaborating. Most participants expressed their willingness to continue with the exercise and so did we as facilitators. Amanda wrote on a flip chart a few of the issues derived from the views expressed that she thought were relevant for participants (she was then using her power as a facilitator to 'move on' in the workshop). The rest of participants then focused on agreeing/disagreeing on the list of issues being identified and giving a more positive slant to their contributions. As for myself, I could see we had opened a possibility for action which responded more to my own concerns of 'helping'. As will be seen later in the chapter, I could also use some power available as a facilitator.

### Continuing with the Engagement: 'What We Want to Shape'

During the lunch break we as facilitators decided to 'speed up' the process of selecting the most relevant issues to work on. It was a decision I decided to go along with,[3] given the pressures of time. To speed up selection of issues, we would then distribute colored stickers among participants. When participants came back from lunch we asked them to take stickers and place them next to each of the issues that they considered most important (red) and most urgent (yellow). Those issues with the most stickers placed next to them would be selected as the most relevant to be tackled. With this exercise participants were shaping the definition of potential future actions to improve their situation.

By the end of the exercise, the two most relevant issues in terms of both urgency and importance were:

- Voluntary organizations and the CVS should improve their management practices and become more accountable and sustainable.
- More information about funding opportunities should be shared among organizations, so they could work together and improve their chances of getting funding and thus becoming sustainable.

With the above issues we proceeded to invite remaining participants (some of them had left before lunch[4]) to define, in two smaller groups, activities that could contribute to address each issue. Following the ideas of SSM, we initially intended to facilitate the definition of conceptual models of activity, but (again) given the pressures of time we decided to quickly show participants an example of a conceptual model, and ask them to go on directly to list activities deemed as essential for each issue. We also asked participants about the type of support they would require from CVS in relation to activities to be defined, and include any possibility that could be supported by existing electronic information resources (for instance the CVS website).

During the presentation of activities by each subgroup, the CVS information manager took notes about the suggestions, and assessed their feasibility, also in technical terms. She also suggested other activities which would meet the aims desired by each of the subgroups. The CVS director also provided his own suggestions for action which he considered feasible given the existing situation of the CVS. Acting as a facilitator and 'expert researcher', I also gave advice as someone who had been acquiring experience in searching for funding in a university environment.[5]

As a result of presentations and discussions on possibilities for improvement, it was agreed that some actions would be explored. These included:

- Making available a web-based government tool which would enable organizations to look for potential partners in the preparation of funding bids.
- Encouraging the use of existing procedures and support mechanisms to facilitate the creation of voluntary organizations so that they would comply with financial and legal requirements. These mechanisms could also be made available to existing organizations. The CVS website was to be enriched with information and useful contact points to help them become administratively solid.

With these possibilities we finished the workshop. The CVS director and information manager as well as some participants expressed to us their satisfaction with the process and outcomes and with the usefulness of suggestions for improving their current situation. In addition, they encouraged us to write about this experience.

### Power 'Outside': The Unintended and Unforeseen

Six months after we did the above exercise we contacted the CVS information manager to ask her about any progress being made in relation to the suggestions that came up. She let us know that due to a new emergency in the city of Hull (due to floods in the days after our exercise took place), the CVS and some member organizations had been called to support the local council in providing assistance to people who needed it. The suggestions for action had not been implemented. Instead voluntary organizations were reinforcing their 'own' power by doing what they were doing best (helping people in need). However, there were still tensions with government organizations. CVS members were in the process of becoming more knowledgeable about new legislation that was affecting them; some were responding to the need to get funding to survive. This can be seen as a new scenario.

This new situation would mean that there is a continuous process of power development, so a picture of power scenario could be portrayed. Power–ethics formations analysis could be conducted if we decide to enter into relations with the CVS again. However, this scenario can have other interpretations. As far as we know, the UK government has continued using information technologies to invite service organizations (profit and non-profit oriented) to get involved in ensuring that service provision is transparent and accountable. We know for instance of the Alito[6] portal (http://scms.alito.co.uk/ accessed in December 2008) in which any organization can register as service providers (e.g. suppliers), get access to potential funding opportunities and appropriately respond to them. Alito has been seen by some organizations as a system that encourages collaboration whilst at the same time developing a culture of transparency on the side of regional governments and of excellence in service delivery on the side of supplier organizations. For other organizations, it is a way of 'controlling them' via the development of a culture in which transparency is only developed in the provision of information and the creation of an 'elite' group of service organizations.

At the time of writing about Alito, it remains to be seen how helpful it has been for different parties involved and in which degree or ways. It also remains to be seen how voluntary organizations have been teaming up or partnering with other organizations to seek funding available through Alito. What we know so far and from first-hand experience is that some (small) profit organizations see their own future survival in direct connection with Alito and government funding.[7] For us, this means that the dynamics of power are unpredictable and a new scenario of 'society as a network' is emerging. The fact that electronic information services like Alito are already being deployed speaks about how the network society vision is developing in possibly more sophisticated ways (in this case having a more transparent and accountable exchange of information by different organizations). So it seems we are back to square one (Chapter 2)!

This could constitute a new scenario for our practice. Now we know that organizations and individuals are called to take part in new networks of flow of information, in other words to engage. Those who do not take part might be in danger of having to look for opportunities for their survival elsewhere. Thus it is essential for organizations to adopt visions, shaping them up and making their (our) own ethical stance about them. This could be a new scenario of society as a collective.

We seem to continue to find the same phenomena of interest and thinking patterns in the information society. But we now know that this also has to do with our own ethics, and how we decide to act according to what we think needs to be done. The above tells us that, as discussed in Chapter 2, the network society is here to stay, whether we like it or not. The dynamic nature of network development requires us to keep an eye on the 'outside' of our own area of practice, and get ready to act because the 'outside' can affect us as individuals or organizations. We also get this message after engaging with systems-thinking in our practice.

If we live and work in the information society we need to continue asking the questions that our scenario-based framework have proposed: what should (a society) be; what do we want (of it); and who do we want to be (in society). For organizations like the CVS, these questions gain relevance given that they need to respond to 'visions' in order to survive (and also to make their role useful in society); they need to keep an eye on what happens, continually engage their members in deciding action to improve their situation, and act according to what they think is right. For ourselves as individuals and practitioners, we need to continually make sense of what happens, in order to decide what type of ethics we want to live and in which type of society we want to live.

The invitation is then to make these questions an essential part of our practice. This chapter began by raising the issue of us having to 'think on our feet' in daily life and help others do the same. The information society is here to stay and it continually changes in many ways. We need to keep an eye on what we want do to and who we want to be in it. To help us 'think on our feet', at least we know how we can think about the information society, and how we need to think again tomorrow.

## Chapter Summary

This chapter has presented a framework to complement the patterns of thinking and action which we have developed for our practice in the information society. We have considered the temporality of our societies and our possibilities to 'intervene' in them. The issue of time has been mentioned as a challenge for systems thinkers. Together with challenges for the information society (in particular the economic drive as mentioned in Chapter 2) they have constituted a departure point for the development of ways of thinking to guide our information systems practice with the help of systems methodologies.

In this chapter we have gone one more step by suggesting that we need to think on our feet in every activity of our practice. This means that we need to continually adapt to different scenarios, many of which could appear in single events of our practice. We have suggested a framework to help us formulate and address key questions in three different types of scenarios:

- Society as a network: What should a society be?
- Society as a collective: What do we want to do in society?
- Society as a picture of power: Who do we want to become?

These questions could help us to situate our practice in daily life and in the ways we think about the information society.

## Key Messages

*   Temporality of practice is an issue. Our ways of thinking need to be flexible to respond to the dynamics of a situation.
*   There are key questions to help us thinking: what should a society be; what do we want to achieve as a collective; and who do we want to become as practitioners.
*   The information society keeps changing, we need to respond to this change according to what we think is best for ourselves and other people.

## Questions / Exercises

*   In relation to the framework to guide practice defined in this chapter, in which most common scenario do you see yourself operating in daily life at work or elsewhere?
*   How will you manage your practice in other types of scenarios?
*   What educational activities can be suggested to help information systems or systems practitioners improve their practice and their chances of contributing to improve the development of the information society?

## Further Reading

Dunleavy *et al.* (2006). A comprehensive study of the new dynamics between information systems, technology providers and government institutions in what is now called 'digital era governance'. New forms of networking are emerging.

# 9   Conclusions

So it seems like the end of a journey. Hopefully for the reader it will just be the beginning of his/her own! This final chapter aims to round up the discussion on the information society and systems-thinking. As we have seen in this book these two can be together through *practice* in different types of activity.

The information society has been presented and studied as a new manifestation of the idea of having a 'networked' society. This idea has appealed to many audiences (technological, political, social, etc) throughout history. Recently, it has been regarded as *new* societal order because now the presence of information and communication technologies is stronger than ever. They help us see 'how' a networked type of society can be made reality, with new examples emerging by the day. We are connected and continue developing connections across the world.

This 'new' order brings us both positive and negative impacts. On the one hand, more people can become information literate; they get access to opportunities for education and progress whilst also creating new ones. Claims to efficiency, democracy and transparency have been made in society and in many cases these have lived up to expectation. The information society offers possibilities, and whilst doing so, it encourages individuals to go beyond them. Access to electronic information can generate knowledge, which in turn generates power to do things in many ways (Toffler, 1992). It is up to 'us' as individuals to make the best of this one-lifetime chance whilst avoiding being overloaded by information, knowledge, systems and technologies.

On the other hand, this is precisely one of the main sources of general concern for people who are living and working in the information society. Information brings issues of access and privilege, and by doing so it revives existing debates or generates new ones in relation to social inclusion and participation. Those groups of individuals advocating egalitarianism or community-based orientations for the information society argue that information needs to become a public asset (Menzies, 1996). Otherwise its use will reinforce existing class, power and political conflicts. These people see that their argument gains force when the socio-economic gaps widen between those individuals who are information literate and those who are not. People and organizations with the appropriate knowledge see these gaps as opportunities for offering products and services; they seem to have reaped most of the benefits of the information society. And due to this initial advantage, it is likely that they could obtain more benefits in the future than anyone else. Widening gaps between socio-economic groups seem to confirm that those who were/are better off will continue being better off, to the detriment of those who are/ were not.

The dynamics of the information society could lead us to assert the above in simple terms (e.g. 'black and white', 'good' or 'bad', 'technology-based' or 'not'). But the reality is more complex than that. Even in advanced societies where the concept of an information-based society has been pioneered we still see gaps. Before we can completely accept or reject a 'new' societal order, this book has provided a middle-ground set of perspectives (or patterns) that, whilst allowing us to think of *how* we relate our practice to the information society, have also opened opportunities for challenging and improving such practice in different realms.[1]

In practical terms, the above means that:

- We can make the information society more 'digestible' and 'humane' through the use of the patterns being proposed in our practice. There could be many other ways of understanding information society phenomena, but in principle, we can see the information society as: (1) developing visions and transforming ways of living in society (idealist pattern); (2) co-constructing and shaping visions with concerns and values in mind (strategic pattern); or (3) allowing people to operate in society regarding constraints and possibilities about what is 'acceptable' to do and/or to 'be' (power-based pattern). In all these we see possibilities for use of information systems and communication technologies.
- Systems-thinking and systems methodologies have allowed us to imagine how the above patterns could be followed in our practice. Methodologies have allowed us to engage in defining and suggesting ways to take patterns to practice. The end result is a new type of systems practice. It can open further opportunities for research and reflection which could help both information systems and systems-thinking.
- Whilst we have become more aware of how we can improve our practice with systems-thinking in the information society we have also become more aware of the *commitments* that the different patterns bring. In each pattern there is a set of assumptions and implications which it is necessary to be conscious of when engaging at different levels of activity. We have used commitments of critical systems-thinking to identify and address a number of challenges that emerge when we bring systems methodology use: time, problem solving orientation and limited scope. These challenges bear similarities with the challenges identified for the development of the information society. We have been able to address these challenges in practice (see Chapters 5 to 8).
- We have also considered that practitioners dealing with temporality in information society situations need to 'think on their feet', and be able to make their thinking more flexible so as to respond to what we see unfolding in situations (see Chapter 8). We are conscious that we need to adapt to the dynamics of situations and be able to address different questions with the help of methodologies and critical thinking about power and ethics issues. The end result has been a framework that could help our thinking and that integrates the use of different patterns of thinking. The framework intends to complement rather than replace the use of the defined patterns.

These considerations led us to think that we have a number of ways of thinking and acting in the information society. It is now time to take stock to reflect on how far we have gone in promoting systems practice in the information society. We now summarize each of the patterns defined throughout the book. We draw some implications of the use of these patterns for systems practice and for management. We finish the chapter by raising a number of suggestions for the education of future practitioners.

## The Idealist Pattern Revisited

Human beings like to imagine future states of life. Either at a personal or professional level, we continually imagine how our life will be. Through history, we have generated a view about society as a network in which we are able to communicate and exchange information. This type of network is said to offer any one of us opportunities to pursue our own goals, and ultimately to become better (possibly more knowledgeable and wiser) human beings.

Whilst many ancient cultures attributed the achievement of wisdom to possibly supernatural factors (or innate gifts), it was the Ancient Greeks who regarded the acquisition of knowledge as a condition to achieve wisdom. In a network type of society, knowledge can be helped by the provision of information and its exchange via communication. Information can now be captured, represented, processed and exchanged as streams of 'bits'. From the time in which communication processes could be represented and modeled, information became inevitably embedded in such processes. The rest (what one can do with information) is left to individuals, their purposes and motivations.

An idealist pattern assumes that we can all envision our future through a vision and work to make it happen through a number of transformations. If the above idea is followed (we can acquire and use information), the aim of remaining activities of our practice is to generate and implement visions. We already have some visions lined up:

*   making organizations 'information-based', more flexible and responsive to customers needs;
*   making public and private institutions more 'citizen-centered', efficient and accountable;
*   making individuals more 'autonomous', with more choices for their lives. This applies to employees, citizens and information/systems practitioners themselves.

These visions of 'making', lead us to think that as practitioners, we need to make sure that we contribute to making them reality. In the idealist pattern, achieving these visions requires us to work on establishing a number of preconditions or transformations. From our practice, these preconditions are about projects that need to be in place. These projects range from making sure that information can easily circulate (and therefore there is a technical infrastructure supporting it) to changing organizational structures so that people become more empowered to serve others much better. Information systems and technologies can help us to deliver the transformations required; their use needs to make sense to people involved and affected.

### *The Contributions of Systems-thinking*

Systems-thinking can help the idealist pattern in relation to visions and transformations. It can do so by helping supporting the definition of visions through considering different aspects in discussion. It is often the case that traditionally this type of discussion never happens, or if it does, it is only to clarify how the idea should happen, without considering fully a variety of aspects and, more importantly, what people can make out of a vision.

Systemic-thinking helps us to refine our perceptions about the vision. It can provide us with different ways of thinking about the vision, each way bringing different requirements and possibilities. It can also help us to debate about the vision, so that we might consider alternatives to it. These alternatives are:

*   not implementing the vision;
*   implementing the opposite to what the vision defines;
*   implementing a variation of the vision.

In practice, and with the help of methodologies like strategic assumption surface testing (SAST) (Mason and Mitroff, 1981) we find that we can generate visions which make more sense to people involved, and by doing so we find that they can feel more empowered to face the future. Systems methodologies have helped us to justify visions in people's own terms, and to generate their own vision within the vision.

Systems methodologies can also help us to design systems to meet visions by supporting the definition of transformations required to make a vision reality. With methodologies like Ackoff's (1981) interactive planning (IP), we have seen that designs of how the vision could work as a system can be produced. With this, a vision can be refined or firmed up to something that is technologically feasible, operationally viable, and most important, something that gives people the possibility of living their core values.

Under the idealist pattern of practice, we have used other methodologies to support or redefine transformations required. Soft systems methodology (SSM) (Checkland, 1981) helps us to make sense of a transformation (e.g. project) that is required to achieve a vision (often by implementing preconditions for the vision). This methodology also helps us to facilitate understanding of such a transformation, as well as consideration of several aspects that need to be taken into account in plans or initiatives.

### *Implications for Practice*

Envisioning future states or required transformations can help people gather around common goals, and put their energy into defining how these would happen. If an idealist pattern of practice is followed, practitioners (information systems professionals, policy makers, others) would need to be able to contribute to the definition or refining of visions about the information society. They will need to foster creativity and participation. They will need to know what information and communication technologies (ICTs) and information systems (IS) can do for such visions, and ensure that different elements are addressed in projects or initiatives.

Moreover, the idealist pattern is about enthusing other people with the content of visions, and making sure that visions are accepted by them. In many societies, visions like the 'bits-based' one presented in Chapter 5, can 'dazzle' people and convince them. In others, they do not make sense. Visions need to be the 'right ones'. They need to be grounded into what people see they can do with them. If this cannot be fully achieved and needs further debate on not only how to implement a vision but also how to shape it in terms of people's values, a different pattern of thinking is required: that of enabling people to express their concerns, values and beliefs, and to shape future ICT use with them.

### The Strategic Pattern Revisited

Not only do we as human beings like to define or take visions to completion. We also like to engage with others in their definition or implementation; this seems to be part of our lives in collectives and societies. As individuals, we like to shape the form of things in groups, so as to make them ours, in other words to *own them*. We like to get the support of our communities in deciding and taking any action. We like to learn from other people. Existing cultures, traditions, values, and ways of living influence how we see the world around us. We like to preserve or 'keep' valuable things, or to incorporate what we have in the development of new visions and perspectives.

The strategic pattern of practice assumes that the use of ICTs is shaped by, among other things, people's existing values, beliefs and ways of living. In Chapter 6 we presented the case in which technologies fit for a single purpose (e.g. a bicycle) get adopted in different ways, and one particular technology is finally accepted. Moreover, the same technology can produce different results in different contexts or organizations. Examples of the latter are many but we highlight two: (1) the rate of usage (and noise) of mobile technology is greater in societies where explosive conversation is part of people's way of life; (2) the appearance of websites is influenced by what people 'look and feel' in different parts of the globe. These examples show how people shape ICT use according to what they think is important to them and/or others. People and technology produce different and often unexpected configurations. We now have web services for dating, baby-sitting, travelling, counseling and even car repairing![2]

The shaping of information and communication systems and technologies also takes place given that we as individuals like to participate and be taken into account in decisions; we will be the ones using systems and technologies. In societies where there are conditions favorable for participation (so-called democratic environments for decision making), inclusion of people is often taken for granted. Not only this, but participation is also used to 'assess' other types of societies in their advancement towards implementing information society initiatives.[3] This sort of 'substratum' needs to be investigated and understood by us as practitioners. This could give us insights as to how people participate in defining their affairs and how they take decisions together.

Out of engagement and participation, it might be possible to generate visions about the information society, as well as localized strategies or initiatives to implement them. The shaping of visions according to people's concerns and values can result in adding new elements to visions including:

- different groups of people being served by initiatives;
- ICT serving (rather than inhibiting the achievement of) people's needs, and being used widely;
- inclusive decision making.

The Javeriana case we presented in Chapter 6 has shown how engagement with people can be facilitated and can lead us to consider issues of culture and values of solidarity and care for each other in society (Córdoba, 2002). These issues will have an impact on the definition and use of systems and technologies. We can guide the definition and implementation of plans related to information technology use by addressing these issues as a 'whole system of enquiry' with people involved and affected.

### The Contributions of Systems-thinking

As seen in Chapter 4, a particular strand of systems-thinking embeds the inclusion of stakeholder groups as part of the phenomena to be studied; in other words people are part of the larger system in which ICT is to be implemented. After the emergence of systems theories we have seen developments which use the idea of a system as a human construction to enable us to see and debate about situations. The idea of a systems boundary has been useful to help people define their concerns and how other elements (other people, other concerns) could be included so as to address situations of exclusion or marginalization. This is a key issue in the information society and systems-thinking has helped us to address it when talking to people about their concerns, values and interests about society. We can use the idea of a system as an enquiring and debating device in situations where we see a diversity of perceptions and views from stakeholders.

Approaches like soft systems methodology (SSM) and critical systems heuristics (CSH) (Ulrich, 1983) have been used in practice to facilitate representation of concerns about a current situation. CSH has also been used to define an 'ought' mode of such a situation. With this being defined (as a more local type of vision), SSM and other approaches (e.g. Ackoff's interactive planning or IP) can be used to support people in shaping the definition of any improvement of their situation. In activities of design, the role of information systems and technologies has been considered as that of mainly *supporting* people's concerns about their societies. Systems methodologies allow them first to define their desired (meaningful) situation, and then debate about role(s) of ICT to support desired activities. We have defined interesting and insightful suggestions to improve a situation with the help of ICT.

Moreover, reflection on systems boundaries has also been useful to facilitate continual debate on and identification of concerns from people, and to reflect on consequences of any decision to be made. This has helped our practice activities to become explicitly aware of issues of ethics (one of them being the inclusion of people in initiatives). Exerting critical thinking about boundaries has enabled practitioners to accept that not everything can be possible, and that given this, as Ulrich (1983) suggests, it is essential to secure (at least temporarily) agreements about decisions and their consequences. Systems-thinking enables practice to become more continually reflective about people, issues and consequences. It has put practitioners in the wider scheme of things, where their (our) actions have impacts. They might acknowledge the importance of becoming more aware of their actions and their ethics as part of the situations they are trying to improve.

### Implications for Practice

With a strategic pattern of practice, it becomes possible to design 'whole' plans, in other words, plans that contemplate different aspects of changes to be made to make sense of the information society. The use of systems methodologies 'throws' practitioners into a wider arena of activity. With methodologies practitioners can facilitate reflection and debate on issues that are not necessarily related to the use of information systems and technologies. In the examples presented, these issues include things like:

- goals of organizations;
- cultural constraints, values and possibilities;
- co-ordination of efforts (e.g. projects, initiatives, plans);
- what we think about each other.

These issues would also make practitioners more conscious of the importance of fitting any new initiative with what is already in place, and being conscious of the 'ways things are done' in a particular context. This could become a facilitating element for improvement, but also an inhibiting one, in particular if people and organizations stick to the idea that what they do is what they will continue doing. To the existence of this type of generalization, it was suggested that practitioners need to become more critical of their own and other people's sweeping generalizations, so as to explore ways of challenging them in case they are not helping in the adoption of alternative ways of doing things.

Critical awareness on issues of power and ethics was suggested when these generalizations do not allow for any alternative to be considered or 'force' people involved to assume particular roles which bring ethical implications. This led to the definition of a third pattern of thinking for practice in the information society.

## The Power-based Pattern Revisited

In the example presented in Chapters 6 and 7 and from other experiences in our practice we have found that it is often the case that people stick to the idea that 'the ways we do things' should not be subjected to change. We find that this idea gains momentum and uncritical acceptance if it is related to ethical issues, thus making it challenging to even talk about the information society (let alone thinking of designing plans to implement any related action).

The 'ways we do things' influences practice, but can also be influenced by it; it generates intended and unintended impacts; and it influences our ethical stances to situations. To consider both and embrace them together we have defined a pattern by which people can relate their actions to other actions. It is a pattern that situates us as subjects of forms of power and ethics that operate in our relations with ourselves and others. By doing so, they influence what we consider 'right' or 'wrong' to do. We need to identify and reflect on these forms if we want to frame any improvement on relations between people.

### *The Contributions for Systems-thinking*

The 'way we do things' has been looked at from the perspective of power–ethics. Using Michel Foucault's ideas on power and ethics, we have been able to enrich our practice with a perspective that considers how actions influence other actions. Although this is not explicitly a systems idea, Foucault's work has previously been incorporated in systems-thinking. One of the aims behind this is to facilitate critical reflection on how action for improvement can be adequately defined.

Systems-thinkers have argued that any attempt to improve situations needs to consider the operation of power at different levels, so as to facilitate exploration of future possibilities, one of them being the 'liberation' of suppressed 'knowledges' as Flood (1990) (a systems-thinker) would call them. Power analysis has been focused on the 'micro' operation as Flood calls it. Little has been said about power explicitly influencing individuals' ethics, and how power relations can account for the 'unintended' consequences of action, including the use of information and communication technologies.

This is one reason why we develop a pattern that considers both power and ethics in practice. Analysis of how power operates plays an important part in relation to what can be achieved if the previous two patterns guide practice. It might give us clues as to how and why certain visions (and not others) are defined (idealist pattern), as well as how and why certain ways of working (e.g. by co-ordinating efforts) do (not) succeed (strategic pattern). We have defined an element of analysis of power and ethics (power–ethics formations) to help practitioners become more aware of how to act in relation to power and their own ethical purposes. This could be of interest to practitioners if they want to gain clues about how their actions and those of others are framed within a wider perspective of things. These clues could well complement their use of systems methodologies.

Moreover, Foucault's work can inspired a stronger and deeper degree of reflection on the relation between power and ethics, and how we (individuals) become the subjects of *both* in our practice. Foucault suggests that it is impossible to escape from power. Not only are its 'juridical' forms present in societies; ways of knowing, behaving and acting that influence individuals' perceptions about themselves are also part of power in society. Power is the by-product of history, and is part of the information society.

If the idea of unintended uses of information and communication technologies is taken seriously by practitioners, this would mean that we can still (as individuals or groups), and despite the apparently 'negative' consequences of systems and technology, operate within power and find ways of becoming the subjects they want to become. A deeper degree of reflection on issues of power and ethics can lead us as practitioners to enquire about how actions influence other actions, and how systems and technologies get deployed or rejected in society. It can also lead us to consider our own ethics, and how they are also the by-product of relations with ourselves and others. This type of reflection can complement systems methodology use. *Methodologies also influence power and ethics.* Their use becomes part of a network of relations and hence we can decide to use them according to our own ethical purposes (Córdoba, 2006). Analysis of power should lead us to find possibilities to live our own ethics and use systems and technologies for our own ethical purposes.

At a 'macro level', we have argued that the information society could be altering the balance of power, either by reinforcing control over individuals, or by making more explicit the ways in which information can play at their (dis)advantage. Despite this 'overall' influence of power, individuals have the possibility of creating new ways of being and behaving whilst living in the present times. This seems to be a key call for people to act upon. It is a call that encourages all of us to use what we have at our disposal, what actions we can influence and what actions we would like to be influenced by. The information society as a new order can present people with opportunities and challenges. At least we have both, so by knowing them we can use our freedom more critically.

### *Implications for Practice*

Research in information systems practice has in the last decade seen the use of different theories and approaches to explain phenomena. With new social theories being imported into the field of information systems, the possibilities are endless. But this book is not only about creating another possibility, which could be about using Foucault's ideas to enrich critical perspectives on studying information systems phenomena.

With the power-based pattern, it has been said that a richer type of analysis can be conducted about practice, and with it, a better view of possibilities and constraints for ethically-guided action could be mapped. However, there is more. The power-based pattern is an invitation for practitioners to re-think *who they are*. Through a more critical interpretation of practice, they can also explore and assess the ways in which they have become practitioners, and how they are recreating such ways in their daily activities.

The main implication for practice under a power-based pattern is the fact that practitioners are also the result of our choices. The power-based pattern makes us more conscious of the how and the why of such choices. But it does not fully define the *what* of our choices, in other words it does not fully define who we want to become. This is a task we need to undertake. We *must* define who we want to become, and encourage other people to do the same. If we decide not to do anything, this would mean leaving out the possibility of owning our own ethical behavior and ultimately, our own ethical future.

The hope of this book is that by the end of reading it practitioners might acknowledge the fact that we are all part of the information society and that we can become useful if we put our heart into it at any stage of what we call our practice.

### The Future: Educating Practitioners

The book has been an attempt to provide an alternative slant on the practice of information systems in the information society. Although general in this attempt, it has been conceived of as an invitation to encourage systems practitioners to look at their activities with a more critical but hopeful eye.

The final framework in the last chapter can orient the activities of practitioners on a day-to-day basis. Moreover, we think it also makes us more aware of the issue of temporality of the information society, and how we can react to it. This leads us to suggest a view on how education in information systems and systems practice could be further developed. We now propose some possibilities for education for the future. We first summarize some lessons from the book in relation to education, and we suggest some strategies to take these lessons to practice.

### Lessons Learned

The book has been about improving practice in the information society by giving tools to practitioners to:

1   *Become more creative and active in developing the information society.* An idealist pattern of practice should encourage practitioners to become more creative and proactive in exploring ways of benefiting people with the use of ICT. Systems-thinking has helped to foster creativity. New methodologies, techniques, approaches, and ways of developing new 'bits-based visions' should be created to help people with visions and transformations.
2   *Become more 'engaging' with people*, so as to foster dialogue, participation, joint exploration, and ultimately shaping up use of information systems and technologies in different realms of life in the information society. Systems methodologies can help in this regard by encouraging a more open and reflective type of education for practitioners. Still, more needs to be done in bringing these and other methodologies closer to activities of participation when it comes to educating practitioners on how to decide on possibilities of systems and technology use. Information systems and systems practitioners need to be supported in order to enabling conversations, debates, and design of initiatives.
3   *Become more 'ethically aware'.* The information society is a complex phenomenon worldwide, and that includes us as individuals. Ideas about the network paradigm, gradual development and adoption of systems and technologies and power–ethics relations have invited us to think about who we want to be and how we want to live. In the light of the dynamics of the information society, ethics need to be continually thought through, bearing in mind that we are not alone, and that we can work with other people. We still have opportunities to construct society according to what we think should be done. Education for hope, for exploring what we can really do, and for venturing in doing it, should be made possible and should become a useful way of constructing our own future.

Bearing in mind these three areas of activity, we now suggest three different strategies for education in the information society.

### Strategies to Take Lessons to Practice

From the above, it becomes clear that (a) creativity, (b) engagement and (c) ethical awareness are three elements whose development can be fostered via education. The use of systems methodologies can help in this regard. Complementary to methodology use, we suggest the following elements:

•   *Teaching creative thinking to 'firm up' visions.* De Bono (2004) has been regarded as a very inspirational thinker for systems researchers. He offers a number of techniques and methods to help 'expand' our thinking to consider different possibilities when taking a decision. De

*Table 9.1* Thinking hats for an 'access for all' initiative

| Color of hat (De Bono, 2004) | 'Access for all' policy |
| --- | --- |
| **White: Information**. What [information] do we have? What do we need? How are we going to get the information we need? | How many is 'all'? How many computer access points are we planning? |
| **Red: The warm**. Feelings, emotions, intuition. What are our feelings about the situation? | Do we genuinely feel this decision will generate good impact? |
| **Black: Caution**. What faults or weaknesses are there? What might go wrong and why might things not fit? | Is this a feasible plan according to available financial resources or restrictions? Any contingencies in case of not succeeding? |
| **Yellow: The positive**. Values, benefits, how something can be done, why it should work | What signs in the public can we see that prompt us to consider this possibility? |
| **Green: Creativity**. Explore alternatives and possibilities collectively. | Are there other ways of providing access? How can we imagine people accessing internet? |
| **Blue: Organization of thinking**. What is the end goal? Why we are here? What have we achieved? | What steps need to be taken to ensure we implement any decision? What is the final result of the discussion? Where can we go next with our decision/plan? |

Bono proposes that when a group of individuals are to solve a problem, they need to transit through different 'thinking modes' or 'hats'. A hat is a set of features that we highlight about a potential solution. We can employ different types of hats at different times and according to the nature of a decision. What is important is for everyone participating to have the same hat at the same time.

In Table 9.1, following De Bono (2004), if for instance, we're deciding on a policy to provide internet access to 'all', we could gather a number of different individuals involved in the decision and go together through the different hats. With the table, we convey the idea that we need to be more creative if we are going to firm up visions to bring the information society into place; and this would require us to leave a particular role or source of expertise to think as a whole group. Knowledge of potential uses of ICTs to support the exchange of electronic information and bits is only part of what we need to do. We need to creatively *challenge* our thinking if the information society is to give us the benefits we could be envisaging.

In the case of a bits-based vision (Chapter 5), using 'hats' could help us enhance a vision by generating ideas by which the vision or parts of it could be implemented. Within an idealist pattern of practice, what might be needed is just an act of creation to trigger different activities on different fronts. Policy makers might find this useful in defining a vision-based set of policies. Practitioners might like some clarification of the new technology or system that is about to be implemented. In this type of creative activity many aspects and possibilities for the use of information systems and technologies in society can be aired, explored or (re)defined.

- *Developing 'soft' skills*. Engaging people in shaping up systems and technology use requires practitioners to go outside their 'comfort zone' and be able to talk to others. Talking to people is about listening first of all, and understanding what people are saying, and confirming what was said or expressed (hence the usefulness of feedback in Shannon's communication model, presented in Chapter 2). It is also about mediating between people and finding shared spaces of concern so that people agree on taking things forward (or agree to disagree). Practitioners should develop their soft skills; talk to other people from different disciplines; and convey clear messages about what they do and what they think. From our experience, this has been a challenge for both information systems and systems practitioners and is related to practitioners' language.

In practice we find that organizations nowadays need to deal with the complexities of inter-connecting different types of information systems applications and technologies. Whilst technologies can help them perform almost any type of transaction, when it comes to changing a system there are difficulties in matching users' requirements with functionalities of systems and making systems flexible to changes and new requirements. Companies that have addressed this situation find it useful to engage both systems experts and users in a joint process of modeling core activities or capabilities. To do so, they provide some shared modeling tools so that any change in functionality can be more easily translated into changes in systems functionalities. This is very valuable and gives us a good start. Complementary to the availability of 'tools', what seems to be missing from this strategy is the importance of educating both systems and users in talking to each other, going beyond their 'silos' and focusing on a problem. This suggests that education on negotiation and managing change becomes paramount. Techniques that help people put themselves in the other's shoes and help them appreciating the complexities of a 'whole' operation could be valuable. Good consultants in information systems have known this for some time; maybe we can learn from them!

- *Becoming 'authentic' as practitioners.* We want to develop practitioners who are true to themselves. This means that by considering the influence of power in their practice, they use it according to their own ethics. Although ethics can be considered as a by-product of power, practitioners can still shape power relations and (re)develop themselves continually through their activities. Opportunities should be given for practitioners and other people to become more sensitive to the operation of power; to be able to quickly analyze it (e.g. 'think on their feet') and draw potential constraints and implications; and to continually reflect as human beings who they want to become.[4] Career and self-development opportunities can be taken to a deeper degree of reflection. People can see themselves as works of art in the making, and continue doing so either in one job or another. For people as human beings, this is where their authenticity resides. Being human as practitioners, and encouraging other people to do the same should be part of our career plans wherever we are.

With these elements, we hope that our practice in the information society offers us more and better chances to make this society better for all. We need to create and maintain these chances and invite other people to do the same. In doing so, we should be hoping for the best, and we should be trying our best.

As people, we are part of the big systemic concert that the information society has brought to us. The days of practice as a closed type of activity are long gone. The information society tells us that our actions will inevitably have an effect on this concert and in ourselves as part of society as a whole system. It is better that we join them with the best we can: our (systems-based) thinking and our practice.

# Notes

## 1 Introduction

1 These individuals are human beings, and would like to live in a better type of society than is currently the case. However, their work responsibilities require them to focus on specific issues and ignore their own values.

## 2 The Information Society

1 Shannon mentions that other researchers at that time like Norbert Wiener were using ideas on communication to study communication processes in living beings. In his seminal paper (1948), Shannon also introduces an example of a communication system with a 'correction' channel that allows an observer to modify the message being received according to the message s/he observed being sent.

2 This would also include supporting initiatives by proposing ideas and innovations on how information products could be better researched, developed and used in society.

3 Castells (1996) would argue that there have been particular social milieu that facilitate the development of technologies. Such milieus promote certain values through key individuals from different types of institutions. For instance, Castells cites Silicon Valley as one such milieu which to many was driven by values of innovation, experimentation and reaction against the establishment.

4 According to Castells, this term speaks more strongly about the pervasiveness of the logic of information and knowledge manipulation in every realm of society than that of the information society.

5 Masuda regards communities of people as essential to support the initiative of the information society. Communities would support individuals when for instance needing information about job opportunities or training in the use of technologies. Without communities, the implementation of initiatives would be difficult. In Japan, communities of entrepreneurs and government organizations have been regarded as key actors who facilitate innovation and technological development.

6 For instance, the Zapatista movement in Mexico; a virtual city for Amsterdam; or even a 'mirrored' website of a city council to oppose the 'official' website.

## 3 Systems-thinking

1 Orthogonal is a term borrowed from Bilson's (2007) work on autopoiesis. This means promoting conversations that impact on other conversations by challenging their assumptions.

## 4 Applied Systems-thinking

1 In practice we have found that the definition of a meaningful transformation can be done with people before they are divided into groups, or refined at the stage of assumption surfacing and rating.

2  It is difficult to argue that scientists from different countries had (or still have) the same motivations to develop alternatives to systems analysis or systems engineering.

3  These are systems that have meaning and reflect the human purpose of people involved in and affected by a related situation.

4  These commitments have been re-defined by different authors. Here we present a version by Midgley (2000).

5  In the realm of information systems, Clarke (2007) suggests rethinking the nature of strategy in organizations and with it the role of information systems. He uses the commitments of critical systems-thinking to build awareness in activities of information and knowledge generation. His use of systems methodologies also helps people to gain a better understanding of the 'wider' system of people in which information systems and communication technologies are to be deployed.

6  According to Midgley (2000), the terms 'sacred' and 'profane' are not meant in a purely religious sense, but indicate the valued or devalued status of marginalized elements.

## 5   The Idealist Pattern for Practice in the Information Society

1  For instance, the latest European Union policy documents propose sharing electronic information between countries. This will surely change the ways in which countries relate to one another.

2  Work by projects has become very popular, and project management has become a discipline. In this area we have seen an increasing interest by systems thinkers.

3  As an anecdote, when involved in defining a set of policies for the information society in Colombia several years ago, I decided to draw a map of the different systems that in my view (having been to some meetings) were needed. The map contained an education system, a policy making system and an industry system, all interconnected. When I showed this to the meetings co-ordinator of a Forum to talk about the role of technologies in the country, she said she liked it but that we needed to focus on a particular aspect of the discussion (role of technologies in industry and education). A few years later I joined another of the forum's meetings. Discussions were stilled focused on only a few of the emerging issues that I perceived as being interconnected.

4  Even in situations where there is no democratic space, it can be said that definitions take place in conversations, regardless of how unidirectional or bidirectional these conversations are, or the factors which influence the development of conversations. In Western societies, it is commonly assumed that there is a democratic background for discussion of plans and initiatives. (Un)fortunately, information society initiatives inherit these assumptions. In the next chapter the issue of engagement with people will be tackled head on.

5  The name has been changed for confidentiality reasons.

6  I would like to thank Philip Shields for the invitation to participate in the planning exercise reported in this section.

7  I would like to thank Dr. Amanda Gregory from Hull University Business School in the UK for her invaluable help in preparing and facilitating the workshop reported here.

8  SWOT: Strengths, Weaknesses, Opportunities and Threats.

9  We invited participants to think of combining options and produce a new one, as we understand the meaning of synthesis in chemistry.

## 6   The Strategic Pattern for Practice in the Information Society

1  I would like to thank Diego Torres and Alexandra Bohorquez for their collaboration in the project reported in this chapter.

2  In another design exercise, as soon as we started presenting the enriched picture, one of the participants (a project manager) stood up and argued that a 'similar' exercise of planning had been conducted at the institution a few years ago with the purpose of defining institutional plans for the next five years. He encouraged people to follow these plans instead of inventing new ones. Although we argued that our project intended to be a bottom-up exercise (in contrast with what appeared to be a top-down institutional process), he found it difficult to consider alternatives to existing plans and it proved difficult to help the group engage in what we had planned. This type of generalization (sticking to the institutional plans) was difficult to challenge.

## 7 The Power-based Pattern for Practice in the Information Society

1 The introduction and use of information systems and technologies in different realms of societal life has inspired me to reflect on different patterns.
2 As mentioned before, the use of ICTs to support administrative processes and transactions has pervaded local, regional and national government departments.
3 In the next chapter a more detailed presentation of a combined use of patterns of thinking is developed.
4 That image had to do with the nature of academic departments at the university. If I was working with the computer science engineering department, my own discourse needed to be 'technically' orientated. This also shows the operation of power as influencing how we should present ourselves as members of a group.
5 In the interview with the senior research manager, I was asked about my 'commitment' to Javeriana in relation to the purpose of my visit. Also in the final workshop I was reminded that I needed to continue 'following up' on activities if I wanted to provide a 'good' contribution to the institution.

## 8 A Dynamic Practice Framework for Living and Working in the Information Society

1 Many public service organizations are examples of this. New 'administration' means new plans, projects, and people to undertake them. What was envisaged in the previous administration needs to be replaced.
2 This is of course a more articulated post-hoc analysis. During the exercise reported above my initial thought was that we needed to do something to help participants rather than simply accepting the constraints being imposed upon us. This is what led me to express my own ethical views.
3 There was disagreement between us. Amanda was knowledgeable about the technique we adopted (using stickers to define relevant issues) whereas I preferred to ask people directly to select the issue. We had a discussion but given the pressure of time we selected her preferred technique. It can also be said that she used her power of persuasion and authority to convince me! This was another scenario: a picture of power. I felt I needed to 'agree' in order to continue guiding the workshop. However, I also played another role: that of an expert in funding, which within the possibilities given by the use of soft systems methodology, allowed me to contribute and influence the definition of actions for improvement.
4 This also included one of the 'local' participants who had raised concerns about the usefulness of the workshop.
5 A possible interpretation of this was that we moved back into a temporary 'picture of power' scenario in which existing relationships among participants (including me) allowed us to give advice to shape up improvements.
6 Alito is a UK consortium of government and non-government organizations that aims to facilitate the exchange of information to make public tendering for service delivery more transparent and efficient. Government bodies make available information for contracts and service organizations can apply 'online' to be awarded such contracts.
7 During 2007, for a project with Juan-Gabriel Cegarra of Universidad Politécnica de Cartagena (Spain), we interviewed a number of small business owners in the Humberside and Lincolnshire region of the UK. Small businesses see opportunities in getting government funding to provide services to government organizations or undertaking particular work. This is the case for services like printing or computer recycling which small companies can undertake. In the UK this is also supported by the fostering of public private partnerships in the delivery of services for the community. We would like to thank the small business owners who took part in this project for their insights on how they make sense of new forms of 'networking' in the information society.

## 9 Conclusions

1 his book hopes to inspire, although not necessarily in the same ways, information systems planners, designers, managers, researchers and policy makers to enrich their practice with critical thinking about how the information society is currently being deployed, and how they could generate new and better ways of contributing to such deployment.

2  I was surprised a few weeks ago to find a website which offers expert advice about the mechanical problems of cars. If a mechanic is available online, s/he will give you advice on what to do to repair a problem you report. See the website at http://uk-car.justanswer.com (accessed December 2008).

3  The latest example I have come across is in the area of electronic government. There are indicators (also defined by the United Nations) of 'readiness' to adopt electronic government which are based on the democratic, inclusive and transparent nature of government institutions. See for example the United Nations report of 2005: http://www2.unpan.org/egovkb/global_reports/05report.htm, accessed December 2008.

4  This is different from asking practitioners to find their 'true selves', which according to Foucault, will never be achieved, as there is no such thing.

# References

Ackoff, R. (1981) *Creating the Corporate Future: Plan or To Be Planned For,* New York, John Wiley.

Barinaga, E. (2008) The information society: A global discourse and its local translation into regional organisational practices. In Jemielniak, D. and Kociatkiewicz, J. (Eds.) *Management Practices in High-Tech Environments.* Hershey, PA, Information Science Reference.

Beck, E., Madon, S. and Sahay, S. (2004) On the margins of the 'Information Society': A comparative study of mediation. *The Information Society,* 20, 279–90.

Bijker, E., Hughes, T. and Pinch, T. (Eds.) (1987) *The Social Construction of Technological Systems: New Directions in the Sociology and History of Technology,* Cambridge, MA, MIT Press.

Bilson, A. (2007) Promoting compassionate concern in social work: Reflections on ethics, biology and love. *British Journal of Social Work,* 37(8):1371–86.

Castells, M. (1996) *The Rise of the Network Society,* Cambridge, MA, Blackwell.

Castells, M. (2001) *The Internet Galaxy: Reflections on Internet, Business and Society,* Oxford, Oxford University Press.

CEC (1997) Green paper on the convergence of the telecommunications, media and information technology sectors, and the implications for regulation: Towards an information society approach. Brussels, Commission of the European Communities (CEC).

Checkland, P. (1981) *Systems Thinking, Systems Practice,* London, John Wiley.

Checkland, P. and Poulter, J. (2006) *Learning for Action: A Short Definitive Account of Soft Systems Methodology and Its Use for Practitioners, Teachers and Students,* Chichester, John Wiley.

Checkland, P. and Winter, M. (2006) Process and content: Two ways of using SSM. *Journal of the Operational Research Society,* 57, 1435–41.

Churchman, C. W. (1968) *The Systems Approach,* New York, Delacorte Press.

Clarke, S. (2001) *Information Systems Strategic Management: An Integrated Approach,* London, Routledge.

Clarke, S. (2007) *Information Systems Strategic Management: An Integrated Approach,* London, Routledge.

Córdoba, J. R. (2002) A Critical Systems Thinking Approach for the Planning of Information Technology in the Information Society. PhD thesis. Centre for Systems Studies, University of Hull, UK.

Córdoba, J. R. (2006) Using Foucault to analyse ethics in the practice of problem structuring methods. *Journal of the Operational Research Society,* 57, 1027–34.

Córdoba, J. R. and Midgley, G. (2006) Broadening the boundaries: An application of critical systems thinking to IS planning in Colombia. *Journal of the Operational Research Society,* 57, 1064–1080.

De Bono, E. (1976) *Teaching Thinking,* London, Penguin.

De Bono, E. (2004) *How to Have a Beautiful Mind,* London, Vermillion.

DOT Force (2000) Okinawa Charter on Global Information Society, Declaration of the G8. Okinawa, Japanese Government.

Dreyfus, H. and Rabinow, P. (1982) *Michel Foucault: Beyond Structuralism and Hermeneutics,* Brighton, Harvester Press.

Dunleavy, P., Margetts, H., Bastow, S. and Tinkler, J. (2006) *Digital Era Governance: IT Corporations, the State, and E-Government,* Oxford, Oxford University Press.

Flood, R. L. (1990) *Liberating Systems Theory,* New York, Plenum Press.

Foucault, M. (1977) *The History of Sexuality, Volume 1: The Will to Knowledge,* London, Penguin.

Foucault, M. (1982) Afterword: The subject and power. In Dreyfus, H. and Rabinow, P. (Eds.) *Michel Foucault: Beyond Structuralism and Hermeneutics.* Brighton, Harvester Press.

Foucault, M. (1984a) The ethics of the concern of the self as a practice of freedom. In Rabinow, P. (Ed.) *Michel Foucault: Ethics Subjectivity and Truth: Essential Works of Foucault 1954–1984.* London, Penguin.

Foucault, M. (1984b) *The History of Sexuality, Volume 2: The Use of Pleasure,* London, Penguin.

Foucault, M. (1984c) What is enlightenment? In Rabinow, P. (Ed.) *The Foucault Reader: An Introduction to Foucault's Thought.* London, Penguin.

Freeman, C. (1997) Technical change and economic growth: The case of 'catch-up'. In Fase, M. M. G., Kanning, W., Walker, D. A. and Heertje, A. (Eds.) *Economics, Welfare Policy and the History of Economic Thought: Essays in Honour of Arnold Heertje.* Cheltenham, Edward Elgar.

Gates, B. (2001) *Business @ The Speed of Thought,* Harlow, Pearson.

Gregory, A. (2007) The state we are in: Insights from autopoiesis and complexity theory. *Management Decision,* 44, 962–972.

Hammer, M. and Champy, J. (1995) *Re-engineering the Corporation: A Manifesto for Business Revolution,* London, Nicholas Brealey.

Heeks, R. (2005) e-government as a carrier of context. *Journal of Public Policy,* 25, 51–74.

Henderson, J. and Venkatraman, N. (1999) Strategic alignment: Leveraging information technology for transforming organisations. *IBM Systems Journal,* 38, 472–84.

Ivanov, K. (1991) Critical systems thinking and information technology: Some summary reflections, doubts and hopes through critical thinking critically considered, and through hyper systems. *Journal of Applied Systems Analysis,* 18, 39–55.

Jackson, M. C. (1985) Social systems theory and practice: The need for a critical approach. *International Journal of General Systems,* 10, 135–51.

Jackson, M. C. (1992) An integrated programme for critical thinking in information systems research. *Information Systems Journal,* 2, 83–95.

Jackson, M. C. (2003) *Creative Holism: Systems Thinking for Managers,* Chichester, John Wiley.

Kapra, F. (1997) *The Web of Life: A New Synthesis of Mind and Matter,* London, Flamingo.

Kauffman, S. (1996) *At Home in the Universe: The Search for Laws of Complexity,* London, Penguin.

Luhmann, N. (1996) *Social Systems,* Stanford, CA, Stanford University Press.

Mansell, R. (Ed.) (2002) *Inside The Communication Revolution: Evolving Patterns of Social and Technical Interaction,* Oxford, Oxford University Press.

Mansell, R. and Steinmueller, W. (2000) *Mobilizing the Information Society: Strategies for Growth and Opportunity,* Oxford, Oxford University Press.

Mason, R. and Mitroff, I. (1981) *Challenging Strategic Planning Assumptions: Theory, Cases and Techniques,* New York, John Wiley.

Masuda, Y. (1980) *The Information Society as Post-Industrial Society,* Tokyo, Institute for the Information Society.

Maturana, H. and Varela, F. (1987) *The Tree of Knowledge: The Biological Roots of Human Understanding,* Boston, MA, Shambala.

Mendoza, J. M. (2006) *Innovación por lo Alto: Imaginación y Acción en la Empresa,* Bogotá, Asesores del 2000.

Menzies, H. (1996) *Whose Brave New World? The Information Highway and the New Economy,* Toronto, Between the Lines.

Midgley, G. (2000) *Systemic Intervention: Philosophy, Methodology and Practice,* New York, Kluwer Academic/Plenum.

Mingers, J. (1984) Subjectivism and soft systems methodology: A critique. *Journal of Applied Systems Analysis,* 11, 85–113.

Ministerio de Comunicaciones (1997) *Bases para una política nacional de informática.* [*Foundations for the Formulation of National Policies of Information Technology in Colombia*]. Bogotá, Ministry of Communications.

Negroponte, N. (1995) *Being Digital,* Boston, MA, MIT Press.

Orlikowski, W. (1992) The duality of technology: Rethinking the concept of technology in organisations. *Organization Science,* 3, 398–427.

Perez, C. (1983) Structural change and assimilation of new technologies in the economic and social systems. *Futures,* 15, 357–75.

Porat, M. U. (1977) *The Information Economy: Definition and Measurement,* Washington DC, Government Printing Office.

Porter, M. and Millar, V. (1985) How information gives you competitive advantage. *Harvard Business Review,* 63, 149–160.

Poster, M. (2003) The good, the bad and the virtual: Ethics in the age of information. In Wyschogrod, E. and McKenny, G. (Eds.) *The Ethical.* Oxford, Blackwell Publishing.

Robey, D. and Boudreau, M. (1999) Accounting for the contradictory organizational consequences of information technology: Theoretical directions and methodological implications. *Information Systems Research,* 10, 167–85.

Shannon, C. E. (1948) A mathematical theory of communication. *The Bell System Technical Journal,* 27, 379–423.

Steiner, G. (1969) *Top Management Planning,* Basingstoke, Macmillan Press.

Toffler, A. (1992) *Power Shift: Knowledge, Wealth and Violence at the Edge of the 21st Century,* London, Bantam Books.

Turner, F. (2006) *From Counterculture to Cyberculture: Stewart Brand, the Whole Earth Network, and the Rise of Digital Utopianism,* Chicago, IL, University of Chicago Press.

Ulrich, W. (1983) *Critical Heuristics of Social Planning: A New Approach to Practical Philosophy,* Berne, Haupt.

Ulrich, W. (2001a) Critically systemic discourse: A discursive approach to reflective practice in ISD (part 2). *Journal of Information Technology Theory and Application,* 3, 85–106.

Ulrich, W. (2001b) A philosophical staircase for information systems definition, design and development. *Journal of Information Technology Theory and Application,* 3, 55–84.

Von Bertalanffy, L. (1968) *General System Theory: Foundations, Development, Applications,* New York, Brazilier.

Walsham, G. (1993) Ethical issues in information systems development: The analyst as a moral agent. In Avison, D., Kendall, J. E. and De Gross, J. I. (Eds.) *Human, Organisational and Social Dimensions of Information Systems Development.* North Holland, Elsevier Science.

Weil, S. (1998) Our Concerns as Researchers: Action Research Methods to Develop Critical Reflection. Research Training Workshop. University of Hull, UK.

Wickham, J. (1997) Where is Ireland in the global information society? *Economic and Social Review,* 28, 277–94.

Willcocks, L. (2004) Foucault, power/knowledge and information systems: Reconstructing the present. In Mingers, J. and Willcocks, L. (Eds.) *Social Theory and Philosophy for Information Systems.* Chichester, John Wiley.

Winograd, T. and Flores, F. (1987) *Understanding Computers and Cognition: A New Foundation for Design,* London, Addison Wesley.

Zuleta, E. (2005) Elogio de la dificultad. In Zuleta, E. (Ed.) *Elogio de la dificultad y otros ensayos.* Medellín, Colombia, Hombre Nuevo Editores & Fundación Estanislao Zuleta.

# Index

Figures are indicated by **bold** page numbers, tables by *italic* numbers.